Essentials of Psychology

Study Guide

D1530367

Jeffrey S. Nevid

CENGAGE
Learning

Australia • Brazil • Japan • Korea • Mexico • Singapore • Spain • United Kingdom • United States

CENGAGE Learning

Essentials of Psychology: Study Guide,

Jeffrey S. Nevid

Senior Manager, Student Engagement:

Linda deStefano

Janey Moeller

Manager, Student Engagement:

Julie Dierig

Marketing Manager:

Rachael Kloos

Manager, Production Editorial:

Kim Fry

Manager, Intellectual Property Project Manager:

Brian Methe

Senior Manager, Production and Manufacturing:

Donna M. Brown

Manager, Production:

Terri Daley

Essentials of Psychology: Concepts and Applications, 4th Edition
Jeffrey S. Nevid

ISBN-13: 978-1-305-00668-3

ISBN-10: 1-305-00668-2

WCN: 01-100-101

Cengage Learning

5191 Natorp Boulevard
Mason, Ohio 45040
USA

Cengage Learning is a leading provider of customized learning solutions with office locations around the globe, including Singapore, the United Kingdom, Australia, Mexico, Brazil, and Japan. Locate your local office at: **international.cengage.com/region.**

Cengage Learning products are represented in Canada by Nelson Education, Ltd.
For your lifelong learning solutions, visit **www.cengage.com/custom.**
Visit our corporate website at **www.cengage.com.**

Printed in the United States of America

Brief Contents

Name:________________________ Class:________________ Date:________

Essentials of Psychology Chapter 1

1. According to the text, all but which of the following are emerging specialty areas in psychology?
   a. sport psychology
   b. geropsychology
   c. consumer
   d. forensic psychology
   e. neuropsychology

2. Dr. Greenberg is an industrial/organizational psychologist. In his job at Acme Corporation, he is likely to work on all but which of the following tasks?
   a. Use psychological tests to determine the fit between a job applicant's abilities and available positions in the company.
   b. Identify leadership qualities that are most effective in increasing worker productivity.
   c. Examine ways to make computer systems easier to use.
   d. Conduct a survey to determine employees' job satisfaction.
   e. Conduct a survey to determine which consumers are most likely to buy Acme's products.

3. Which of the following is the newest movement in contemporary psychology?
   a. Cognitive psychology
   b. Positive psychology
   c. Sociocultural psychology
   d. Humanistic psychology
   e. Social-cognitive psychology

4. Regarding the psychodynamic perspective, which of the following statements is FALSE?
   a. This perspective remains a vibrant force in psychology today.
   b. Compared to Freud, neo-Freudians place less emphasis on basic drives.
   c. Psychodynamic principles and ideas are found in our popular culture.
   d. Today, only people formally trained in Freudian psychology endorse the belief that psychological problems may be rooted in childhood.
   e. This perspective focuses on the inner life of fantasies, wishes, dreams, and motives.

5. A school psychologist would be most likely to
   a. help teachers develop new instructional techniques.
   b. study how groups affect individuals.
   c. evaluate a student for placement in a special education program.
   d. make suggestions as to how managers could improve employee morale.
   e. investigate the relationship between childhood obesity and self-esteem.

Essentials of Psychology Chapter 1

6. Your psychology professor asks a student volunteer to concentrate on eating an apple and then describe the individual elements of that experience. Your professor is demonstrating the technique of _______, which is a technique used by investigators of ________.
   a. stream of consciousness; functionalism
   b. introspection; structuralism
   c. introspection; Gestalt
   d. introspection; humanism
   e. stream of consciousness; structuralism

7. Anna works for Federal Motors Corporation in the Human Factors Division. Her job is to identify ways in which engineers can design the instrumentation of the onboard navigational system to be easiest for their customers to use. Anna is most likely which type of psychologist?
   a. Consumer
   b. Industrial/organizational
   c. Environmental
   d. Clinical
   e. Geropsychologist

8. In a study of the effects of various brands of ice cream on weight gain, the type of ice cream consumed represents the
   a. dependent variable.
   b. independent variable.
   c. placebo.
   d. control variable.
   e. random variable.

9. Psychology is best described as a science that studies
   a. the role of the mind in explaining behavior.
   b. how the mind controls our behavior.
   c. observable behavior only.
   d. mental processes only.
   e. behavior and mental processes.

10. Dr. Fiennes, a psychological researcher, studies the biological bases of memory problems in the elderly using animal research subjects. Fiennes is a(n) ______ psychologist.
   a. comparative
   b. biological
   c. environmental
   d. health
   e. physiological

Essentials of Psychology Chapter 1

11. Developmental psychologist Arthur Chang watches children in a daycare center through a one-way mirror. Chang is utilizing which form of research?
    a. case study
    b. correlational
    c. survey
    d. experimentation
    e. naturalistic observation

12. Dr. Jameson's research question is, "What kind of music will put people in the mood to purchase more products?" Dr. Jameson is most likely a(n) ________ psychologist.
    a. industrial-organizational
    b. physiological
    c. environmental
    d. consumer
    e. business

13. The behaviorist emphasis on observable events as the focus of inquiry can be traced to which philosopher?
    a. Socrates
    b. Plato
    c. Aristotle
    d. Rosseau
    e. Confucius

14. An emphasis on the unconscious and early childhood experience characterizes which school of psychology?
    a. Behaviorism
    b. Structuralism
    c. Empiricism
    d. Psychodynamic
    e. Humanism

15. A factor that varies in an experiment is called a
    a. theory.
    b. statistic.
    c. constant.
    d. hypothesis.
    e. variable.

16. The approach that studies the relationships between biological processes and behavior is termed
    a. cognitive-behavioral therapy.
    b. Gestalt psychology.
    c. structuralism.
    d. introspection.
    e. physiological psychology.

Essentials of Psychology Chapter 1

17. ______ psychologists have worked to identify the cluster of psychological characteristics and behaviors that distinguish people.
    a. Educational
    b. Personality
    c. Experimental
    d. School
    e. Developmental

18. The major proponent of behaviorism for much of the 20th century was
    a. Watson.
    b. Skinner.
    c. James.
    d. Wertheimer.
    e. Freud.

19. A placebo effect would be most likely to account for changes in
    a. blood pressure.
    b. blood sugar.
    c. pupil dilation.
    d. pain intensity.
    e. body temperature.

20. The use of the survey method is limited by which types of biases?
    a. social desirability bias and volunteer bias
    b. random sampling bias and population bias
    c. case study bias and observational bias
    d. survey bias and volunteer bias
    e. method bias and population bias

21. Regarding Mary Whiton Calkins, which of the following statements is FALSE?
    a. She was the first female pioneer in psychology, having completed her doctorate requirements at Johns Hopkins University in 1882.
    b. She was the first female president of the American Psychological Association, in 1905.
    c. Although she completed all of her doctoral requirements at Harvard, the school denied her a doctorate.
    d. She conducted important research on learning and short-term memory.
    e. She was a student of William James.

22. A developmental psychologist would most likely
    a. study the psychological crises people experience at different ages.
    b. conduct research to determine if a high school graduation test predicts success in college.
    c. study how prejudice develops.
    d. design a program to help people avoid risky sexual behaviors.
    e. administer tests to children to determine their eligibility for gifted education programs.

23. Ethics review committees are typically composed of
    a. laypersons only.
    b. professionals only.
    c. samples of research participants from the population under study.
    d. both professionals and samples of research participants.
    e. both professionals and laypersons.

24. Dr. Sears gives a lecture on positive psychology. Which psychologist's work will she be most likely to highlight in her lecture?
    a. Abraham Maslow
    b. William James
    c. Martin Seligman
    d. John B. Watson
    e. Carl Rogers

25. Dr. Burlington works with Ivy University's basketball team, where he helps the athletes handle competitive pressures. He is also conducting a study to determine the most important factors influencing athletic performance anxiety. Burlington is probably a(n) ______ psychologist.
    a. personality
    b. sport
    c. clinical
    d. educational
    e. applied athletic

26. Which term best captures the meaning of the word 'gestalt'?
    a. Unconscious
    b. Introspection
    c. Pattern
    d. Observation
    e. Feeling

Name:____ Class:_________________________ Date:_____________

Essentials of Psychology Chapter 1

27. Wundt is to ______ as James is to ______.
    a. structuralism; Gestalt
    b. structuralism; functionalism
    c. behaviorism; Gestalt
    d. behaviorism; functionalism
    e. functionalism; psychoanalysis

28. A movement with modern psychology that applies principles from Darwin's theories is called
    a. humanistic psychology.
    b. evolutionary psychology.
    c. cognitive psychology.
    d. behavioral psychology.
    e. sociocultural psychology.

29. Dr. Samuelson conducts research on the relationship between strokes and speech problems. He is probably a(n) ______ psychologist.
    a. experimental
    b. health
    c. neuro
    d. social
    e. gero

30. A researcher adhering to the behavioral perspective would likely believe that
    a. unhealthy eating habits are learned and can be unlearned.
    b. aggression results when people are blocked from pursuing their goals.
    c. depression is related to changes in brain chemistry.
    d. depression is linked to social stresses like poverty.
    e. aggression is related to unconscious impulses.

31. All of the following would be exhibited by neo-Freudians EXCEPT
    a. reduced emphasis on sexual and aggressive urges.
    b. increased emphasis on the unconscious.
    c. increased emphasis on self-awareness.
    d. increased emphasis on self-direction.
    e. increased emphasis on conscious choice.

32. Which of the following correlations represents two variables with the strongest relationship?
    a. +0.80
    b. -0.95
    c. +0.85
    d. -0.75
    e. answer cannot be determined with information given

33. Dr. Mingus keeps a very detailed record of a series of interviews with an individual who is suffering from a rare brain disorder. This is an example of which research method?
    a. Experiment
    b. Correlational
    c. Case study
    d. Naturalistic observation
    e. Survey

34. Which of the following relationships would most likely have the weakest correlation?
    a. a school child's age and vocabulary
    b. a building's height and weight
    c. number of fingers on a person's hand and intelligence
    d. air temperature and number of air conditioners being used
    e. amount of snowfall and number of skiers

35. Social desirability bias and volunteer bias are problems typically associated with which research method?
    a. naturalistic observation
    b. experiments
    c. case studies
    d. field studies
    e. surveys

36. In her dissertation research, a graduate student finds a correlation of +0.95 between two of the variables being studied. How should she interpret this correlation coefficient?
    a. There is no relationship between the variables.
    b. The variables have a moderate, positive relationship.
    c. The variables have a strong, negative relationship.
    d. The variables have a moderate, negative relationship.
    e. The variables have a strong, positive relationship.

37. An ethical guideline intended to protect a research participant's privacy involves
    a. obtaining informed consent.
    b. maintaining confidentiality.
    c. ensuring anonymity.
    d. obtaining prior approval by an ethics review panel.
    e. destroying research records after participation.

38. An extension of the behavioral perspective that incorporates the study of mental processes is termed ________.
    a. social-cognitive theory
    b. evolutionary psychology
    c. Gestalt psychology
    d. humanism
    e. neuropsychology

Essentials of Psychology Chapter 1

39. Which perspective is most responsible for bringing issues related to diversity to the forefront of psychological research?
    a. Cognitive
    b. Behaviorism
    c. Psychodynamic
    d. Sociocultural
    e. Humanistic

40. A correlation coefficient of 0.00 means
    a. there is no relationship between the variables.
    b. as one variable increases, the other variable increases.
    c. as one variable decreases, the other variable decreases.
    d. as one variable increases, the other variable decreases.
    e. the variables are dependent.

41. Christine Ladd-Franklin is credited as being
    a. the first woman to receive a Ph.D. in psychology.
    b. the first African-American woman to conduct research in psychology.
    c. the earliest woman pioneer in psychology.
    d. the first person to receive a Ph.D. in psychology from Yale University.
    e. the first female president of the APA.

42. A strong belief that the environment molds the behavior of humans and other animals is characteristic of which school of psychology?
    a. Psychodynamic
    b. Behaviorist
    c. Structuralist
    d. Gestalt
    e. Humanist

43. Dr. Spires talks with some students before psychology class begins. Spires says, "I believe that mental experience is best understood as a whole, rather than in terms of its parts." Her students recognize that Spires describes which school of thought?
    a. Gestalt
    b. Humanism
    c. Psychodynamic
    d. Structuralism
    e. Functionalism

Essentials of Psychology Chapter 1

44. Developmental psychologists study which aspects of development across the lifespan?
   a. Physical and cognitive
   b. Social and personality
   c. Physical, personality, and cognitive
   d. Social, cognitive, and physical
   e. Physical, social, cognitive, and personality

45. This early pioneer in psychology, who developed a new theory of color vision, received his/her Ph.D. several decades after completing all of the requirements for the degree.
   a. Mary Whiton Calkins
   b. Margaret Floy Washburn
   c. Christine Ladd-Franklin
   d. Francis Sumner
   e. Gilbert Haven Jones

46. All of the following are steps in the scientific method EXCEPT
   a. drawing conclusions.
   b. developing a hypothesis.
   c. ignoring contradictory evidence.
   d. gathering evidence.
   e. generating a research question.

47. Regarding behaviorism, which of the following statements is FALSE?
   a. Watson believed that, with control of their environments, he could shape infants to be any kind of adult.
   b. B.F. Skinner conducted most of his research with humans.
   c. In the early 20th century, behaviorism was the dominant force in psychology.
   d. B.F. Skinner presented ideas and techniques for rewarding and punishing behavior.
   e. Behaviorists rejected introspection as a research method.

48. All of the following are steps in the scientific method EXCEPT
   a. drawing conclusions.
   b. developing a hypothesis.
   c. drawing conclusions based on gathering expert opinions.
   d. gathering evidence.
   e. generating a research question.

49. ______ describes the attempt to duplicate research findings reported by other scientists.
   a. Variability
   b. Replication
   c. Hypothesis testing
   d. Empiricism
   e. Theorizing

Name:________________________________ Class:____________________ Date:__________

Essentials of Psychology Chapter 1

50. The "third force" in psychology is more formally known as
    a. social-cognitive theory.
    b. humanistic psychology.
    c. the psychodynamic perspective.
    d. evolutionary psychology.
    e. the physiological perspective.

51. Which of the following pioneers of psychology was a therapist?
    a. Wundt
    b. Skinner
    c. James
    d. Watson
    e. Freud

52. Which of the following statements would be made by a humanist?
    a. Unhealthy eating habits lead to obesity.
    b. Aggression results when people are blocked from pursuing their goals.
    c. Depression is related to changes in brain chemistry.
    d. Aggression is related to unconscious impulses.
    e. Obesity is best understood in its cultural context.

53. A statistical measure of the association between two variables is called a(n)
    a. independent variable.
    b. dependent variable.
    c. control variable.
    d. correlation coefficient.
    e. placebo.

54. Every participant in an experiment has an equal chance of receiving one of the treatments. This is called
    a. control assignment.
    b. random selection.
    c. a placebo effect.
    d. random assignment.
    e. control selection.

55. A researcher adhering to the psychodynamic perspective would likely believe that depression
    a. represents anger turned inward.
    b. stems from a sense of purposelessness.
    c. is influenced by genetic factors.
    d. is more common among certain groups because of social stresses more prevalent in those groups.
    e. can be treated through changes in reinforcement patterns.

Essentials of Psychology Chapter 1

56. The ethical code of psychologists is based on all but which of the following ideas?
    a. People have a basic right to make their own decisions.
    b. Research participants or clients must not be harmed.
    c. People's dignity and welfare must be respected.
    d. People have a basic right to exercise choice.
    e. Determination of ultimate truth outweighs individual cost.

57. What is the most common doctoral degree awarded in the field of psychology?
    a. Ph.D.
    b. Psy.D.
    c. M.A.
    d. Ed.D.
    e. B.A.

58. What makes psychology a scientific discipline?
    a. Its discounting of tradition and folklore.
    b. Its focus on testing theories, beliefs, and assumptions.
    c. Its emphasis on mental, as opposed to behavioral, processes.
    d. Its valuing of scholarly opinions over laboratory tests.
    e. Its reliance on popular opinion.

59. One of the main reasons that information published in scientific journals is trustworthy is because
    a. these journals pay for fact checkers to verify information before it is published.
    b. these journals generally post information online before it is published so others can review it.
    c. the articles are peer-reviewed by other professionals prior to publication.
    d. the articles are written by researchers who have proven themselves to be reliable.
    e. none of the above.

60. You see a journal article entitled, "Injection of Happystuff Causes a Reduction in Symptoms of Depression in Adult Males." This tells you that the independent variable
    a. is the injection of Happystuff.
    b. is the reduction in symptoms of depression.
    c. is the population of adult males.
    d. is the construct of depression.
    e. cannot be determined.

61. Regarding functionalism, which of the following statements is FALSE?
    a. William James contributed to both psychology and philosophy.
    b. William James did not use the technique of introspection.
    c. Compared to structuralism, functionalism focuses on the "why" of behavior.
    d. The functionalists believed that people develop habits because the habits help them adapt to the demands of living.
    e. William James believed that conscious experience could not be parceled into discrete units.

62. Which of the following early pioneers of psychology was a poor student and was required to repeat a grade?
    a. Fechner
    b. von Helmholtz
    c. James
    d. Wundt
    e. Titchener

63. Dr. Williamson works with the FBI to develop personality profiles of rapists. Williamson is probably a(n) ______ psychologist.
    a. social
    b. forensic
    c. industrial/organizational
    d. physiological
    e. health

64. The work of ______ psychologists often overlaps with the work of psychiatrists.
    a. experimental
    b. clinical
    c. developmental
    d. educational
    e. counseling

65. In an experiment, the factor that changes in response to some other factor is referred to as the
    a. independent variable.
    b. dependent variable.
    c. control variable.
    d. random variable.
    e. placebo.

66. Which of the following does NOT belong?
    a. Mental structures
    b. Structuralism
    c. Introspection
    d. Functionalism
    e. Wundt and Titchener

67. Your dog is demonstrating some unacceptable behavior. You are able to go back in time to talk to one of the pioneers of psychology. Who would be the best choice to help with your problem?
   a. Sigmund Freud
   b. Wilhelm Wundt
   c. Edward Titchener
   d. William James
   e. B.F. Skinner

68. The concept of behavior in the definition of psychology incorporates ALL but which of the following?
   a. thinking.
   b. dreaming.
   c. quiet reading.
   d. making yourself a sandwich.
   e. secretion of insulin by the pancreas.

69. As scientists, psychologists have confidence in theories that
   a. have stood the test of time.
   b. reveal the true nature of human behavior.
   c. are tied to observable evidence.
   d. do not rely simply on observation.
   e. are accepted by the majority of leading scholars.

70. Cognitive psychologists would be interested in all of the following EXCEPT
   a. concept formation.
   b. language processes.
   c. problem solving.
   d. decision making.
   e. instincts.

71. Which type of psychologist might administer an intelligence test to your 12-year-old child to determine if he or she should be in special education classes?
   a. school
   b. educational
   c. counseling
   d. clinical
   e. personality

Essentials of Psychology Chapter 1

72. A method of developing knowledge based on the evaluation of evidence from experiments and careful observation is called the ______ approach.
    a. intuitive
    b. statistical
    c. empirical
    d. theoretical
    e. eclectic

73. ______ is a growing movement in psychology directed toward studies of human experience such as hope, happiness, and altruism.
    a. Positive psychology
    b. Neo-behaviorism
    c. Eclecticism
    d. Evolutionary psychology
    e. Sociocultural psychology

74. Dr. Schultze conducts research on the effects of a new drug on obsessive-compulsive disorder. In his study, neither Schultze nor the participants knows who is receiving the active drug and who is receiving the placebo. This example describes
    a. random sampling.
    b. a double-blind study.
    c. a single-blind study.
    d. a control factor.
    e. a social desirability bias.

75. As a humanist, Dr. Randall is most likely interested in all but which of the following questions?
    a. How do people select and pursue goals that are meaningful?
    b. Is depression related to threats to one's self-image?
    c. Does food provide special meaning to obese people?
    d. Can a lack of purpose influence a person's depression?
    e. How do aggressive people direct the unconscious impulses?

76. Which subspecialty represents the largest group of psychologists?
    a. Industrial/organizational
    b. Clinical
    c. Counseling
    d. School
    e. Experimental

Essentials of Psychology Chapter 1

77. Agreement to participate in a study following disclosure of information about its purposes and potential risks and benefits is called
    a. confidentiality.
    b. critical thinking.
    c. informed consent.
    d. ethics review.
    e. replication.

78. Graduate student Felicity Farraday has just completed her dissertation entitled, "The Role of Observational Learning in the Development of Prejudice." What is Farraday's likely major in college?
    a. Health psychology
    b. Environmental psychology
    c. Experimental psychology
    d. Developmental psychology
    e. Social psychology

79. Dr. Holder is a psychologist working from the sociocultural perspective. In her research, which variable is Dr. Holder LEAST likely to study?
    a. Income level
    b. Unconscious motives
    c. Gender
    d. Disability status
    e. Sexual orientation

80. Which theorists are associated with humanistic psychology?
    a. John B. Watson and B.F. Skinner
    b. Wilhelm Wundt and Edward Titchener
    c. William James and Charles Darwin
    d. Max Wertheimer and Sigmund Freud
    e. Abraham Maslow and Carl Rogers

81. Dr. Chen finds in her study of people's charitable habits that individuals overestimate the amount of money they give to their churches and private schools. Dr. Chen's results may reflect
    a. over-representation bias.
    b. social desirability bias.
    c. poor random sampling.
    d. large sample bias.
    e. volunteer bias.

Essentials of Psychology Chapter 1

82. Which of the following statements is NOT true of a correlation?
    a. Correlations can range from -1.0 to +1.0.
    b. Negative correlations indicate relatively weak relationships.
    c. Correlations can indicate possible causal factors.
    d. Correlations can identify high-risk groups.
    e. Negative correlations indicate inverse relationships.

83. All but which of the following are cognitive factors that influence behavior?
    a. the value placed on different objects in the environment
    b. rewards and punishments
    c. the value placed on different personal goals
    d. expectancies about the rewards of particular behaviors
    e. expectancies about the possible punishments associated with particular behaviors

84. Your psychology professor refers to a research study and says the results were "statistically significant." Which step in the scientific method does this apply?
    a. Drawing conclusions
    b. Developing a research question
    c. Gathering evidence
    d. Replicating results
    e. Forming a hypothesis

85. ______ was the first African American to receive a doctorate in psychology in the United States, and ______ was the first African American to publish research findings in a major journal.
    a. Kenneth Clark; Richard Suinn
    b. J. Henry Alston; Kenneth Clark
    c. Gilbert Haven Jones; Francis Sumner
    d. Mary Whiton Calkins; Margaret Floy Washburn
    e. Francis Sumner; J. Henry Alston

86. Dr. Finnegan, a psychological researcher, ensures that he maintains the privacy of his research records. Which ethical principle does this example describe?
    a. informed consent
    b. ethical review
    c. random assignment
    d. confidentiality
    e. social desirability bias

Essentials of Psychology Chapter 1

87. Which of the following psychologists is most likely to study how humans process information?
    a. Dr. Alvarez, a behaviorist
    b. Dr. Benitez, a humanist
    c. Dr. Carlson, a cognitive psychologist
    d. Dr. Dimitri, a neo-Freudian
    e. Dr. Elrod, a physiological psychologist

88. _____ psychologists study the relationship between psychological factors and the prevention and treatment of physical illness.
    a. Consumer
    b. Clinical
    c. Educational
    d. Developmental
    e. Health

89. Which type of psychologist would evaluate whether overcrowding in urban areas is associated with increased violent crimes?
    a. Evolutionary
    b. Consumer
    c. Environmental
    d. Clinical
    e. Personality

90. Who is generally recognized as the founder of American psychology?
    a. Hall
    b. James
    c. Wundt
    d. Freud
    e. Watson

91. A humanist would give which explanation for aggression?
    a. Brain abnormalities explain violent behavior in some people.
    b. Social conditions give rise to drug use that, in turn, causes aggressive behavior.
    c. Aggression results from unconscious impulses.
    d. Aggression increases when people become frustrated by not being able to meet their goals.
    e. Aggression is learned through observing others and through reinforcement.

92. The American Psychological Association was founded in which year?
    a. 1875
    b. 1923
    c. 1909
    d. 1971
    e. 1892

Essentials of Psychology Chapter 1

93. Humanistic psychologists stress all of the following EXCEPT
    a. individuals' abilities to make meaning and purpose in their lives.
    b. self-awareness and free will.
    c. unconscious forces.
    d. being true to oneself.
    e. becoming an authentic person.

94. In 1970, women accounted for about what proportion of new doctorates in psychology?
    a. one-tenth
    b. one-fifth
    c. one-half
    d. two-thirds
    e. three-fourths

95. You read a news story about a psychologist who provided expert testimony during a criminal case. This sort of activity is characteristic of which type of psychologist?
    a. Developmental
    b. Forensic
    c. Educational
    d. Consumer
    e. Industrial/organizational

96. Regarding training to work in the field of psychology, which of the following statements is FALSE?
    a. The primary difference between the Ph.D. and the Psy.D. is that the Psy.D. focuses more on practitioner skills than on research skills.
    b. Those who pursue doctorate-level work in schools of education typically earn a Doctorate in Education, or Ed.D.
    c. A dissertation requires the completion of an original research project.
    d. The Bachelor's degree is recognized as the entry-level degree for professional work in some specialty areas like school psychology and industrial/organizational psychology.
    e. The Doctor of Philosophy is the most common doctoral degree.

97. Women now account for about what proportion of doctorates in psychology?
    a. one-third
    b. one-half
    c. two-thirds
    d. four-fifths
    e. nine-tenths

Essentials of Psychology Chapter 1

98. Dr. Vickers just took a position as an educational psychologist with the Blackstone School System. Of the following tasks, which is Vickers LEAST likely to do in this position?
   a. Develop a test to measure students' academic potential.
   b. Train teachers in the use of a new instructional method.
   c. Administer intelligence tests to students.
   d. Develop a new instructional method for use in the classroom.
   e. Conduct research on student motivation.

99. Psychology is a scientific discipline in that it focuses on
   a. the pursuit of truth, not simply opinion.
   b. testing opinions and assumptions in the light of evidence.
   c. systematically building theories to explain phenomena.
   d. behavioral, as opposed to mental, processes.
   e. accumulated wisdom of scholars.

100. Your professor stated that stress can lead to heart disease. She cited several medical studies to show that stress was linked to heart disease. Therefore, she said we should avoid all forms of stress in order to ensure living a long and healthy life. The professor needs to rethink advice based on which of the following features of critical thinking?
   a. avoiding oversimplification
   b. considering alternative explanations
   c. confusing correlation with causation
   d. avoiding overgeneralization
   e. all of the above

101. The word 'psychology' comes from two Greek roots that mean
   a. knowledge and mind.
   b. emotion and mind.
   c. emotion and spirit.
   d. mind and emotion
   e. knowledge and spirit.

102. Which of the following mental health professionals is most likely a behavior therapist?
   a. Dr. Angelo helps clients learn techniques for changing maladaptive thoughts.
   b. Dr. Barney uses techniques based on learning principles to help clients alter maladaptive patterns of action.
   c. Dr. Childers helps her clients uncover unconscious motives and desires.
   d. Dr. Diaz prescribes drugs for his patients that suffer from anxiety disorders.
   e. Dr. Evans helps her patients understand how their culture influences their maladaptive behaviors.

Essentials of Psychology Chapter 1

103. The Gestalt school of psychology was founded by_________.
   a. Wundt
   b. Kafka
   c. Kohler
   d. Darwin
   e. Wertheimer

104. In the psychodynamic view, the _____ is an area of the mind that lies beyond the reach of ordinary consciousness.
   a. preconscious
   b. subconscious
   c. conscience
   d. personal conscious
   e. unconscious

105. Dr. von Waldner conducts research on depression. His hypothesis is that depression results from maladaptive thought patterns. From which perspective is von Waldner working?
   a. Cognitive
   b. Humanistic
   c. Psychodynamic
   d. Sociocultural
   e. Physiological

106. In a drug study, group one receives an inactive pill and group two receives a pill that is believed to be effective in treating depression. Group two is the
   a. control group.
   b. placebo group.
   c. independent group.
   d. dependent group.
   e. experimental group.

107. Which perspective in psychology would suggest that depression is related to changes in brain chemistry?
   a. Psychodynamic
   b. Physiological
   c. Cognitive
   d. Humanistic
   e. Behavioral

108. Which of the following is NOT a benefit of correlational research?
   a. It can establish cause-and-effect relationships.
   b. It can identify high-risk groups.
   c. It can allow prediction of one variable on the basis of the other.
   d. It can help increase understanding of relationships between variables.
   e. It can offer clues to underlying causes.

Essentials of Psychology Chapter 1

109. Which type of psychologist would be interested in memory loss in elderly individuals?
   a. Social psychologist
   b. Health psychologist
   c. Counseling psychologist
   d. Forensic psychologist
   e. Geropsychologist

110. In survey research, _______ are segments of the total group who are the subject of interest to the researcher.
   a. populations
   b. volunteers
   c. control groups
   d. samples
   e. committees

111. The founder of behaviorism was
   a. Watson.
   b. Skinner.
   c. James.
   d. Pavlov.
   e. Freud.

112. Animal trainer Bob Jeffers uses rewards to teach his animals to perform circus tricks. Jeffers's techniques are based on principles from which school of psychology?
   a. Behaviorism
   b. Structuralism
   c. Psychodynamic
   d. Functionalism
   e. Humanism

113. Ajit is a graduate student in psychology who is conducting research on the effectiveness of two types of therapy in the treatment of phobias. Ajit is at the stage where he uses statistics to analyze the data he has collected in order to determine if his initial hypothesis is supported by the research. At which stage of the scientific method is Ajit working?
   a. Drawing conclusions
   b. Developing a research question
   c. Gathering evidence
   d. Replicating results
   e. Forming a hypothesis

Essentials of Psychology Chapter 1

114. Dr. Kavanaugh has noticed that many of her students are having difficulties understanding the basic parts of a nerve cell (neuron) but don't seem to have the same problems understanding most of the different regions of the brain. Dr. Kavanaugh wonders if her lectures have some bearing on this situation, and has posed a question she intends to purse in her research—whether the ways in which information is presented affects student interest and memory of the material. If she is interested in pursuing this research question further, Dr. Kavanaugh's next step in the scientific method would be
   a. to develop a research question.
   b. to form a hypothesis.
   c. to gather evidence.
   d. to manipulate the way she delivers lectures.
   e. to draw conclusions.
   f. generating a research question.

115. Dr. Wilmington is a social psychologist who studies the topic of love. He goes to a variety of places where couples are found and watches how they interact with each other. Which research method is Dr. Wilmington using for his study?
   a. Case study
   b. Survey
   c. Correlational
   d. Experiment
   e. Naturalistic observation

116. In an experiment, the ______ group receives the manipulation of the independent variable.
   a. control
   b. experimental
   c. independent
   d. dependent
   e. random

117. Trustworthy online information is most likely to be provided by all but which of the following?
   a. government agencies
   b. APA and APS
   c. scientific journals
   d. professional organizations
   e. private corporations

118. Psychology made the transition from philosophy to science with which event?
   a. William James changed the field's focus from structuralism to functionalism.
   b. Plato died and interest in the philosophical aspects of psychology died with him.
   c. G. Stanley Hall founded the American Psychological Association.
   d. Titchener brought methods of introspection to the U.S.
   e. Wundt opened his laboratory in Leipzig.

Name:______________________ Class:______________________ Date:______________

Essentials of Psychology Chapter 1

119. Who is the only African American to have served as president of the American Psychological Association?
 a. Kenneth Clark
 b. J. Henry Alston
 c. Gilbert Haven Jones
 d. Francis Sumner
 e. Richard Suinn

120. The ethical guideline requiring that information about a research study be disclosed to potential research participants before they participate is referred to as
 a. prior approval.
 b. prior consent.
 c. informed consent.
 d. ethical approval.
 e. informational disclosure.

121. Your psychology professor refers to a research study and says the results were "statistically significant." What does this mean?
 a. The results can be generalized from the sample to the population.
 b. The results have been replicated.
 c. The hypothesis proves the theory it was testing.
 d. The results were unlikely to have been due to chance or other random factors.
 e. The results do not suffer from a social desirability bias.

122. Which of the following is NOT a concern regarding animal research?
 a. justification of intended benefits of the research
 b. protection from unnecessary harm
 c. some advances in medical science depend on animal research
 d. informed consent
 e. approval from institutional review boards

123. You eavesdrop as a group of psychologists eats lunch together. After reading the first chapter in your psychology textbook, you can correctly identify which psychologist as a behaviorist?
 a. Dr. Tsui says, "I'm excited about my new research project. I'll be studying how creativity helps people solve problems."
 b. Dr. Lightman says, "I believe that early learning experiences have shaped my actions as an adult."
 c. Dr. Melfi says, "I have a client who has a lot of unresolved unconscious conflicts with his mother. I think we'll be working together a long time."
 d. Dr. Fraser says, "Looking back at my life at midlife, I recognize how my goals have given me a sense of meaning."
 e. Dr. Reeves says, "I'm delivering my favorite lecture today – the role of heredity in language development."

Essentials of Psychology Chapter 1

124. Your friend asks if there is any evidence that ADHD (Attention-Deficit Hyperactivity Disorder) might be due to abnormal brain structures. You might suggest that she take a course in
   a. cognitive psychology.
   b. physiological psychology.
   c. personality psychology.
   d. evolutionary psychology.
   e. geropsychology.

125. Regarding the major contemporary perspectives in psychology, which of the following statements is FALSE?
   a. The behavioral perspective focuses on observable actions and the influences of learning processes in behavior.
   b. The humanistic perspective emphasizes the importance of subjective conscious experience and personal responsibility and freedom.
   c. The physiological perspective examines how behavior and mental experience is shaped by biological processes and the workings of the brain and nervous system.
   d. The sociocultural perspective focuses on mental processes that allow us to gain knowledge about ourselves and the world.
   e. The psychodynamic perspective suggests that our psychology is shaped by unconscious motives and conflicts outside the range of ordinary awareness.

126. Which of the following is NOT a characteristic of critical thinking?
   a. a questioning attitude
   b. avoidance of oversimplification and overgeneralization
   c. an open mind
   d. reliance on common sense
   e. considering alternative explanations

Name:____________________ Class:________________ Date:__________

Essentials of Psychology Chapter 2

1. The brain has ______ major parts and they are called the ______.
   a. 4; frontal, parietal, occipital, and temporal lobes
   b. 2; sympathetic and parasympathetic regions
   c. 3; amygdala, hippocampus, and thalamus
   d. 3; hindbrain, midbrain, and forebrain
   e. 3; medulla, pons, and cerebellum

2. Releasing factors are secreted by the
   a. hypothalamus.
   b. hippocampus.
   c. pituitary gland.
   d. pineal gland.
   e. pancreas.

3. Associative neuron is another name for
   a. sensory neuron.
   b. motor neuron.
   c. interneuron.
   d. efferent neuron.
   e. somatic neuron.

4. In a split-brain research study, what will happen when a pencil is presented in the patient's visual field?
   a. The patient will be able to pick out the pencil from a group of objects, but not be able to say "pencil" regardless of which visual field the pencil is presented to.
   b. The patient will be able to say "pencil," but will not be able to pick out pencil from a group of objects regardless of which visual field the pencil is presented to.
   c. The patient will be able to say "pencil" when the pencil is presented to the right visual field, but not when presented to the left visual field.
   d. The patient will be able to say "pencil" when the pencil is presented to the left visual field, but not when presented to the right visual field.
   e. The patient will be able to pick out the pencil from a group of objects, but not be able to say "pencil" when the pencil is presented to the right visual field.

5. Which of these best identifies the soma's function?
   a. Sending signals to other neurons
   b. Controlling metabolic processes
   c. Producing myelin
   d. Receiving signals from other neurons
   e. Releasing neurotransmitters to other neurons

Essentials of Psychology Chapter 2

6. The fundamental building block of the nervous system is the ________.
   a. nerve
   b. brain
   c. neuron
   d. spinal cord
   e. pituitary gland

7. Regarding the human genome, which of the following statements is FALSE?
   a. Scientists have decoded the human genome.
   b. The focus today in gene research is understanding how genes work and identifying specific genes involved in various disorders.
   c. Most psychologists today agree that both heredity and environment interact to shape human behavior and mental processes.
   d. Each cell in the human body contains the full complement of human genes.
   e. Genes are composed of deoxyribonucleic acid, and they are linked together on long strands called chromosomes.

8. Which chemicals are described as both neurotransmitters and hormones?
   a. estrogen and progesterone
   b. insulin and melatonin
   c. norepinephrine and epinephrine
   d. ACTH and cortical steroids
   e. oxytocin and testosterone

9. Which brain structure is described as the connection between the two cerebral hemispheres?
   a. cerebrum
   b. basal ganglia
   c. hippocampus
   d. brain stem
   e. corpus callosum

10. Which of the following is NOT true of action potentials?
   a. They are generated according to an all-or-none principle.
   b. They all travel at the same speed.
   c. They are electrical charges that shoot down the axon.
   d. They are initiated when the axon is depolarized sufficiently.
   e. They are followed by a refractory period.

Essentials of Psychology Chapter 2

11. Regarding the frontal cortex, which of the following statements is FALSE?
    a. The frontal lobes control voluntary movements of specific parts of the body.
    b. The frontal lobes contain the motor cortex and the somatosensory cortex.
    c. The frontal lobes enable humans to suppress impulses.
    d. Of the brain lobes, the frontal lobes are the ones best described as containing "you."
    e. The frontal lobes are involved in processing emotional states.

12. Sonal is at a brain research center, participating in a study. She is hooked up to a machine that measures electrical activity in her brain through the use of electrodes attached to her scalp. This description best characterizes which of the following techniques?
    a. computed tomography
    b. electroencephalography
    c. positron emission tomography
    d. magnetic resonance imaging
    e. lesioning

13. Charlize is excessively anxious and irritable. Charlize probably has an excess of which type of hormone?
    a. thyroid
    b. melatonin
    c. ACTH
    d. insulin
    e. cortical steroids

14. All but which of the following describe the reticular formation?
    a. contains nerve pathways that connect the hindbrain with the forebrain
    b. regulates attention
    c. regulates arousal
    d. controls heartbeat
    e. screens irrelevant visual and auditory information

15. Phineas Gage showed severe personality changes following an accident that damaged his
    a. temporal cortex.
    b. hypothalamus.
    c. hippocampus.
    d. prefrontal cortex.
    e. cerebellum.

16. After a neuron fires, about how long is its refractory period?
    a. one-thousandth of a second
    b. one-hundredth of a second
    c. one-tenth of a second
    d. one second
    e. one-thousandth of a minute

Essentials of Psychology Chapter 2

17. The fatty layer of cells that is wrapped around many axons is called the
    a. myelin sheath.
    b. synaptic cover.
    c. dendritic wrap.
    d. terminal button.
    e. nerve.

18. A lesion is
    a. an electrode that is placed in the brain to stimulate neurons.
    b. an electrode that is placed in the brain to record neural activity.
    c. a portion of the brain that has been purposefully damaged.
    d. a doughnut-shaped device used to produce an image of the brain.
    e. an image generated by a PET scan.

19. Which of the following neurotransmitters prevents neurons from overly exciting adjacent nerve cells?
    a. Gamma-amniobutyric acid (GABA)
    b. Glutamate
    c. Dopamine
    d. Norepinephrine
    e. Serotonin

20. During his first three years of life, Jason has developed many motor skills like crawling, walking, and running that require his muscles to move efficiently and smoothly. In terms of brain function, Jason's motor development is the result of which process?
    a. Stripping of the nodes of Ranvier
    b. Development of the myelin sheath
    c. Depolarization
    d. Development of action potentials
    e. Regulation of hormones

21. In neural communication, ______ is to key as ______ is to lock.
    a. axon; dendrite
    b. neuron; glial cell
    c. neurotransmitter; receptor site
    d. synapse; soma
    e. action potential; resting potential

Essentials of Psychology Chapter 2

22. Which technique can best be described as using the measurement of radioactive isotopes to evaluate the activity of the brain?
    a. electroencephalography
    b. computed tomography
    c. lesioning
    d. magnetic resonance imaging
    e. positron emission tomography

23. Actor Michael J. Fox and boxing great Muhammad Ali have a disease that leads to progressive loss of their motor functioning. This condition results from a shortage of
    a. epinephrine.
    b. norepinephrine.
    c. dopamine.
    d. gamma-amniobutyric acid (GABA).
    e. serotonin.

24. Which of the following best describes a synapse?
    a. A tiny gap separating one neuron from another through which messages are carried
    b. The tubelike part of a neuron that carries messages to other neurons
    c. Rootlike structures that receive neural impulses from other neurons
    d. Body organs or structures that produce secretions
    e. A bundle of axons from different neurons that transmit nerve impulses

25. Who was a pioneer in the discovery of the language areas of the brain?
    a. Roger Sperry
    b. Michael Gazzaniga
    c. Phineas Gage
    d. Oliver Sacks
    e. Paul Broca

26. Dr. Williamson conducts research examining the effects of electrical stimulation in certain parts of the brain. Dr. Williamson has found that stimulation of this part of the brain in laboratory rats will result in changes to the rats' mating, eating, and socialization behaviors. Based on this description, which part of the brain is Dr. Williamson most likely to be studying?
    a. hypothalamus
    b. medulla
    c. pons
    d. cerebrum
    e. amygdala

Essentials of Psychology Chapter 2

27. Shelley drinks two caffeinated grande lattes every morning. In terms of neurotransmission, what is happening in Shelley's body?
    a. Caffeine in the coffee serves as an agonist that suppresses the actions of glutamate and enhances the actions of dopamine.
    b. Caffeine in the coffee serves as an agonist that suppresses the actions of dopamine.
    c. Caffeine in the coffee serves as an antagonist that enhances the actions of glutamate.
    d. Caffeine in the coffee serves as an agonist that increases the availability of glutamate.
    e. Caffeine in the coffee serves as an antagonist that suppresses the actions of dopamine.

28. Glial cells do all but which of the following?
    a. form the myelin sheath
    b. assist neurons in communicating with each other
    c. remove waste products from neurons
    d. nourish neurons
    e. produce neurotransmitters

29. Regarding the relationship between the nervous system and the endocrine system, which of the following statements is best described as FALSE?
    a. The systems are integrated, in that the brain regulates the activity of the endocrine system.
    b. Both are considered communication systems.
    c. The nervous system uses neurotransmitters as messengers, whereas the endocrine system uses hormones.
    d. The endocrine system functions at a slower pace than the nervous system.
    e. Both convey their messages through a network of nerves.

30. Two psychologists debate the nature-nurture problem. What is the topic of their debate?
    a. The relative role of the endocrine system and the central nervous system in reflexive responses
    b. The ethical concerns of using invasive experimental techniques in studying the brain
    c. The pros and cons of the sympathetic versus parasympathetic nervous systems
    d. The role of hemispheric lateralization in the development of handedness
    e. The influence of genetics versus environment in human behavior

31. Delta Epsilon fraternity sponsors a Beer Fest every October, where party-goers consume large amounts of alcohol. At the neurotransmitter level, what is happening to the party-goers?
    a. Alcohol decreases sensitivity of receptor sites for serotonin.
    b. Alcohol increases sensitivity of receptor sites for gamma-amniobutyric acid (GABA).
    c. Alcohol increases sensitivity of receptor sites for serotonin.
    d. Alcohol mimics the effects of endorphins.
    e. Alcohol decreases sensitivity of receptor sites for gamma-amniobutyric acid (GABA).

Essentials of Psychology Chapter 2

32. Which part of a neuron may range in size from a few thousandths of an inch to several feet long?
    a. axon
    b. synapse
    c. myelin
    d. soma
    e. There are no parts of a neuron that are this size.

33. In a neuron, _____ is to sending as ______ is to receiving.
    a. soma; synapse
    b. terminal button; synapse
    c. axon; dendrite
    d. terminal button; soma
    e. dendrite; axon

34. A _____ is an automatic, unlearned response to a stimulus.
    a. phenotype
    b. reticular formation
    c. nerve
    d. synapse
    e. reflex

35. The knoblike swellings at the ends of axons are called
    a. terminal buttons.
    b. synapses.
    c. soma.
    d. dendrites.
    e. nodes of Ranvier.

36. Which type of study provides the clearest way to address the nature-nurture question?
    a. twin study
    b. adoptee study
    c. split-brain study
    d. familial association study
    e. human genome study

37. Scientists use the term ______ to describe the division of functions between the right and left hemispheres of the brain.
    a. all-or-none principle
    b. plasticity
    c. split-brain
    d. handedness
    e. lateralization

Essentials of Psychology Chapter 2

38. After a motorcycle accident in which she wasn't wearing a helmet, Vanessa has difficulty responding emotionally to unpleasant stimuli. Vanessa most likely experienced damage to which brain structure?
   a. medulla
   b. amygdala
   c. thalamus
   d. hippocampus
   e. cerebellum

39. What is the job of a dendrite?
   a. to send signals to other neurons
   b. to receive signals from other neurons
   c. to synthesize neurotransmitters
   d. to control metabolic functions
   e. to generate action potentials

40. Following brain trauma, Takami has difficulty processing auditory stimuli. Based on this description, Takami probably suffered damage to which portion of her brain?
   a. frontal lobe
   b. parietal lobe
   c. temporal lobe
   d. occipital lobe
   e. somatosensory lobe

41. The majority of the cerebral cortex is made up of the
   a. frontal lobes.
   b. parietal lobes.
   c. corpus callosum.
   d. association areas.
   e. occipital lobes.

42. What is the approximate resting potential of a neuron?
   a. –50 mV
   b. –70 mV
   c. +50 mV
   d. +70 mV
   e. 0 mV

43. Regarding Parkinson's disease, which of the following statements is FALSE?
   a. Scientists believe that genetic factors are involved.
   b. It is a degenerative brain disease.
   c. Symptoms include tremors, muscle rigidity, and difficulty controlling finger and hand movements.
   d. It affects about 1.5 million Americans.
   e. It involves an excess of the neurotransmitter glutamate.

Essentials of Psychology Chapter 2

44. The two subdivisions of the autonomic nervous system are
    a. the peripheral nervous system and the central nervous system.
    b. the somatic nervous system and the peripheral nervous system.
    c. the parasympathetic and sympathetic nervous systems.
    d. the involuntary and the voluntary nervous systems.
    e. the sympathetic and the somatic nervous systems.

45. Which part of a neuron could best be described as a "docking station"?
    a. myelin sheath
    b. axon
    c. soma
    d. synapse
    e. dendrite

46. Split-brain patients are the result of an operation that severs the
    a. cerebrum.
    b. cerebellum.
    c. corpus callosum.
    d. cerebral cortex.
    e. reticular formation.

47. White matter refers to
    a. clusters of glial cells.
    b. myelinated axons.
    c. clusters of synapses.
    d. nodes of Ranvier.
    e. unmyelinated axons.

48. In the cerebral cortex, ______ is to vision as ______ is to hearing.
    a. occipital; parietal
    b. temporal; frontal
    c. frontal; parietal
    d. parietal; temporal
    e. occipital; temporal

49. The cerebral cortex accounts for approximately what percentage of the brain's total mass?
    a. 25%
    b. 40%
    c. 50%
    d. 80%
    e. 90%

Essentials of Psychology Chapter 2

50. Shalanda's daughter touches her hand. Sensory receptors in Shalanda's skin transmit information about this sensation to Shalanda's spinal cord and brain. Which type of neuron is responsible for this process?
    a. Motor
    b. Glial
    c. Associative
    d. Efferent
    e. Afferent

51. Which of the following is an antagonist that blocks the actions of a particular neurotransmitter?
    a. Amphetamines that produce states of pleasure.
    b. Caffeine that keeps the central nervous system stimulated.
    c. Antipsychotic drugs that help control hallucinations and delusional thinking.
    d. Alcohol that produces a relaxed feeling.
    e. A tranquilizer like Valium that reduces anxiety in people with panic disorder.

52. All but which of the following techniques are used for recording and/or imaging the brain?
    a. EEG
    b. lesioning
    c. MRI
    d. PET scan
    e. computed tomography scanning

53. Regarding terminal buttons, which of the following is FALSE?
    a. The terminal buttons release neurotransmitters.
    b. Terminal buttons store and release chemicals that carry neural messages to other nearby neurons.
    c. Terminal buttons are the most common type of neuron in the nervous system.
    d. Terminal buttons look like knobby swellings.
    e. The terminal buttons are found at the end of axons.

54. Regarding a neuron's soma, all but which of the following are TRUE?
    a. The soma conducts outgoing messages to other neurons.
    b. The soma is the neuron's cell body.
    c. The soma conducts life-sustaining functions of the cell.
    d. The soma contains the cell's genetic material.
    e. The soma houses the cell's nucleus.

55. Which brain structure is best described as a "relay station"?
    a. Hypothalamus
    b. Thalamus
    c. Basal ganglia
    d. Limbic system
    e. Cerebellum

Essentials of Psychology Chapter 2

56. Regarding the nervous system, which of the following statements is FALSE?
    a. Nerves are not the same as neurons and can be visible to the human eye.
    b. The nervous system has more than one type of neuron.
    c. There are more neurons than glial cells in the nervous system.
    d. A nerve is best defined as a bundle of axons from different neurons.
    e. Glial cells serve to support neurons, as well as to form the myelin sheath on axons.

57. Broca's area is located in the _______ lobe, while Wernicke's area is located in the ______ lobe.
    a. left frontal; left temporal
    b. left frontal; right frontal
    c. right frontal; left temporal
    d. right frontal; right temporal
    e. right temporal; left temporal

58. If you were to look at the structures in the forebrain, you would find that the hippocampus can be described as being shaped like a(n)
    a. pea.
    b. almond.
    c. egg.
    d. web.
    e. seahorse.

59. Of the following people, which is most likely to be relying primarily on the use of the right hemisphere?
    a. Anthony is giving a speech.
    b. Becca is reading a book.
    c. Clarita is writing a story.
    d. Dominic is performing math computations.
    e. Eduardo is listening to music.

60. Chemical messengers that transport nerve impulses from one nerve cell to another are called
    a. hormones.
    b. glials.
    c. synapses.
    d. neurotransmitters.
    e. interneurons.

61. According to research examining the relationship between genetics and shyness (Reiss et al., 2000), parents who are overprotective of a shy child
    a. may accentuate the child's shyness.
    b. may minimize the child's shyness.
    c. may see the child outgrow his/her natural shyness over time.
    d. may also have outgoing children who tend to dominate the shy child.
    e. may have relatively little influence on the child's genetically determined shyness.

Name:______________________________ Class:____________________ Date:__________

Essentials of Psychology Chapter 2

X 62. What best identifies the job of a synapse?

a. to produce neurotransmitters

b. to provide a place in which neurons can communicate with one another

c. to house the neuron's genetic material

d. to allow an attachment between the axon and the cell body

e. to release neurotransmitters

63. Which part of the brain controls balance and coordination?

a. cerebrum

b. cerebellum

c. pons

d. medulla

e. thalamus

64. Afferent neurons

a. transmit information about the outside world to the spinal cord and brain.

b. convey messages from the brain and spinal cord to the muscles of the body controlling movement.

c. convey messages to glands for the release of hormones.

d. connect neurons to other neurons.

e. are also known as motor neurons.

65. The fact that alcohol often causes problems with balance and coordination suggests that it may have an effect on the

a. cerebrum.

b. corpus callosum.

c. cerebellum.

d. thalamus.

e. reticular formation.

66. Recent research suggests that hand preference begins to develop

a. before birth.

b. during the first six months of life.

c. between ages 1 and 2.

d. between ages 3 and 4.

e. around ages 5 or 6.

X 67. Agonists do all of the following EXCEPT

a. increase the availability of neurotransmitters.

b. increase the effectiveness of neurotransmitters.

c. block reuptake of neurotransmitters.

d. mimic the action of neurotransmitters.

e. block receptor sites.

Essentials of Psychology Chapter 2

68. Besides the neuron, the other main type of cell in the nervous system is the ________ cell.
   a. glial
   b. synaptic
   c. nerve
   d. somatic
   e. myelin

69. Regarding premenstrual syndrome (PMS), which of the following statements is FALSE?
   a. About 75% of women experience some form of premenstrual syndrome.
   b. PMS involves physical as well as psychological symptoms.
   c. PMS is caused by an imbalance of hormones—too much or too little estrogen or progesterone.
   d. PMS can be influenced by sociocultural factors.
   e. Some research has linked PMS to disturbances in the functioning of serotonin.

70. Which of the following is NOT released by the adrenal glands?
   a. norepinephrine
   b. epinephrine
   c. cortical steroids
   d. adrenaline
   e. melatonin

71. Which of the following DOES NOT describe functions of the autonomic nervous system?
   a. It operates without conscious direction.
   b. It transmits messages between the central nervous system and sensory organs and muscles.
   c. It consists of the parasympathetic and sympathetic nervous systems.
   d. It regulates involuntary bodily processes.
   e. It regulates respiration.

72. Which brain structure regulates such bodily functions as thirst and hunger, fluid concentrations, and body temperature?
   a. reticular formation
   b. hippocampus
   c. thalamus
   d. medulla
   e. hypothalamus

73. Somatosensory information is processed by which lobe?
   a. occipital
   b. frontal
   c. temporal
   d. parietal
   e. reticulartal

Essentials of Psychology Chapter 2

74. Jackson had an operation in which his corpus callosum was severed. It is most likely that Jackson had which disease?
    a. Epilepsy
    b. Parkinson's disease
    c. Huntington's disease
    d. Alzheimer's disease
    e. Multiple sclerosis

75. Simon "sees stars" after being hit on the head. Based on this description, Simon's experience is the result of actions in his
    a. frontal lobe.
    b. somatosensory lobe.
    c. temporal lobe.
    d. occipital lobe.
    e. parietal lobe.

76. Approximately how thick is your cerebral cortex?
    a. one-tenth inch
    b. one-eighth inch
    c. one-quarter inch
    d. one-half inch
    e. one inch

77. The part of the nervous system that enables you to make sense of the world around you is the
    a. the autonomic nervous system.
    b. the perceptual nervous system.
    c. the sympathetic nervous system.
    d. the central nervous system.
    e. the central processing system.

78. In the autonomic nervous system, _______ is to release, as _______ is to replenish.
    a. peripheral; central
    b. sympathetic; parasympathetic
    c. spinal cord; brain
    d. central; peripheral
    e. parasympathetic; sympathetic

79. Melatonin, which is secreted by the pineal gland, plays a role in regulating
    a. glucose.
    b. releasing factors.
    c. growth hormones.
    d. coping mechanisms.
    e. sleep.

Essentials of Psychology Chapter 2

X

80. Regarding handedness, which of the following statements is FALSE?
   a. Prenatal hormones, genetics, and social factors all influence the development of handedness.
   b. Males are more likely than females to be left-handed.
   c. About 95% of fetuses suck their right thumbs.
   d. When one parent is left-handed and one parent is right-handed, the chances of their offspring being left-handed are 1 in 2.
   e. Around 5% of the population is left-handed.

X

81. Which part of the brain is best described as responsible for piecing together sensory input to form meaningful perceptions of the world?
   a. frontal lobe
   b. association areas
   c. temporal lobe
   d. parietal lobe
   e. occipital lobe

X

82. Which technique can best be described as taking snapshots of the brain in action?
   a. computed tomography
   b. electroencephalography
   c. CT scan
   d. magnetic resonance imagery
   e. functional magnetic resonance imaging

83. In contrast to agonists, antagonists are drugs that
   a. increase the availability of neurotransmitters.
   b. increase the effectiveness of neurotransmitters.
   c. block receptor sites.
   d. mimic the action of neurotransmitters.
   e. speed up the transmission of neural impulses.

84. Which parts of the forebrain are sometimes described as the "executive center" and can be likened to the central processing unit of a computer?
   a. frontal lobes
   b. temporal lobes
   c. reticulartal lobes
   d. parietal lobes
   e. occipital lobes

85. Which hormone is involved in regulating blood sugar levels?
    a. noradrenaline
    b. insulin
    c. adrenaline
    d. glucose
    e. oxytocin

86. Which gland is best described as the "master gland"?
    a. the pineal
    b. the pituitary
    c. the adrenals
    d. the thyroid
    e. the hypothalamus

87. The term lateralization refers to
    a. divisions of the brain into hindbrain, midbrain, and forebrain.
    b. the division of functions between the right and left hemispheres.
    c. the cross-wiring of the brain.
    d. the connections between Broca's area and Wernicke's area.
    e. the observation that split-brain patients have trouble naming objects that they touch but do not see.

88. When split-brain patients are shown pictures of objects presented on the left side of the visual field, they can frequently identify the object by touch, even though they cannot name the object verbally. This illustrates
    a. the importance of the right hemisphere in producing language.
    b. the importance of the left hemisphere in processing tactile stimulation.
    c. the importance of the left hemisphere in producing language.
    d. the normalcy of information processing in split-brain patients.
    e. the hemispheric divisions of the eye and brain connections.

89. The body's master control unit describes
    a. the autonomic nervous system.
    b. the somatic nervous system.
    c. the central nervous system.
    d. the sympathetic nervous systems.
    e. the central processing system.

90. Endorphins are similar in chemical structure to which drug?
    a. Cocaine
    b. Amphetamines
    c. Caffeine
    d. Alcohol
    e. Heroin

Essentials of Psychology Chapter 2

X

91. Which of the following is NOT part of the hindbrain?
   a. cerebellum
   b. reticular formation
   c. medulla
   d. pons
   e. brainstem core

92. Of the following hormones, which can we describe as most likely to be related to aggressive behavior?
   a. insulin
   b. melatonin
   c. testosterone
   d. progesterone
   e. estrogen

93. Trina has recently been having trouble staying awake throughout the day. Which area of Trina's brain is related to her difficulty?
   a. cerebellum
   b. pons
   c. medulla
   d. cerebrum
   e. hippocampus

94. The sympathetic nervous system does each of the following EXCEPT ________
   a. increase heart rate.
   b. release glucose.
   c. increase respiration.
   d. draw stored energy from bodily reserves.
   e. promote digestion.

95. Prolonged neurotransmitter activity is prevented by all of the following functions EXCEPT
   a. reuptake.
   b. release of excitatory neurotransmitters.
   c. breakdown of neurotransmitters by enzymes.
   d. regulation of sensitivity to neurotransmitters.
   e. release of neuromodulators.

96. Which of the following statements about spinal reflexes is FALSE?
   a. They are unlearned reactions.
   b. They bypass the brain.
   c. They allow very quick responses.
   d. They always involve three neurons.
   e. They are automatic.

Name:______________________ Class:______________________ Date:______________

Essentials of Psychology Chapter 2

97. In a neuron, the cell's metabolic functions are performed by the
    a. soma.
    b. axon.
    c. terminal button.
    d. synapse.
    e. dendrite.

98. Regarding the limbic system, which of the following statements is FALSE?
    a. The limbic system is located in the forebrain.
    b. The limbic system is more evolved in mammals than in lower animals.
    c. The limbic system includes the amygdala, hippocampus, and basal ganglia.
    d. The limbic system plays a role in emotional processing.
    e. The limbic system is involved in the regulation of memory.

99. In a twin study, an investigator compares concordance rates of fraternal and identical twins. A concordance rate is best described as
    a. the degree of genetic similarity between the twins.
    b. the degree of environmental similarity between the twins.
    c. the degree to which twins resemble their parents.
    d. the percentage of shared traits or disorders.
    e. the percentage of genetic overlap.

100. Which portion of the central nervous system serves as the link between the brain and the peripheral nervous system?
    a. The forebrain
    b. The lower brain
    c. The midbrain
    d. The hindbrain
    e. The spinal cord

101. Depolarization occurs when the neuron becomes
    a. less negative due to the influx of sodium ions.
    b. more negative due to the influx of sodium ions.
    c. more negative due to the influx of potassium.
    d. less negative due to the outflow of sodium ions.
    e. more negative due to the outflow of sodium ions.

102. Damage to Broca's area can lead to
    a. Alzheimer's disease.
    b. paralysis.
    c. schizophrenia.
    d. Parkinson's disease.
    e. aphasia.

Essentials of Psychology Chapter 2

103. After a car accident, Brandon lost some of his visual abilities. Based on this description of his injuries, which portion of Brandon's cerebral cortex was probably damaged in the accident?
   a. Somatosensory lobe
   b. Temporal lobe
   c. Parietal lobe
   d. Frontal lobe
   e. Occipital lobe

104. On a camping trip, Eleni accidentally steps on a hot coal from the campfire. Upon touching the coal, her foot reflexively withdraws from the coal. What is the sequence of response in Eleni's neurons?
   a. Sensory neuron – interneuron – motor neuron
   b. Sensory neuron – motor neuron – interneuron
   c. Motor neuron – interneuron – sensory neuron
   d. Motor neuron – sensory neuron – interneuron
   e. Interneuron – sensory neuron – motor neuron

105. Your anatomy professor states that today's lecture will be about the central nervous system. Which parts of the body do you expect to learn about?
   a. the brain
   b. the spinal cord
   c. the brain and spinal cord
   d. the brain, spinal cord, and all other nerves
   e. the brain, spinal cord, and the sensory organs

106. Wernicke's area is associated with _____, whereas Broca's area is associated with _____.
   a. language production; language comprehension
   b. left-handedness; right-handedness
   c. hemispheric specialization; lateralization
   d. language comprehension; language production
   e. speech aphasia; visual aphasia

107. The brain and the spinal cord make up the
   a. nervous system.
   b. somatic nervous system.
   c. peripheral nervous system.
   d. autonomic nervous system.
   e. central nervous system.

Essentials of Psychology Chapter 2

108. Twenty-three-year-old Thomas has schizophrenia. Familial association studies suggest that which of Thomas's relatives is most likely to also have schizophrenia?
   a. one of his parents
   b. one of his grandparents
   c. his sibling
   d. his dizygotic twin
   e. his monozygotic twin

109. Scientists consider the ______ to be the "seat of intelligence."
   a. somatosensory cortex
   b. corpus callosum
   c. prefrontal cortex
   d. motor cortex
   e. hippocampus

110. Which technique helps scientists understand why people cannot tickle themselves?
   a. functional MRI
   b. MRI
   c. PET scan
   d. EEG
   e. lesioning

X 111. Which of the following is the best definition of genotype?
   a. structures in a cell's nucleus that house a person's genes
   b. observable physical and behavioral characteristics
   c. a trait influenced by multiple genes interacting in complex ways
   d. basic unit of heredity that contains a person's genetic code
   e. an organism's genetic code

X 112. The resting potential of a neuron is a result of the
   a. high concentration of sodium ions outside the cell.
   b. high concentration of sodium ions inside the cell.
   c. low concentration of potassium ions outside the cell.
   d. high concentration of potassium ions inside the cell.
   e. balanced concentration of sodium ions and potassium ions inside the cell.

113. ______ are also called neural impulses.
   a. Enzymes
   b. Refractory periods
   c. Action potentials
   d. Resting potentials
   e. Neuromodulators

Essentials of Psychology Chapter 2

114. Which lobe processes information related to touch and body movement?
   a. occipital
   b. temporal
   c. parietal
   d. frontal
   e. reticulartal

115. Positron emission tomography (PET) scans work by
   a. measuring the reflection of a narrow X-ray beam as it passes through the brain.
   b. tracing the amount of glucose used in different parts of the brain.
   c. measuring the signals emitted by the brain when placed in a strong magnetic field.
   d. destroying parts of the brain to observe the effects on behavior.
   e. using mild electrical currents to observe the effects of stimulating parts of the brain.

116. Sharon is a long-distance runner. After a certain point in her workout, she begins to feel a natural "high" instead of pain. This feeling is likely the result of chemicals in her brain called
   a. stimulants.
   b. enzymes.
   c. endorphins.
   d. adrenalines.
   e. hormones.

117. Which hormone stimulates the adrenal cortex to secrete other hormones that promote muscle development?
   a. melatonin
   b. epinephrine
   c. norepinephrine
   d. ACTH
   e. progesterone

118. All of the following senses are routed through the thalamus EXCEPT
   a. touch.
   b. taste.
   c. smell.
   d. vision.
   e. hearing.

119. Which of the following situations is the type of physical functioning primarily influenced by the parasympathetic nervous system?
   a. Aaron's body releases glucose when he stands up to the bully at school.
   b. Betty meditates and visualizes positive outcomes every morning upon awakening.
   c. Chan's pupils dilate when he tells a lie to his father.
   d. Dawn's heart beats faster as she prepares to take her first psychology exam.
   e. Evan's breathing rate increases while giving a speech.

Essentials of Psychology Chapter 2

120. Regarding neurons, which of the following is NOT true?
   a. Each is a single cell.
   b. They transmit electrical impulses.
   c. They contain genetic material.
   d. They are the only cells found in the nervous system.
   e. They come in three types – motor, sensory, and interneuron.

121. Adoptee studies describe efforts to
   a. examine similarities between adopted children and non-adopted children.
   b. examine similarities between adopted children and their biological or adoptive parents.
   c. measure the genetic similarity between adopted children.
   d. assess the extent to which adopted children share similar characteristics as non-adopted children raised in the same household.
   e. examine similarities between adopted children and the general population.

122. The limbic system includes all but which of the following?
   a. amygdala
   b. hippocampus
   c. pons
   d. parts of the hypothalamus
   e. parts of the thalamus

123. Glial cells function most like which of the following?
   a. staples
   b. tape
   c. paper clips
   d. fasteners
   e. glue

124. In twin studies, the ______describes the percentages of cases in which both members of twin pairs share the same trait or disorder.
   a. genotype
   b. concordance rate
   c. phenotype
   d. polygenic trait rate
   e. plasticity percentage

Essentials of Psychology Chapter 2

X

125. The ______ is located just behind the amygdala and can be described as playing an important role in the formation of memories.
   a. hypothalamus
   b. thalamus
   c. hippocampus
   d. cerebellum
   e. pons

X

126. Regarding the organization of the brain and its function, which of the following statements is FALSE?
   a. The midbrain plays an important role in the regulation of memory and emotions.
   b. The brain is divided into three major parts.
   c. The hindbrain contains structures that control basic bodily functions like breathing.
   d. The midbrain contains nerve pathways for relaying messages between the hindbrain and forebrain.
   e. The forebrain is the largest part of the brain.

127. During the past hour, nine-month-old Heather has engaged in each of the following actions. Which action was NOT controlled by her medulla?
   a. She had an accelerated heart beat when her older brother frightened her.
   b. She coughed after breathing in some dust particles.
   c. She swallowed formula from her bottle.
   d. Wind caused her mobile to move, and she smiled.
   e. Developing allergies caused her to sneeze.

128. In the endocrine system, _____ is to the pineal gland as _____ is to the pancreas.
   a. ACTH; oxytocin
   b. melatonin; insulin
   c. epinephrine; norepinephrine
   d. melatonin; oxytocin
   e. insulin; melatonin

129. Regarding the organization of the cerebral cortex and cerebrum, which of the following statements is FALSE?
   a. The cerebral cortex is divided into four parts, with the occipital and parietal lobes in the right hemisphere and the frontal and temporal lobes in the left hemisphere.
   b. In general, each of the cerebral hemispheres controls feeling and movement on the opposite side of the body.
   c. The cerebral hemispheres are connected by the corpus callosum.
   d. The cerebrum consists of two large masses, called the left and right hemispheres.
   e. The cerebral cortex forms the thin, outer layer of the largest part of the forebrain, the cerebrum.

Essentials of Psychology Chapter 2

130. Anxiety disorders such as panic disorder may be due to reduced levels of
   a. dopamine.
   b. glutamate.
   c. serotonin.
   d. gamma-amniobutyric acid (GABA).
   e. fluoxetine.

131. In neurons, efferent is to ______ as afferent is to ______.
   a. sensory; motor
   b. motor; sensory
   c. motor; interneuron
   d. interneuron; sensory
   e. sensory; interneuron

132. A familial association study is used to determine
   a. the degree of environmental similarity between twins raised apart.
   b. the extent to which adopted children share the same characteristics as their adoptive parents.
   c. the extent to which the same disorders or traits are shared among family members.
   d. the extent to which family members have different traits or characteristics.
   e. the extent to which family members participate in shared activities.

133. Cocaine and amphetamines increase the availability of which neurotransmitter?
   a. Glutamate
   b. Serotonin
   c. Norepinephrine
   d. Dopamine
   e. Gamma-amniobutyric acid (GABA)

134. There are ______ types of neurons in the human nervous system and these are called ______.
   a. 2; axons and dendrites
   b. 2; interneurons and glial cells
   c. 3; afferent, efferent, and associative cells
   d. 3; glial cells, nerves, and myelin cells
   e. 3; nodes of Ranvier, glial cells, and myelin cells

135. Psychologists believe that irregularities in ______ transmission may help explain symptoms of schizophrenia.
   a. glutamate
   b. dopamine
   c. norepinephrine
   d. epinephrine
   e. gamma-amniobutyric acid

Name:______________________ Class:______________ Date:________

Essentials of Psychology Chapter 2

136. Damage to which portion of the cerebral cortex would most likely interfere with a person's hearing?
   a. temporal lobe
   b. occipital lobe
   c. parietal lobe
   d. frontal lobe
   e. somatosensory lobe

137. Among five sets of identical twins, how many pairs are predicted to share the same hand preference?
   a. one pair
   b. two pair
   c. three pair
   d. four pair
   e. All of the pairs will share the same hand preference.

138. Which of the following does NOT occur during the refractory period?
   a. Sodium gates close.
   b. Positively charged ions are pumped out.
   c. Electrochemical balance is restored.
   d. Neurotransmitters are pumped in.
   e. The neuron cannot fire.

139. ______ is the brain's ability to adapt and reorganize itself following trauma or surgical alteration.
   a. Aphasia
   b. Plasticity
   c. Lateralization
   d. Concordance
   e. Depolarization

140. All of the following are components of a neuron EXCEPT the
   a. soma.
   b. axon.
   c. medulla.
   d. dendrite.
   e. cell body.

141. Your heartbeat, digestion, and pupil contractions are ______ processes regulated by the ______ nervous system.
   a. involuntary; somatic
   b. involuntary; autonomic
   c. controllable; somatic
   d. voluntary; somatic
   e. voluntary; autonomic

Essentials of Psychology Chapter 2

142. Humans have _____ chromosomes.
    a. 23 pairs of
    b. 23
    c. 2
    d. 30,000 to 40,000
    e. more than 3 billion

143. What is the most common type of neuron found in your nervous system?
    a. sensory
    b. motor
    c. somatic
    d. afferent
    e. interneuron

144. Juan eats a meal full of sugar and starches. In response, his pancreas releases insulin into the bloodstream which stimulates his cells to draw more glucose from his blood. This decreases the level of glucose in Juan's body and, eventually, the pancreas reduces its insulin secretion. Juan's endocrine system is engaging in which process?
    a. plasticity
    b. homeostasis
    c. aphasia
    d. concordance
    e. lateralization

145. Fourteen-year-old Anton takes Prozac for his depression. Chemically speaking, Prozac works for Anton primarily by increasing the availability of ______ in his brain.
    a. dopamine
    b. gamma-amniobutyric acid (GABA)
    c. norepinephrine
    d. glutamate
    e. serotonin

Name:______________________ Class:______________ Date:________

Essentials of Psychology Chapter 3

1. The minimal difference between two stimuli that people can reliably detect is the
   a. absolute threshold.
   b. difference threshold.
   c. perceptual threshold.
   d. sensitivity threshold.
   e. Weber's constant.

2. ______ cells are nerve cells in the back of the eye that transmit neural impulses in response to light stimulation.
   a. Bipolar
   b. Optic
   c. Foveal
   d. Retinal
   e. Ganglion

3. Rebecca tells Tom that he is singing "off pitch." Rebecca is referring to which physical property of sound?
   a. Amplitude
   b. Frequency
   c. Loudness
   d. Speed
   e. Decibel

4. Shaun holds his finger up in front of his eyes at arm's length and focuses on the image. He slowly moves the finger toward his eyes, focusing his eyes to maintain a single image. As he does this, Shaun experiences muscular tension in his eyes. This is an example of which depth perception cue?
   a. retinal disparity
   b. shadowing
   c. convergence
   d. relative size
   e. interposition

5. The process of sensation enables us to _________, where the process of perception enables us to _________.
   a. detect the world around us; make sense of the world around us
   b. make sense of the world around us; detect the world around us
   c. form meaningful representations of sensory information; experience the rich tapestry of colors and sounds
   d. transform sensory signals into sensations; convert external stimulation into neural signals
   e. convert external stimulation into neural signals; transform sensory signals into sensations

6. Jack has the most common form of color blindness. What type of color blindness does he have?
   a. blue-green
   b. red-yellow
   c. red-green
   d. blue-yellow
   e. blue-red

7. Limiting attention to certain stimuli and filtering out other stimuli is called
   a. sensation.
   b. perception.
   c. selective attention.
   d. perceptual set.
   e. habituation.

8. People who only see in black and white are called
   a. monochromats.
   b. dichromats.
   c. trichromats.
   d. gray tones.
   e. partially color blind.

9. Tony observes an oval bowl on a table from several different perspectives. Although the image on his retina changes, he continues to perceive the bowl as oval. Tony's experience is an example of ______.
   a. brightness constancy
   b. retinal disparity
   c. size constancy
   d. linear perspective
   e. shape constancy

10. When the full moon appears near the horizon, 6-year-old Mallory says, "The moon is bigger tonight than last night." Last night, Mallory saw the moon later in the night, when it was high in the sky. Mallory's experience is an example of the
   a. apparent movement illusion.
   b. stroboscopic effect.
   c. Müller-Lyer illusion.
   d. Ponzo illusion.
   e. moon illusion.

11. ______ is the visual process by which the lens changes its shape to focus images more clearly on the retina.
   a. Convergence
   b. Retinal disparity
   c. Habituation
   d. Accommodation
   e. Closure

12. Joseph has been assisting the team doctor in his treatment of relatively minor but painful injuries for his football team. The doctor has carefully instructed Joseph to alternate between applying hot compresses and cold packs to the injured area. This treatment may be effective because both heat and cold send competing messages through the spinal cord that may temporarily block pain messages. This technique is known as
    a. meditation
    b. biofeedback
    c. distraction
    d. changing thoughts
    e. creating a bottleneck

13. Neurons that respond to specific characteristics of the visual stimulus are called
    a. photoreceptors.
    b. ganglion cells.
    c. bipolar cells.
    d. optic neurons.
    e. feature detectors.

14. High-frequency sounds cause the greatest vibration of
    a. hair cells in the middle of the basilar membrane.
    b. hair cells nearest the oval window.
    c. hair cells nearest the auditory nerve.
    d. hair cells farthest down the basilar membrane from the oval window.
    e. the membrane of the eardrum.

15. Which of the following is an example of the depth cue of relative clarity?
    a. Tall buildings appear farther away when viewed from a distance on a smoggy day compared to a fair day.
    b. The texture of sand beneath your feet is more detailed than the texture of sand 30 feet in front of you.
    c. Lines on the sides of the road appear to come together in the distance.
    d. Two buildings are known to be the same size, but the one that is closer appears larger.
    e. In a photograph, patterns of light and dark create the appearance of three-dimensional objects, even though the photo is flat.

16. In human hearing, the auditory receptors are _____ and approximately ______ are in each ear.
    a. hair cells; 15,000
    b. hair cells; 5,000
    c. follicles; 5,000
    d. follicles; 15,000
    e. hair cells; 150,000

Essentials of Psychology Chapter 3

17. Austin experiences motion sickness on his first cruise vacation. From which two senses has Austin received conflicting information?
    a. kinesthesis and visual
    b. kinesthesis and olfactory
    c. vestibular and visual
    d. vestibular and olfactory
    e. audition and olfactory

18. The study of relationships between the characteristics of external stimuli and sensations is called
    a. psychophysics.
    b. perception.
    c. parapsychology.
    d. subliminal perception.
    e. sensory adaptation.

19. Graduate student Shalanda Huffman studies how physical sources of stimulation relate to the physical experience of these stimuli. Huffman's field of study is called
    a. subliminal perception.
    b. perception.
    c. parapsychology.
    d. psychophysics.
    e. sensory adaptation.

20. When you are watching a movie, what type of apparent movement gives you the perception of a "moving picture"?
    a. retinal disparity
    b. opponent process
    c. stroboscopic
    d. linear perspective
    e. relative size

21. According to Weber's Law, a person would be most sensitive to changes in which sensation?
    a. the loudness of sounds
    b. the heaviness of weight
    c. the saltiness of food
    d. brightness of lights
    e. the pitch of sounds

Essentials of Psychology Chapter 3

22. Regarding vision, which of the following statements is FALSE?
    a. Nearsightedness and farsightedness result from abnormalities in the shape of the eye.
    b. The fovea is the part of the retina that corresponds to the center of one's gaze, and it provides the sharpest vision.
    c. The fovea contains both rods and cones.
    d. The far ends of the retina contain only rods, no cones.
    e. Bipolar cells connect photoreceptors to ganglion cells.

23. A piece of chalk placed in the shade on a sunny day reflects less light than a black hockey puck placed directly in the sunlight. Yet we perceive the chalk to be brighter than the hockey puck. We can explain this perceptual phenomenon based on the principle of
    a. brightness constancy.
    b. color constancy
    c. relative reflectance.
    d. retinal disparity.
    e. contrast effects.

24. Regarding pheromones, which of the following statements is FALSE?
    a. Evidence suggests that pheromones play a large role in influencing sexual attraction among humans.
    b. Among humans, researchers have shown that exposure to male sweat may lead women to feel more relaxed.
    c. Pheromones are found in bodily secretions, and they allow animals to mark their territories and establish dominance.
    d. Humans have receptors in the nose that may allow them to sense pheromones.
    e. Pheromones are detected through the sense of smell or taste.

25. When Harold first enters his swimming pool, the water feels uncomfortably cold. Five minutes later, it feels comfortable to Harold. This is an example of
    a. convergence.
    b. sensory adaptation.
    c. selective attention.
    d. accommodation.
    e. just-noticeable difference.

26. Weber's constant for brightness of lights is
    a. one-seventh.
    b. one-tenth.
    c. one-sixtieth.
    d. one-fiftieth.
    e. one-twentieth.

Essentials of Psychology Chapter 3

27. When you are presented with the following visual information, "A," your brain sees a series of lines and angles in a particular format and interprets this visual information as the letter "A." This is an example of which concept from perception?
    a. perceptual set
    b. bottom-up processing
    c. top-down processing
    d. selective attention
    e. habituation

28. Other factors being equal, which person is most likely to be a supertaster?
    a. Yuan, an Asian man
    b. Yuna, an Asian woman
    c. Lenny, a European-American man
    d. Betty, a European-American woman
    e. None of these; there are no racial or gender differences among supertasters

29. All but which of the following are examples of monocular cues for depth perception?
    a. interposition
    b. texture gradient
    c. shadowing
    d. linear perspective
    e. convergence

30. Salvador is a stage magician. As part of his act, Salvador identifies the written contents of a sealed envelope. This aspect of Salvador's performance is called
    a. psychokinesis.
    b. telepathy.
    c. subliminal perception.
    d. clairvoyance.
    e. precognition.

31. The study of events that cannot be explained by known psychological, physical, or biological mechanisms is referred to as
    a. precognitive psychology.
    b. clairvoyance.
    c. telepathy.
    d. parapsychology.
    e. psychophysics.

32. Which sense is especially effective at stimulating emotional memories?
    a. smell
    b. taste
    c. hearing
    d. vision
    e. touch

33. The optic nerve consists of the axons of the _____ cells and exits the eye in the _____.
    a. bipolar; fovea
    b. bipolar; blind spot
    c. ganglion; fovea
    d. ganglion; blind spot
    e. optic; blind spot

34. Which of the following describes the pupil?
    a. opening through which light enters the eye
    b. part of the eye that adjusts its shape to view objects at varying distances
    c. transparent covering at the front of the eye
    d. part of the eye that contains the photoreceptors
    e. structure responsible for peripheral vision

35. In the process of sensation, the sensory receptors
    a. make sense of external stimulation.
    b. assemble information from various sensory organs into meaningful patterns.
    c. form meaningful representations of sensory information.
    d. transform sensory signals into neural signals.
    e. interpret the meaning of sensory data.

36. Some birds must return to roost as darkness approaches. This is because their eyes contain
    a. cones, but no rods.
    b. rods, but no cones.
    c. too many cones.
    d. too many rods.
    e. more rods than cones.

37. All of the following are basic tastes EXCEPT
    a. sweet.
    b. salty.
    c. sour.
    d. savory.
    e. bitter.

38. In the study of sensory system functioning, ______ is to absolute threshold as ______ is to difference threshold.
    a. Gustav Fechner; Ernst Weber
    b. Ernst Weber; Gustav Fechner
    c. Wilhelm Wundt; Ernst Weber
    d. Max Wertheimer; Thomas Young
    e. Gustav Fechner; Wilhelm Wundt

39. Regarding cross-cultural research on visual perception, which of the following has been found?
    a. Westerners and East Asians both tend to focus more on categorization than on contextual information in their visual processing.
    b. Westerners and East Asians both tend to focus more on contextual information than on categorization in their visual processing.
    c. Westerners tend to focus more on categorization in their visual processing, whereas East Asians tend to focus more on contextual information.
    d. East Asians tend to focus more on categorization in their visual processing, whereas Westerners tend to focus more on contextual information.
    e. Both East Asians and Westerners demonstrate a pattern of balancing categorization with context in their visual processing.

40. Brenda only has one eye. Which of the following depth cues is she unable to use?
    a. relative size
    b. retinal disparity
    c. interposition
    d. texture gradient
    e. linear perspective

41. Regarding the theories of color vision, which of the following is TRUE?
    a. Trichromatic theory is supported by the behavior of cells lying between the cones and the occipital lobe of the cerebral cortex.
    b. Opponent-process theory is supported at the receptor level.
    c. Most authorities today suggest that color vision includes elements of both trichromatic and opponent-process theories.
    d. Trichromatic theory is based on Hering's work with afterimages.
    e. Helmholtz showed that three primary colors of light could be mixed in different ways to create any color.

42. When Clara interacts with her sister, Shirley, Clara's interpretations of Shirley's behavior and comments are influenced by preconceptions and expectations from their previous experiences. Which term describes this dynamic?
    a. perceptual set
    b. selective attention
    c. divided attention
    d. perceptual constancy
    e. habituation

Essentials of Psychology Chapter 3

43. Grouping disconnected pieces of information into a meaningful whole describes the Gestalt principle of
    a. similarity.
    b. closure.
    c. connectedness.
    d. proximity.
    e. continuity.

44. All of the following are true of cones EXCEPT
    a. they are responsible for peripheral vision.
    b. they provide color vision.
    c. they allow discernment of fine details in bright light.
    d. they are less sensitive to light than are rods.
    e. there are fewer cones than rods in the human eye.

45. Regarding hearing loss, which of the following is FALSE?
    a. Cochlear implants can help correct damage to the auditory nerve.
    b. Exposure to loud sounds, disease, and aging can cause nerve deafness.
    c. People with conduction deafness can sometimes benefit from hearing aids that amplify sound waves.
    d. Hearing loss in later life is not inevitable.
    e. Loud noise can impair learning ability.

46. The smallest amount of a stimulus that a person can reliably detect is called
    a. absolute threshold.
    b. difference threshold.
    c. just-noticeable difference.
    d. perceptual constancy.
    e. Weber's constant.

47. Depth cues that require the use of both eyes are called
    a. monocular cues.
    b. binocular cues.
    c. stroboscopic cues.
    d. dichromatic cues.
    e. convergence cues.

48. Which two cues are used in the perception of movement?
    a. monocular and binocular
    b. changing size and the path of the image crossing the retina
    c. relative size and relative clarity
    d. linear perspective and shadowing
    e. retinal disparity and convergence

Essentials of Psychology Chapter 3

49. Chemical senses include
    a. touch only.
    b. taste only.
    c. smell only.
    d. both touch and taste.
    e. both taste and smell.

50. Difference thresholds are determined by a constant fraction of the magnitude of the original stimulus. This is the premise of
    a. Weber's law.
    b. selective attention theory.
    c. Gestalt laws of perceptual organization.
    d. signal-detection theory.
    e. the volley principle.

51. Regarding the experience of sound, which of the following statements is FALSE?
    a. Sound waves travel slower than light waves.
    b. The amplitude of sound waves determines their perceived loudness and is measured in decibels.
    c. Humans hear by sensing sound waves that result from changes in molecular vibration.
    d. Pitch is the perception of how high or low a sound seems, which corresponds to the frequency of the sound wave's vibration.
    e. Women's voices are usually higher than men's because their vocal cords are longer and tend to vibrate more slowly than men's.

52. In a research experiment, participants are shown a series of drawings before seeing an ambiguous picture that could be perceived as a rat or a man. Group 1 sees drawings of animals, while Group 2 sees drawings of humans. Perceptual set suggests which of the following results when participants are shown the ambiguous picture?
    a. Both groups will report seeing a man.
    b. Both groups will report seeing a rat.
    c. Group 1 will report seeing a rat, while Group 2 will report seeing a man.
    d. Group 1 will report seeing a man, while Group 2 will report seeing a rat.
    e. Neither group will see a rat or a man, since the picture is ambiguous.

53. Regarding perceptual processing, which of the following statements is FALSE?
    a. The human brain is more efficient than computer systems at facial recognition.
    b. Facial recognition is an example of bottom-up processing.
    c. Top-down processing helps explain why humans can recognize handwriting of all different styles.
    d. Top-down processing is based on acquired experience and knowledge with patterns.
    e. Both top-down and bottom-up processing are ways the brain recognized meaningful patterns.

Essentials of Psychology Chapter 3

54. Dustin suffers from chronic back pain as the result of an old injury. Any time he is required to sit for long periods, he makes sure to bring a music player into the treatment room with him, because he has found that listening to his favorite music helps him cope with the pain. Dustin is using the pain control technique of
 a. creating a bottleneck at the "gate."
 b. biofeedback.
 c. obtaining accurate information.
 d. meditation.
 e. distraction.

55. The tendency to perceive properties of an object as remaining the same despite changes in its retinal image is called
 a. gestalt organization.
 b. perceptual constancy.
 c. habituation.
 d. perceptual stability.
 e. closure.

56. Humans can hear frequencies between about ______ cycles per second.
 a. 100,000 and 200,000.
 b. 50,000 and 100,000.
 c. 20,000 and 50,000
 d. 20 and 20,000
 e. 1 and 20

57. Regarding subliminal perception, which of the following statements is FALSE?
 a. People can perceive stimuli below the threshold of awareness.
 b. The effects of subliminal perception are strong.
 c. Motivational states may influence the effects of subliminal perception.
 d. Advertisers have used tactics that attempt to subliminally persuade people's opinions.
 e. The majority of Americans believe that subliminal perception exists.

58. Evelyn walks past the cafe, which is emitting odors of fresh-brewed coffee. Evelyn smells the odors, and her brain tells her she wants a cup of the delicious brew. Which of the following is responsible for carrying impulses from odor receptors in Evelyn's nose to her brain?
 a. olfactory bulb
 b. olfactory nerve
 c. taste buds
 d. pheromones
 e. vestibular organ

Essentials of Psychology Chapter 3

59. Sound from which of the following should produce the most danger to hearing upon brief exposure?
    a. a ringing telephone
    b. a jet airplane
    c. a lawn mower
    d. a jack hammer
    e. speakers at a rock concert

60. Regarding the skin senses, which of the following statements is FALSE?
    a. The skin is the body's largest sensory organ.
    b. All skin receptors respond to more than one type of stimulation.
    c. There are close to one-half million receptors for touch and pressure distributed throughout the body.
    d. The part of the cerebral cortex that processes information from the skin receptors is called the somatosensory cortex.
    e. There are specific receptors in the skin for warmth and cold.

61. Which sense monitors the position of your body in space and helps maintain balance?
    a. vestibular
    b. kinesthesis
    c. gustation
    d. audition
    e. olfaction

62. The perception of stimuli that are presented below the threshold of conscious awareness is called
    a. clairvoyance.
    b. extrasensory perception.
    c. telepathy.
    d. subliminal perception.
    e. precognition.

63. Sebastian's eyeball is shorter than normal. Light from nearby objects is focused behind his retina instead of on his retina. What condition does Sebastian have?
    a. Nearsightedness
    b. Blindness
    c. Monochromatic color blindness
    d. Red-green color blindness
    e. Farsightedness

64. In terms of where visual processing begins, ______ processing is to parts as _____ processing is to whole.
    a. bottom-up; top-down
    b. bottom-down; top-up
    c. top-down; bottom-up
    d. top-up; bottom-down
    e. up-down; bottom-top

Essentials of Psychology Chapter 3

65. A recipe requires 10 grams of salt. According to Weber's constant for saltiness, which is 1/5, how much *more* salt must a chef add to make the recipe noticeably saltier?
    a. 1/5 of a gram
    b. 2 grams
    c. 5 grams
    d. 10.5 grams
    e. 1/5 of a gram squared

66. According to the carpentered-world hypothesis, people living in cultures in which right-angled structures are rare are less prone to which visual illusion?
    a. Müller-Lyer illusion
    b. Ponzo illusion
    c. Moon illusion
    d. Impossible figures illusion
    e. Stroboscopic movement

67. The vestibular sensory system includes
    a. the semicircular canals only.
    b. the vestibular sacs only.
    c. the olfactory receptors only.
    d. both the semicircular canals and the vestibular sacs.
    e. both the olfactory receptors and the vestibular sacs.

68. Repeated exposure to the same stimulus ______ leads to _____ sensitivity in our sensory systems.
    a. always; reduced
    b. always; no change in
    c. sometimes; reduced
    d. sometimes; no change in
    e. sometimes; reduced or no change in

69. The existence of afterimages provides support for the ________ theory of color vision.
    a. trichromatic
    b. feature detection
    c. color constancy
    d. threshold detection
    e. opponent-process

Essentials of Psychology Chapter 3

70. Weber's law suggests that
    a. absolute threshold measurements underestimate true perceptual sensitivity.
    b. difference thresholds are a constant proportion of the original stimulus.
    c. difference thresholds are a constant quantity.
    d. difference thresholds decrease as stimuli increase.
    e. difference thresholds increase as stimuli decrease.

71. Jonathan practices focused attention to induce a relaxed mental and physical state to help cope with stress. This practice represents
    a. biofeedback
    b. meditation
    c. bottlenecking
    d. telepathy
    e. distraction

72. A psychologist Dr. Shonda Romblay is conducting an experiment to determine how different intensities of light affect the sensations these stimuli produce. The field of study she is exploring is called
    a. psychomotor processing.
    b. parapsychology.
    c. psychophysics.
    d. psychochemistry.
    e. psychological adaptation.

73. In the process of perception, the brain
    a. senses the presence of objects in the world.
    b. produces experiences of vision, hearing, and so on.
    c. forms meaningful impressions by piecing together sensory information.
    d. transforms sensory signals into sensations.
    e. converts external stimulation into neural signals.

74. Red, green, and blue-violet light can be combined to create any color of the spectrum. This has been interpreted as supporting
    a. the trichromatic theory of color vision.
    b. the opponent-process theory of color vision.
    c. the feature detection theory of color vision.
    d. the color constancy theory of color vision.
    e. the existence of afterimages.

75. Marlee's right eardrum was punctured in an accident when she was three years old. She is deaf in her right ear, but is helped with a hearing aid that amplifies sound waves. What type of deafness does Marlee have?
    a. nerve
    b. continuity
    c. closure
    d. subliminal
    e. conduction

76. According to a study reported in the text, about what percentage of teenagers show evidence of hearing loss?
    a. less than 10 percent
    b. about 20 percent
    c. about 33 percent
    d. about 50 percent
    e. more than 75 percent

77. Which of the following is a psychological factor that influences a person's threshold for determining a signal?
    a. The sensitivity of their visual system
    b. Their level of fatigue
    c. Their physical health
    d. The sensitivity of their auditory system
    e. Their motivational state

78. According to signal detection theory, the threshold for detecting a signal depends on
    a. the properties of the stimulus, like its intensity.
    b. the amount and type of background noise.
    c. both the properties of the stimulus and the amount and type of background noise.
    d. the biological and psychological characteristics of the perceiver.
    e. the properties of the stimulus, background noise, and biological and psychological characteristics of the perceiver.

79. Regarding subliminal perception, which of the following statements is TRUE?
    a. People can perceive stimuli below the threshold of awareness.
    b. The effects of subliminal perception are strong.
    c. Advertisers have demonstrated that subliminal cues can increase sales of some products.
    d. People can be influenced to change their behaviors by cleverly placed subliminal cues.
    e. Scientists doubt the existence of subliminal perception.

80. Receptors for kinesthesis are located in
    a. joints, ligaments, tendons, skin and muscles.
    b. the skin and hair.
    c. the inner and middle ear.
    d. the eyes.
    e. the mouth and nose.

81. Regarding vision, which of the following statements is FALSE?
    a. Objects are seen most clearly when their images are focused on the fovea.
    b. Cones, which are more sensitive to light than rods, are responsible for peripheral vision and vision in dim light.
    c. Light enters the eye through the cornea and then passes through the pupil and lens, which focuses the light on the retina.
    d. As a form of physical energy, light is the stimulus to which receptors in the eyes respond.
    e. Vision is the process by which light energy is converted into neural impulses that the brain interprets as the experience of sight.

82. Among pitch theories, place theory best explains _______ frequency sounds, frequency theory best explains ______ frequency sounds, and volley principle best explains ______ frequency sounds.
    a. mid-range; high; low
    b. high; mid-range; low
    c. high; low; mid-range
    d. low; high; mid-range
    e. low; mid-range; high

83. Mercedes just stubbed her toe on the edge of her bedpost. In response, her brain will most likely signal the release of
    a. dopamine.
    b. pheromones.
    c. endorphins.
    d. norepinephrine.
    e. serotonin.

84. Hearing loss can occur after prolonged exposure to noise as low as _____ decibels, while hearing loss can result from brief exposure to sounds as low as ______ decibels.
    a. 55; 85
    b. 65; 100
    c. 75; 115
    d. 85; 120
    e. 120; 160

85. Which of the following is the best definition of precognition?
    a. the ability to foretell the future
    b. the ability to move objects without touching them
    c. the ability to read other people's minds
    d. the perception of events not available to the senses
    e. the ability to project one's thoughts into others' minds

Name:____________________ Class:________________ Date:__________

Essentials of Psychology Chapter 3

86. Which of the following absolute thresholds for taste is correct?
   a. Detecting a gram of salt dissolved in five gallons of water
   b. Detecting a difference in tastes between two spots on the tongue, one-eighth of an inch apart
   c. Detecting one teaspoon of sugar dissolved in two gallons of water
   d. Detecting a teaspoon of vinegar mixed in with two gallons of water
   e. Detecting the sweetness of a fruit while blindfolded

87. Pain receptors are located in all but which of the following?
   a. muscles
   b. ligaments
   c. joints
   d. tooth enamel
   e. skin

88. Rico is shown the following stimulus: X. When asked what he sees, Rico reports that he sees two intersecting lines rather than saying he sees four separate lines. Rico's response demonstrates which Gestalt principle?
   a. Closure
   b. Proximity
   c. Similarity
   d. Connectedness
   e. Continuity

89. Which theory of pitch best accounts for the perception of sounds between 1,000 and 4,000 cycles per second?
   a. place theory
   b. gate-control theory
   c. frequency theory
   d. opponent-process theory
   e. volley principle

90. The role of feature detectors is to
   a. compensate for retinal disparity in nearsightedness and farsightedness.
   b. detect color stimuli.
   c. detect black and white stimuli.
   d. respond to particular features of visual stimuli.
   e. regulate the size of the pupil.

91. For the sense of taste, sense receptors are called
   a. taste cells.
   b. taste buds.
   c. gustatory nerves.
   d. taste nodes.
   e. gustatory nodes.

Essentials of Psychology Chapter 3

92. In the human eye, rods are to _____ as cones are to _____.
    a. light; color
    b. color; light
    c. retina; pupil
    d. monochromat; dichromat
    e. dichromat; monochromat

93. Various species emit chemical substances called ______ that play important roles in many behaviors.
    a. olfactory hormones
    b. pheromones
    c. neurotransmitters
    d. natural fragrances
    e. olfactions

94. Regarding the sensation of sound, which of the following statements is FALSE?
    a. The brain determines where a sound originated by comparing the sounds received in each ear.
    b. The hair cells of the ear are not actual hairs.
    c. The auditory cortex is located in the frontal lobes of the cerebral cortex.
    d. For each 10-decibel increase in a sound wave's amplitude, there is a tenfold increase in the loudness of the sound.
    e. Sounds typically reach one ear before the other, with the brain able to detect a difference as small as $1/10{,}000^{th}$ of a second.

95. Regarding color blindness, which of the following statements is FALSE?
    a. More men suffer from red-green color blindness than do women.
    b. Red-green color blindness is more common than blue-yellow color blindness.
    c. People who are monochromats can only perceive the world in shades of gray.
    d. About one in 40,000 people is completely color blind.
    e. Red-green color blindness appears to be carried on the Y chromosome.

96. Dr. Dawson's research program is concerned with how a person's experience changes as the intensity of a sound is increased. Dawson is studying
    a. psychophysics.
    b. subliminal perception.
    c. perceptual constancy.
    d. extrasensory perception.
    e. parapsychology.

97. The process by which the brain interprets stimuli and turns them into meaningful representations of the external world is
    a. sensation.
    b. perception.
    c. attention.
    d. memory.
    e. psychokinesis.

98. Sensations of hotness result from
    a. stimulation of hot receptors.
    b. stimulation of warm receptors.
    c. stimulation of cold receptors.
    d. simultaneous stimulation of warm and cold receptors.
    e. stimulation of pain receptors.

99. Marsha has learned that her tolerance for pain is increased dramatically when she focuses her awareness onto a particular word that she repeats over and over whenever she has to undergo a painful medical procedure. Marsha is using _____ to help control her experience of pain.
    a. meditation
    b. biofeedback
    c. distraction
    d. changing thoughts
    e. creating a bottleneck

100. For the sharpest vision, the image of an object should be focused on the
    a. fovea.
    b. blind spot.
    c. olfactory bulb.
    d. optic nerve.
    e. retina.

101. Hans and Franz lift weights at their local gym. When their trainer adds a two-pound weight to Hans's normal 50-pound load, Hans immediately notices. However, when the same two-pound weight is added to Franz's normal 200-pound load, he isn't aware of the extra weight. The difference in Hans's and Franz's experience is consistent with
    a. absolute threshold theory.
    b. difference threshold theory.
    c. Weber's Law.
    d. signal-detection theory.
    e. Gestalt laws of perceptual organization.

Essentials of Psychology Chapter 3

102. Regarding the scientific evidence on the existence of extrasensory perception (ESP), which of the following statements is TRUE?
    a. We have reliable evidence supporting the existence of telepathy but not clairvoyance.
    b. We have reliable evidence supporting the existence of clairvoyance but not telepathy.
    c. We have reliable evidence supporting the existence of both clairvoyance and telepathy.
    d. We lack reliable evidence supporting the existence of either clairvoyance and telepathy.
    e. We can't say because only a few studies have been conducted on the existence of ESP.

103. An object that reflects primarily long wavelength light would most stimulate which category of cone?
    a. blue-violet
    b. green
    c. red
    d. yellow
    e. black-white

104. The idea that the threshold for sensing a stimulus depends not only on the properties of the stimulus itself but on the level of background stimulation, as well as characteristics of the perceiver, is explained by
    a. Weber's Law.
    b. the volley principle.
    c. opponent-process theory.
    d. signal-detection theory.
    e. sensory adaptation.

105. In color vision, blue-violet cones are most sensitive to _____ wavelengths, red cones to ______ wavelengths, and green cones to ______ wavelengths.
    a. short; middle; long
    b. short; long; middle
    c. long; short; middle
    d. long; middle; short
    e. middle; short; long

106. Dr. Halpern tells his graduate student, Dwight, that he'll need to deliver the lecture in Halpern's psychology class today. When Halpern tells him that the lecture is on olfaction, Dwight knows he'll be talking about which sense?
    a. taste
    b. touch
    c. vision
    d. hearing
    e. smell

Essentials of Psychology Chapter 3

107. Felicia is nearly hit by a car while crossing the street. Even though it is nearly dark and the colors of the cars appear faded, she tells the police officer it was definitely a blue car. Felicia's experience is an example of ______.
   a. brightness constancy
   b. retinal disparity
   c. size constancy
   d. color constancy
   e. shape constancy

108. About what percentage of people are "supertasters"?
   a. 10%
   b. 15%
   c. 25%
   d. 35%
   e. 50%

109. The part of the eye that changes shape to adjust for an object's distance is the
   a. lens.
   b. pupil.
   c. cornea.
   d. retina.
   e. iris.

110. Regarding attention, which of the following statements is FALSE?
   a. Motivational states influence attention.
   b. Repeated exposure to a changing stimulus leads to habituation.
   c. Habituation to certain stimuli is quite common and makes evolutionary sense.
   d. Newborn infants pay more attention to their mothers' voices than to the voices of other women.
   e. Humans pay more attention to stimuli that are meaningful or emotionally significant than those that are not.

111. A foreign object has entered Kiara's eye, leaving a scratch. The part of Kiara's eye that is affected is her
   a. pupil.
   b. iris.
   c. lens.
   d. fovea.
   e. cornea.

112. Compared to fibers that carry signals about temperature and touch, pain fibers associated with dull or throbbing pain are
   a. thinner and faster.
   b. thicker and faster.
   c. thinner and slower.
   d. thicker and slower.
   e. small and reach the brain faster.

Essentials of Psychology Chapter 3

113. If you hold a round plate in your hand and turn it from side to side, the image it casts on your retina changes. Yet you still perceive the plate to be round. This phenomenon can be explained by the principle of
    a. brightness constancy.
    b. shape constancy
    c. size constancy.
    d. retinal disparity.
    e. binocular constancy.

114. Which of the following describes the Gestalt law of connectedness?
    a. A series of stimuli will be perceived as representing a unified form.
    b. Objects near each other will be perceived as belonging to a common set.
    c. Humans tend to piece together disconnected bits of information to perceive whole forms.
    d. Objects positioned together or moving together will be perceived as belonging to the same group.
    e. Objects that are similar will be perceived as belonging to the same group.

115. Regarding figure-ground perception, which of the following statements is TRUE?
    a. Figures have shape, while ground does not.
    b. In the old lady/young lady figure, people most often see the old woman.
    c. In the vase/profile figure, the vase always represents the figure.
    d. Outlines always allow us to distinguish between ground and figure.
    e. Humans tend to perceive objects as ground when they have distinctive coloring.

116. The specialized cells in sense organs that detect external stimuli are called
    a. dichromats.
    b. sensory neurons.
    c. bipolar cells.
    d. ganglion cells.
    e. sensory receptors.

117. To see a dimly lit object at night, the image must fall on your
    a. fovea.
    b. blind spot.
    c. cones.
    d. rods.
    e. optic nerve.

118. Regarding light and vision, which of the following statements is FALSE?
    a. Light is physical energy in the form of electromagnetic radiation.
    b. The visible spectrum that humans perceive represents only a small portion of the full spectrum of "light."
    c. Human vision perceives wavelengths of light between approximately 300 and 750 nanometers.
    d. X-rays, ultraviolet waves, and radio waves are portions of the electromagnetic radiation spectrum that humans cannot "see."
    e. Of the colors, red has the shortest wavelength.

119. In deafness, conduction deafness is to _____ as nerve deafness is to _____.
    a. outer ear; inner ear
    b. inner ear; outer ear
    c. middle ear; inner ear
    d. inner ear; middle ear
    e. middle ear; outer ear

120. Receptors for which of the following are located deepest in the skin?
    a. Hot
    b. Cold
    c. Pain
    d. Light touch
    e. Pressure

121. All but which of the following are part of the perceptual laws of grouping?
    a. similarity
    b. proximity
    c. closure
    d. connectedness
    e. figure-ground

122. Signal detection theory predicts all but which of the following?
    a. Arturro more often notices the aroma wafting from his neighbor's apartment after he has eaten than when he is hungry.
    b. During allergy season, Bettina's sense of smell becomes duller.
    c. When her stereo is on, Carolyn does not notice an increase in her neighbor's television volume, but, when she is reading a book, Carolyn immediately notices the increased volume.
    d. As he has gotten older, David notices that his sense of taste has diminished.
    e. Etyda walks the same route every day. Now that the days are getting shorter and part of her walk is in the dark, Etyda notices more sounds that signal possible danger.

Essentials of Psychology Chapter 3

123. Dr. Rhoden conducts animal experiments on visual perception. Rhoden wants to stop the animal's pupil from changing size, so he paralyzes the
   a. cornea.
   b. iris.
   c. lens.
   d. retina.
   e. pupil.

124. Which of the following is FALSE regarding sensory receptors?
   a. They are specialized cells.
   b. They allow us to detect difference thresholds but not absolute thresholds.
   c. They are located in sensory organs.
   d. They detect stimuli from the environment.
   e. They convert external stimuli into neural impulses used to create sensations.

125. Regarding the sense of smell, which of the following statements is FALSE?
   a. Humans have about 10 million odor receptors in the nostrils.
   b. Human odor receptors are capable of sensing about 10,000 different substances.
   c. Different substances have different shaped molecules that fit into particular odor receptors.
   d. Smell is the only sense in which sensory information does not go through the thalamus on its way to the cerebral cortex.
   e. The limbic system is involved in the processing of smells.

126. Pheromones play a role in which of the following animal behaviors?
   a. mate attraction only
   b. dominance and territorial marking only
   c. aggression only
   d. aggression, dominance, and territorial marking only
   e. aggression, dominance, territorial marking, and mate attraction

127. The process by which we receive, transform, and process stimuli is
   a. sensation.
   b. perception.
   c. telepathy.
   d. habituation.
   e. psychophysics.

128. The text discusses ______ types of perceptual constancy and they are ______.
   a. 2; bottom-up and top-down
   b. 2; figure-ground and grouping
   c. 6; relative size, interposition, relative clarity, texture gradient, linear perspective, and shadowing
   d. 4; shape, size, brightness, and color
   e. 5; proximity, continuity, closure, connectedness, and similarity

Essentials of Psychology Chapter 3

129. In human audition, the vibration of the ossicles is triggered by vibration of the _____ and transmitted directly to the _______.
    a. eardrum; oval window
    b. tympanic membrane; oval window
    c. oval window; auditory nerve
    d. eardrum; tympanic membrane
    e. auditory nerve; tympanic membrane

130. The basis of the place theory of pitch detection is that pitch is determined by the place along the _______ that vibrates the most.
    a. ear drum
    b. basilar membrane
    c. oval window
    d. auditory nerve
    e. ossicles

131. When sensory systems become less sensitive to unchanging stimuli, it is called
    a. accommodation.
    b. sensory adaptation.
    c. precognition.
    d. threshold degradation.
    e. subliminal perception.

132. Even though two lines are of equal length, the one with outward pointing wings looks longer than the one with inward pointing wings. This is an example of the
    a. Ponzo illusion.
    b. apparent movement illusion.
    c. Müller-Lyer illusion.
    d. moon illusion.
    e. impossible figures illusion.

133. Which of the following best describes the organ of Corti?
    a. an auditory receptor that transforms vibration of sound waves into neural impulses
    b. a gelatinous structure in the cochlea that contains the auditory receptors
    c. a sheet of connective tissue separating the outer ear from the middle ear
    d. a shell-shaped organ in the inner ear that contains sensory receptors for hearing
    e. a collection of tiny bones in the middle ear that vibrate in response to vibrations from the eardrum

Essentials of Psychology Chapter 3

134. Which of the following suggests that pitch detection is coded by combining frequencies of neurons firing in alternate succession?
   a. volley principle
   b. place theory
   c. opponent-process theory
   d. frequency theory
   e. gate-control theory

135. Who won the Nobel Prize for discovering that the visual cortex contains nerve cells that respond only to lines of particular orientations?
   a. Ewald Hering
   b. Thomas Young and Hermann von Helmholtz
   c. Ronald Melzack and Patrick Wall
   d. Gustav Theodor Fechner
   e. David Hubel and Torsten Wiesel

136. Psychophysics began with the work of which 19th-century German scientist(s)?
   a. David Hubel and Torsten Wiesel
   b. Hermann von Helmholtz and Ewald Hering
   c. Wilhelm Wundt
   d. Ernst Weber
   e. Gustav Fechner

137. Receptor cells for which sense regenerate within a week to 10 days?
   a. vision
   b. audition
   c. taste
   d. touch
   e. olfaction

138. People with normal color vision are described as
   a. monochromats.
   b. dichromats.
   c. trichromats.
   d. nearsighted.
   e. farsighted.

139. All but which of the following are suggested by opponent-process theory?
   a. Black-white photoreceptors are responsible for detecting differences in brightness.
   b. Continually staring at a green image will result in an afterimage of red.
   c. Continually staring at a yellow image will result in an afterimage of blue.
   d. Red-green receptors simultaneously transmit messages for red and green.
   e. Afterimages are the eye's attempt to maintain equilibrium between receptors.

Essentials of Psychology Chapter 3

140. Regarding the sense of taste, which of the following statements is FALSE?
   a. People without tongues are still able to sense taste.
   b. A food's flavor results from mixtures of basic tastes, and the food's aroma, texture, and temperature.
   c. Taste receptors differ from other neurons in that they regenerate at a faster rate.
   d. Genetic factors play a role in taste sensitivity, but not in taste preferences.
   e. Cats are unable to taste "sweet," whereas pigs are able to do so.

141. The ratio of rods to cones is approximately
   a. 10 to 1.
   b. 1 to 10.
   c. 20 to 1.
   d. 1 to 20.
   e. 1 to 1.

142. In vision, the photoreceptors are called
   a. retina, lens, and pupil.
   b. olfactory bulbs.
   c. semicircular canals and vestibular sacs.
   d. pheromones.
   e. rods and cones.

143. Other factors being equal, which sensory stimulus is least likely to lead to sensory adaptation?
   a. the wail of a loud car alarm
   b. the pressure of wearing a new ring on one's finger
   c. the intense odors of a cattle farm
   d. the pressure of wearing a new bracelet on one's wrist
   e. the temperature of water when entering a pool

144. Dr. Barrington is a cross-cultural researcher in the field of perception. She tests two groups of people to determine their susceptibility to the Müller-Lyer illusion. Group 1 consists of Americans, while Group 2 consists of members of the African tribe of Zulus. Generalizing from previous research, what will Barrington find?
   a. Neither group will be susceptible to the illusion.
   b. Both groups will be equally susceptible to the illusion.
   c. The Americans will be more susceptible to the illusion than the Zulus.
   d. The Zulus will be more susceptible to the illusion than the Americans.
   e. Zulus who have moved to American cities will develop less susceptibility to the illusion.

Essentials of Psychology Chapter 3

145. Regarding acupuncture, which of the following statements is FALSE?
    a. Traditional Chinese beliefs suggest that acupuncture releases the body's natural healing energy.
    b. Scientific evidence has ruled out that acupuncture is merely a placebo effect.
    c. Some studies have demonstrated that acupuncture can be effective in reducing chronic lower back pain.
    d. Acupuncture may work through the release of neurotransmitters with pain-killing effects, caused by the stimulation of acupuncture points.
    e. Acupuncture involves the insertion and rotation of thin needles at certain points on the body.

Name:______________________________Class:____________________Date:__________

Essentials of Psychology Chapter 4

2. Scientists believe that narcolepsy is caused by
   a. an overactive thyroid gland.
   b. loss of brain cells in the hypothalamus.
   c. an underactive thyroid gland.
   d. loss of brain cells in the reticular system.
   e. substance abuse.

10. Other factors being equal, which of the following people should be hardest to awaken?
    a. Mary Esther is in Stage 1 of sleep.
    b. Sarah is in Stage 2 of sleep.
    c. Randy is in Stage 3 of sleep.
    d. Ed has just fallen asleep.
    e. None of these; there are no differences in the ability to awaken in the different stages of sleep.

11. Regarding sleepwalking disorder, which of the following statements is FALSE?
    a. Sleepwalking disorder occurs more often in children than in adults, and about 1 to 5 percent of children have the disorder.
    b. Sleepwalking generally occurs during deep, NREM sleep.
    c. Awakening a sleepwalker can be harmful.
    d. Sleepwalkers do not usually remember their nighttime wanderings.
    e. Sleepwalkers can have accidents during their nighttime wanderings.

12. Christiana alters her consciousness through focusing her attention on her breathing to achieve a peaceful, relaxed state. During this state, Christiana attempts to adopt a nonjudgmental state in which she has awareness of the moment. Which technique best describes what Christiana is doing?
    a. Hypnosis
    b. Transcendental meditation
    c. Mindfulness meditation
    d. Daydreaming
    e. Biofeedback

15. Regarding sleep cycles, which of the following statements is FALSE?
    a. In terms of brain activity, REM sleep is similar to ordinary wakefulness.
    b. As the night progresses, the amount of time spent in REM sleep decreases.
    c. The difference between Stage 3 and Stage 4 sleep is based on the proportion of delta waves present.
    d. During sleep, brain waves vary in terms of intensity as well as speed.
    e. During the night, Stage 4 sleep eventually disappears.

Essentials of Psychology Chapter 4

16. All of the following can help a person develop healthier sleeping patterns EXCEPT
    a. maintaining a regular sleep schedule.
    b. taking naps to make up for lost sleep the preceding night.
    c. exercising regularly.
    d. limiting intake of caffeine.
    e. establishing a regular bedtime routine.

17. Which of the following people is experiencing a state of drifting consciousness?
    a. Chandler is in the dreaming state of sleep.
    b. Phoebe is engrossed in watching a movie.
    c. Joey's consciousness changes as he meditates.
    d. Rachel is having hallucinations from taking drugs.
    e. Ross is daydreaming while he waits to see the dentist.

18. Sleep cycles repeat about every_______minutes, and the typical adult has_______cycles per night.
    a. 60; six to seven
    b. 60; three to four
    c. 90; four to five
    d. 120; two to three
    e. 90; two to three

19. To combat insomnia, all but which of the following are recommended in the text?
    a. Before going to bed, write down any reminders, concerns, or other things that are on your mind.
    b. Picture relaxing scenes in your mind as you go to sleep.
    c. Avoid any activities in bed besides sleeping.
    d. Establish a regular exercise program 1-2 hours before going to bed.
    e. Get out of bed if you have not fallen asleep within 20 minutes.

21. Some nights Chang has problems falling asleep. Other nights, he wakes up several times during the night and has difficulty returning to sleep. Chang likely suffers from which sleep disorder?
    a. insomnia
    b. nightmare disorder
    c. narcolepsy
    d. sleepwalking
    e. sleep apnea

22. Compared to dreams during REM, NREM dreams are
    a. longer.
    b. more frequent.
    c. more thoughtlike.
    d. paradoxical.
    e. both longer and more frequent.

Essentials of Psychology Chapter 4

26. What is the most common sleep disorder?
    a. sleep terror disorder
    b. narcolepsy
    c. sleepwalking disorder
    d. insomnia
    e. sleep apnea

33. In general, nightmare disorder occurs in________sleep, while sleep terror disorder occurs in________sleep.
    a. Stage 1; Stage 2
    b. REM; Stage 2
    c. REM; Stage 4
    d. Stage 2; Stage 3 or 4
    e. Stage 2; REM

35. Regarding sleep deprivation, which of the following statements is TRUE?
    a. Sleep deprivation is relatively uncommon.
    b. Sleep deprivation tends to affect older adults but not young adults of college age.
    c. People are generally not able to "rebound" from REM deprivation.
    d. Loss of sleep impairs reaction times.
    e. Even brief periods of sleep deprivation can increase the risk of developing high blood pressure.

36. During the past hour, Gaylon has been experiencing slow-wave sleep. Based on this description, which stages of sleep has Gaylon likely experienced during this time?
    a. Stages 1 and 2
    b. Stages 4 and REM
    c. Stages 3 and 4
    d. Stages 2 and 3
    e. REM and NREM

37. After repeatedly using a drug over six months, Elian's body chemistry has changed such that it depends on having a steady supply of the drug. Elian has developed
    a. tolerance.
    b. psychological dependence.
    c. physiological dependence.
    d. reverse tolerance.
    e. detoxification.

38. In terms of brain waves, awake and alert is to________as awake and relaxed is to________.
    a. alpha; beta
    b. beta; alpha
    c. delta; alpha
    d. delta; beta
    e. beta; delta

Essentials of Psychology Chapter 4

41. According to the activation-synthesis hypothesis of dreaming, random electrical activity in the_________is interpreted by the_________to create a story line.
    a. brain stem; cerebral cortex
    b. cerebral cortex; brain stem
    c. hippocampus; hypothalamus
    d. hypothalamus; hippocampus
    e. brain stem; thalamus

44. The protective function of sleep refers to the role of sleep in
    a. protecting the organism against disease.
    b. protecting the animal from nighttime predators.
    c. preventing depletion of bodily resources.
    d. preventing the animal from injuring others.
    e. protecting the environment.

54. Regarding circadian rhythms, which of the following statements is FALSE?
    a. Frequent time shifting can wreak havoc on circadian rhythms.
    b. During exposure to light, melatonin production increases, helping us maintain wakefulness.
    c. Light entering through the eye helps keep the body clock in sync with day and night.
    d. Body temperature follows a circadian rhythm in which temperature falls a few degrees during the middle of the night.
    e. Circadian rhythms are found in almost all species, including paramecia and trees.

59. An area of the brain that regulates sleep-wake cycles is the
    a. suprachiasmatic nucleus.
    b. amygdala.
    c. pituitary gland.
    d. hippocampus.
    e. corpus callosum.

62. Beta brain waves are_______, and alpha brain waves are_______.
    a. fast and low-amplitude; slow and rhythmic
    b. slow and low-amplitude; fast and rhythmic
    c. fast and high-amplitude; slow and rhythmic
    d. slow and high-amplitude; fast and rhythmic
    e. large and rhythmic; slow and rhythmic

78. Kendra has a sleep disorder in which she suddenly falls into "sleep attacks" during the daytime. What is the name of Kendra's disorder?
    a. REM sleep disorder
    b. Sleep apnea
    c. Sleep terror disorder
    d. Nightmare disorder
    e. Narcolepsy

Essentials of Psychology Chapter 4

87. Jet lag has shown to be associated with all but which of the following?
    a. disruptions to the sleep-wake cycle
    b. irritability
    c. fatigue
    d. difficulties in concentration
    e. decreases in daydreaming

89. Who suggested that dreams help us sort through possible solutions to everyday problems and concerns?
    a. Ernest Hartmann
    b. Publilius Syrus
    c. Sigmund Freud
    d. William James
    e. Alan Rechtschaffen

92. In which stage do you spend the majority of your sleep time?
    a. Stage 1
    b. Stage 2
    c. Stage 3
    d. Stage 4
    e. REM

103. All but which of the following are reasons that investigators have described for the functions of sleep?
    a. Protection and survival
    b. Energy conservation
    c. Consolidation of newly formed memories
    d. Restoration of bodily processes
    e. Enhancement of ability to alter consciousness

105. Regarding daydreaming, which of the following statements is FALSE?
    a. The majority of daydreams have sexual themes.
    b. People are more prone to daydream when they are bored.
    c. People are more prone to daydream when they are engaged in unstructured activities.
    d. Most daydreams involve the mundane tasks of everyday life.
    e. Daydreaming is a form of consciousness that occurs during a waking state.

116. Dr. Washington, a sleep researcher, looks at the EEG output of a participant from a sleep study. When Washington sees sleep spindles on the output, she indicates________on the paper.
    a. Stage 1
    b. Stage 2
    c. Stage 3
    d. Stage 4
    e. REM

Essentials of Psychology Chapter 4

117. In Freudian theory, the actual events that occur in a dream are referred to as its_______content, while the underlying meaning of a dream is its_______content.
   a. unconscious; conscious
   b. latent; manifest
   c. conscious; subconscious
   d. conscious; sexual
   e. manifest; latent

118. Monica is having a long, detailed dream. In which stage of sleep is Monica most likely to be?
   a. Stage 1
   b. Stage 2
   c. Stage 3
   d. Stage 4
   e. REM

120. Kelsey has a sleep disorder in which she suddenly wakes up in the night with a panicky scream. She is only able to remember fragments of her dream images, and she is dazed and frightened upon awakening. Which sleep disorder does Kelsey most likely have?
   a. Sleepwalking disorder
   b. Nightmare disorder
   c. Narcolepsy
   d. Sleep apnea
   e. Sleep terror disorder

132. Which of the following best describes sleep apnea?
   a. Repeated episodes of intense fear during sleep causing sudden awakening in a terrified state
   b. Sudden unexplained sleep attacks during the day
   c. Difficulty falling asleep, remaining asleep, or returning to sleep
   d. A state of dreaming in which the dreamer is aware that s/he is dreaming
   e. Temporary cessation of breathing during sleep

135. From a Freudian perspective, the purpose of dreams is to
   a. consolidate memories and new learning.
   b. sort through possible solutions to everyday problems.
   c. fulfill underlying wishes.
   d. discard unnecessary information.
   e. reconcile urges.

Essentials of Psychology Chapter 4

136. Which statement best describes effective treatment of sleep disorders?
    a. Sleep medications are the most effective short- and long-term treatment for sleep disorders.
    b. Sleep medications can be used for long periods of time to treat severe sleep disorders.
    c. Cognitive-behavioral techniques are as effective as sleep medication in treating insomnia in the short term, but not in the long run.
    d. Cognitive-behavioral techniques are as effective as sleep medication in treating insomnia, and they are more effective in the long run.
    e. Unknown; researchers have yet to investigate and identify the best methods for treating sleep disorders.

138. Regarding REM sleep, which of the following statements is FALSE?
    a. REM sleep is also called active sleep because the brain is more active during REM than NREM.
    b. During REM sleep, muscle activity is blocked almost to the point of paralysis.
    c. REM sleep is also called paradoxical sleep.
    d. All dreams occur during REM sleep.
    e. During REM sleep, a person's eyes dart about under the closed eyelids.

139. Winston is an eight-year-old child who has recently started having sleep problems. He frequently wakes at night, sitting up in his bed and screaming loudly. His mother reports that he seems dazed, or "out of it," and can rarely remember more than one or two fragmentary dream images that don't seem to make sense. Winston probably is suffering from______.
    a. narcolepsy
    b. sleep apnea
    c. nightmare disorder
    d. sleep terror disorder
    e. sleepwalking disorder

Name:______________________________ Class:____________________ Date:____________

Essentials of Psychology Chapter 5

1. Which of the following is the best definition of reinforcer?
   a. a response that operates on the environment to produce certain consequences
   b. a stimulus or event that increases the probability that the response it follows will be repeated
   c. behavior acquired through coincidental association of a response and a reinforcement
   d. a cue that signals that reinforcement is available if the subject makes a particular response
   e. the introduction of an aversive stimulus after a response occurs

2. Under which condition would Watson's experiments on classical conditioning be replicated today?
   a. If the researchers obtained parental permission to expose the child to intense fear
   b. If the researchers used methods to extinguish the fears after completing their experiments
   c. If the researchers followed the children for several years to make sure they were not "damaged" from their participation in the experiment
   d. If the researchers taught parents how to extinguish their children's fears
   e. The experiments would not be replicated even with the parents' permission

3. Rosa has learned to bring an umbrella with her on overcast days, explaining "I don't want to get wet if it rains." We can explain her behavior as a form of
   a. superstitious behavior.
   b. escape learning.
   c. latent learning.
   d. avoidance learning.
   e. observational learning.

4. The rats in Dr. Rexington's learning laboratory are on an "FR-7" schedule of reinforcement. What does this mean?
   a. The rats will receive a food pellet after every seventh bar press.
   b. The rats will receive a food pellet after an average of every seven bar presses.
   c. The rats will receive a food pellet every seven minutes.
   d. The rats will receive a food pellet an average of every seven minutes.
   e. The rats will receive a food pellet every seven minutes, unless they press the bar seven times in a shorter period of time.

5. Which of the following is demonstrating extinction of an operant response?
   a. Ginny, who learns to dress herself when her mother reinforces her for accomplishing each small step in the process
   b. Ron, who receives praise every time he puts his schoolbooks away
   c. Hermione, who eventually stops raising her hand when Professor Snape fails to call on her
   d. Harry, who learns secret routes that provide an escape from the Dark Forest when he is under attack
   e. Malfoy, who leaves school two days early at Christmas break to avoid the rush of holiday traffic

Name:____________________ Class:________________ Date:________

Essentials of Psychology Chapter 5

6. Each of the following describes a form of cognitive learning EXCEPT
   a. observational learning.
   b. insight learning.
   c. operant conditioning.
   d. latent learning.
   e. vicarious learning.

7. Increasing the number of pairings of the US and CS will
   a. weaken the CR.
   b. strengthen the CR.
   c. weaken the CR at first, and then strengthen it.
   d. strengthen the CR at first, and then weaken it.
   e. have no effect on the CR.

8. Chris has been experiencing a number of problems on the job. In order to get away from his problems for a while, Chris regularly drinks heavily in the evening, after work. We can explain this behavior as a form of
   a. escape learning.
   b. avoidance learning.
   c. positive reinforcement.
   d. negative reinforcement.
   e. punishment.

9. Graduate student Charisse Goldberg conducted operant conditioning trials with a laboratory rat. Goldberg trained the animal to press a lever to earn a food pellet. The rat successfully learned to press the lever. In the language of operant conditioning, what is the animal's learned response called?
   a. a higher-order conditioned response
   b. a vicariously learned response
   c. a reconditioned response
   d. a latent response
   e. an operant response

10. Regarding punishment, which of the following statements is FALSE?
   a. Psychologists and pediatricians encourage parents not to rely on punishment as a primary means of discipline.
   b. Punishment can involve the presentation of an unpleasant stimulus.
   c. Punishment can involve the removal of a reinforcing stimulus.
   d. Punishment can be considered the flip side of reinforcement.
   e. Negative reinforcement is the technical term for punishment.

Essentials of Psychology Chapter 5

11. Regarding Rescorla's views on classical conditioning, which of the following statements is FALSE?
    a. Rescorla believes that classical conditioning depends on how reliably the CS serves as a signal for indicating the occurrence of the US.
    b. Rescorla believes that classical conditioning is the result of repeated pairings of NS and US.
    c. Rescorla's perspective on classical conditioning can be described as cognitive.
    d. Rescorla suggests that the more reliably the CS signals the occurrence of the US, the stronger the conditioned response.
    e. Rescorla believed that classical conditioning has important survival implications for animals.

12. Regarding classical conditioning, which of the following statements is FALSE?
    a. Immune system responses can be classically conditioned.
    b. Drug cravings and taste aversions can be acquired through classical conditioning.
    c. Feelings of nostalgia can be elicited by stimuli that were associated with pleasant experiences in the past.
    d. Taste aversions can be acquired with a single pairing of a food or drink and a nausea-inducing stimulus.
    e. While classical conditioning is effective in creating phobias, its principles are not particularly useful in therapy to address phobias.

13. Which of the following best describes charted data for a variable interval schedule of reinforcement?
    a. slight dip in responses after reinforcement
    b. slow, steady rate of response
    c. responses decrease after an initial steep increase
    d. fast, steady rates of response
    e. responses pause after each reinforcement

14. Modern psychologists refer to the first part of the Law of Effect as _____ and the second part as _____.
    a. classical conditioning; operant conditioning
    b. operant conditioning; classical conditioning
    c. reinforcement; punishment
    d. punishment; reinforcement
    e. trial and error; latent learning

15. ______ is a process by which two people in a relationship list the behaviors of the other that they would like changed, and then they agree to reinforce each other for making the changes.
    a. Behavioral management
    b. Method of successive approximations
    c. Reinforcement scheduling
    d. Cognitive mapping
    e. Contingency contracting

Essentials of Psychology Chapter 5

16. While changing her tire, Marguerite bumped the hubcap and all of the lug nuts fell into a storm sewer. After fretting for several minutes, she suddenly realized she could remove one lug nut from each of the other three tires to temporarily mount the spare until she could get to a service station. This is an example of
    a. superstitious behavior.
    b. insight learning.
    c. spontaneous recovery.
    d. shaping.
    e. latent learning.

17. When Salina was a young girl, a dog viciously attacked her as she was walking along a white picket fence. Since then, she displays intense fear of white picket fences. Salina is demonstrating
    a. a discriminative stimulus.
    b. superstitious behavior.
    c. stimulus discrimination.
    d. a phobia.
    e. spontaneous recovery.

18. Researchers have been able to successfully condition immune system suppression by linking neutral stimuli with a(n)
    a. electrical shock.
    b. drug that induces nausea.
    c. immune-suppressant drug.
    d. previously conditioned response.
    e. immune-suppressant drug and electrical shock.

19. Pavlov found that the strength of a conditioned response increased with the number of pairings of the
    a. CR and UR.
    b. CS and US.
    c. CS and CR.
    d. CS and UR.
    e. CR and US.

20. Karen agrees to replace the toilet paper when it runs out if her roommate, Susan, will wash her dirty dishes every evening after dinner. This is an example of
    a. latent learning.
    b. escape learning.
    c. applying reinforcement.
    d. giving praise.
    e. contingency contracting.

Essentials of Psychology Chapter 5

21. Mentally working through a problem until the sudden realization of the solution occurs is referred to as
    a. observational learning.
    b. trial-and-error learning.
    c. information processing.
    d. insight learning.
    e. latent learning.

22. Based on research presented in the text, which of the following is the best recommendation for disciplining children?
    a. Rely mostly on reinforcement.
    b. Avoid reinforcement; rely mostly on punishment to achieve faster effects.
    c. Use only punishment.
    d. Use only reinforcement.
    e. Try to balance the use of reinforcement and punishment.

23. Marcel sat at a cafe eating the best croissant he had ever tasted. He begins frequenting the café to order the croissants. He hardly notices the jingling of the cash register just before the clerk hands him the croissant. Now every time he hears the same kind of jingling from another cash register, his mouth waters. Marcel's learning is an example of
    a. operant conditioning.
    b. latent learning.
    c. conditioned taste aversion.
    d. classical conditioning.
    e. observational learning.

24. A discriminative stimulus signals that
    a. reinforcement is available for a particular response.
    b. an unconditioned stimulus is about to be presented.
    c. a conditioned stimulus is about to be presented.
    d. a neutral stimulus is about to be presented.
    e. an approximately correct response will receive reinforcement.

25. Regarding characteristics that influence conditioned responses, which of the following statements is FALSE?
    a. In general, the more often the CS is paired with the US, the stronger the CR.
    b. In general, the more often the CS is paired with the US, the more reliable the CR.
    c. The strongest conditioned responses occur when the CS is presented first and remains present throughout the administration of the US.
    d. A stronger US will typically lead to faster conditioning than a weaker one.
    e. A single pairing of the CS and US cannot result in classical conditioning.

Essentials of Psychology Chapter 5

26. Rico attends technical college where he is using technology to study for the GED. His computer guides Rico through an inventory of increasingly more challenging questions. If he answers correctly, the questions increase in challenge; if he answers incorrectly, the questions decrease in difficulty. Rico is using which application of operant conditioning?
   a. the Skinner box
   b. behavior modification
   c. token economy
   d. biofeedback
   e. programmed instruction

27. Stimulus generalization occurs when
   a. the conditioned response reappears after extinction.
   b. the conditioned response is displayed following exposure to stimuli that resemble the conditioned stimulus.
   c. the conditioned response is not displayed following presentation of the conditioned stimulus.
   d. the conditioned stimulus elicits responses that are generally like the conditioned response.
   e. the conditioned stimulus generalizes to other settings.

28. Who is most closely associated with classical conditioning?
   a. E.L. Thorndike
   b. Ivan Pavlov
   c. John Garcia
   d. B.F. Skinner
   e. Robert Rescorla

29. Ivan Pavlov's initial research work was in the study of
   a. learning by association with rabbits.
   b. latent learning with rats.
   c. observational learning with children.
   d. digestive processes in dogs.
   e. conditioning of pigeons.

30. To achieve classical conditioning, you should pair
   a. a neutral stimulus with an unconditioned stimulus.
   b. a conditioned stimulus with an unconditioned stimulus.
   c. a neutral stimulus with a conditioned response.
   d. a conditioned stimulus with a conditioned response.
   e. an unconditioned stimulus with a conditioned response.

Name:______________________________ Class:____________________ Date:__________

Essentials of Psychology Chapter 5

31. Researchers use the method of successive approximations in the process of
    a. insight learning.
    b. higher-order conditioning.
    c. conditioning taste aversions.
    d. shaping.
    e. extinction.

32. Presentation of a rewarding stimulus serves as ______, while removal of an aversive stimulus serves as ______.
    a. positive punishment; negative punishment
    b. negative punishment; positive punishment
    c. negative reinforcement; positive reinforcement
    d. positive reinforcement; negative reinforcement
    e. reinforcement; punishment

33. Velma takes headache medicine to relieve pain. The medicine serves to remove the pain. This is an example of
    a. avoidance conditioning.
    b. conditioned reinforcement.
    c. positive reinforcement.
    d. negative reinforcement.
    e. superstitious behavior.

34. Skinner found that coincidental association of a behavior and a reinforcement may result in
    a. extinction.
    b. superstitious behavior.
    c. stimulus discrimination.
    d. taste aversions.
    e. the development of phobias.

35. Of the following parents giving praise to their child, which is using the most effective strategy?
    a. Abdul tells his daughter, "You're a good girl" when she is polite to the neighbor.
    b. Barney tells his son, "I'm so proud of how well you prepared for your biology test."
    c. Cornelius uses the phrase, "You did a wonderful job" every time he praises his daughter.
    d. Darnell says to his son, "I'm proud of how you played tennis, but maybe next time you'll get more points."
    e. Ed, who after his daughter shows him her artwork, avoids making eye contact but says, "That's a great job you did."

36. Psychologist Albert Bandura believes that children learn aggression through
    a. classical conditioning.
    b. insight learning.
    c. observing and imitating models.
    d. latent learning.
    e. none of these; Bandura believes that aggression is an inborn quality.

37. Thorndike used the ______ in studying animal learning.
    a. Skinner box
    b. token economy
    c. programmed instruction computer
    d. maze
    e. puzzle box

38. What is Rosalie Rayner's role in the history of psychology?
    a. She was a student assistant who helped Pavlov with his experiments on classical conditioning in animals.
    b. She was a colleague who helped Skinner with his experiments on operant conditioning in animals.
    c. She developed a cognitive theory of classical conditioning.
    d. She created the puzzle box used by Edward Thorndike.
    e. She was a student assistant who helped Watson with his experiments on classical conditioning in humans.

39. Which of the following is not one of the processes involved in cognitive learning?
    a. thinking
    b. problem solving
    c. mental imaging
    d. information processing
    e. affective monitoring

40. Learning that occurs without apparent reinforcement and is not revealed in performance when it occurs is referred to as
    a. insight learning.
    b. classical conditioning.
    c. spontaneous recovery.
    d. latent learning.
    e. shaping.

41. The most surprising element in Garcia's research on taste aversion was that
    a. animals were sickened by radiation.
    b. animals would avoid drinking water.
    c. animals would drink even if they were sick.
    d. conditioned taste aversion could be developed even when the CS occurred several hours before the US.
    e. conditioned taste aversion could be developed only when the US immediately followed the CS.

42. When two-year-old Clarice was playing in the basement, a large burst of thunder scared her at the same time she saw a spider. Now Clarice has a spider phobia. Clarice's experience is an example of which type of learning?
    a. Operant conditioning
    b. Observational learning
    c. Vicarious learning
    d. Insight learning
    e. Classical conditioning

Name:______________________ Class:______________ Date:________

Essentials of Psychology Chapter 5

43. Amita was just grounded by her parents. She is not allowed to use her computer or cell phone, or watch television. Which method of punishment are Amita's parents using?
    a. token economy
    b. removal of a reinforcer
    c. verbal reprimand
    d. time-out
    e. removal of a negative reinforce

44. In this type of schedule of reinforcement, a person receives reinforcement for different time periods, and the time periods are not always the same.
    a. fixed-interval
    b. variable-interval
    c. variable-ratio
    d. fixed-ratio
    e. continuous

45. Following his experience in the military, Hans developed a classically conditioned fear response to radio static. After he left the military, the response extinguished. However, after not hearing radio static for several months, Hans again shows the conditioned fear response. Hans's experience is best described by
    a. stimulus generalization.
    b. stimulus discrimination.
    c. reconditioning.
    d. spontaneous recovery.
    e. shaping.

46. An acquired fear response is called
    a. a conditioned emotional reaction.
    b. a reconditioned phobia.
    c. a higher-order conditioned response.
    d. a discriminative response.
    e. a form of superstitious behavior.

47. ______ is the systematic application of operant conditioning to strengthen adaptive behavior and weaken maladaptive behavior.
    a. Biofeedback
    b. Behavior modification
    c. Token economy
    d. Shaping
    e. Programmed instruction

Essentials of Psychology Chapter 5

48. Vlad receives $100 for every ten telemarketing calls he makes. This is an example of a ______ schedule of reinforcement.
    a. fixed ratio
    b. variable ratio
    c. fixed interval
    d. variable interval
    e. 100/10

49. Which of the following is an example of negative reinforcement?
    a. A mother picks up her infant when he cries, which then stops his crying, thereby reducing the mother's level of annoyance.
    b. A father picks up his infant when she cries, thereby increasing the likelihood that she will cry to be picked up again in the future.
    c. A grandmother gives her granddaughter a "time out" when she misbehaves, thereby leading the granddaughter to calm down.
    d. A grandfather gives his grandson $10 for every "A" on his report card, thereby strengthening his grandson's study habits.
    e. A caregiver removes a child from the "block play center" when he is throwing blocks, thereby causing him to cry.

50. A researcher finds that rats avoid drinking from bottles in a room in which they had received exposure to radiation that subsequently made them ill. This demonstrates
    a. stimulus discrimination.
    b. stimulus generalization.
    c. conditioned taste aversion.
    d. fixed interval schedule of reinforcement.
    e. behavior therapy.

51. All but which of the following are examples of the application of principles of operant conditioning?
    a. biofeedback training
    b. behavioral modification
    c. conditioned immune system responses
    d. programmed instruction
    e. token economies

52. In Watson's research with Little Albert, the rat began as the _____ and became the _____.
    a. CR; CS
    b. UR; US
    c. NS; CS
    d. NS; CR
    e. CS; NS

Essentials of Psychology Chapter 5

53. Stimuli that are naturally reinforcing are referred to as ______, while stimuli that develop reinforcing properties through association are called ______.
    a. indiscriminative stimuli; discriminative stimuli
    b. primary reinforcers; secondary reinforcers
    c. positive reinforcers; negative reinforcers
    d. primary stimuli; secondary stimuli
    e. shapers; successive approximators

54. Shawn does extremely well on his spelling test in school. His father praises Shawn for this test score and tells him how smart he is, but he should be able to learn the next list of words even faster. Where giving praise is concerned, Shawn's Dad needs to know about the principle of
    a. "Be specific."
    b. "Connect by making eye contact."
    c. "Don't end on a sour note."
    d. "Avoid empty flattery."
    e. "Reward the effort, not the outcome."

55. Which researcher conducted investigations of latent learning with rats in mazes?
    a. Garcia
    b. Skinner
    c. Thorndike
    d. Tolman
    e. Kohler

56. A child receives a dime for, on average, every 5 dandelions he pulls from the yard. This is an example of a ______ schedule of reinforcement.
    a. fixed ratio
    b. variable ratio
    c. fixed interval
    d. variable interval
    e. continuous reinforcement

57. Although Hannah knows that praise strengthens desirable behavior in children, she is not sure what specific strategies she should use. Which of the following guidelines should Hannah follow?
    a. Reward the outcome, not the effort.
    b. Show a serious expression when giving praise to underscore the importance of the behavior.
    c. Combine physical contact with verbal praise.
    d. Give general praise for all accomplishments to build overall self-esteem.
    e. Repeat praise regularly.

Essentials of Psychology Chapter 5

58. Classical conditioning can explain the development of all of the following EXCEPT
    a. aversions to particular foods.
    b. phobias.
    c. positive or negative emotions.
    d. drug cravings during withdrawal.
    e. complex, voluntary behaviors.

59. Primary reinforcers are
    a. the first reinforcers an animal learns.
    b. the most powerful reinforcers an animal learns.
    c. intrinsically rewarding.
    d. reinforcers that are learned through classical conditioning.
    e. also called conditioned reinforcers.

60. Which pattern best describes what happens once classical conditioning occurs?
    a. UR elicits the US.
    b. CS elicits the CR.
    c. NS leads to no response.
    d. NS + US leads to UR.
    e. US + CS leads to UR.

61. Rescorla applies a cognitive perspective in explaining classical conditioning. He focuses on the extent to which the CS __________ the US.
    a. interferes with
    b. predicts
    c. follows
    d. reduces
    e. is elicited by

62. Mr. Bonoir gives students stars on their homework when it is done well. A student can exchange 10 stars for a treat. This is a form of
    a. token economy.
    b. biofeedback.
    c. shaping.
    d. insight learning.
    e. programmed instruction.

Essentials of Psychology Chapter 5

63. Which of the following psychologists is most likely to apply a cognitive perspective to research on classical conditioning?
    a. Dr. Amir, who believes that the stronger the CS, the stronger the CR.
    b. Dr. Harding, who believes the frequency of the pairings of the CS and US are the most important factor explaining strength of the CR.
    c. Dr. Rivers, who believes that conditioned stimuli are signals or cues organisms use to make predictions about the environment.
    d. Dr. Smithers, who believes that reducing the interval between the CS and US will help strengthen the CR.
    e. Dr. Runes, who believes that the ability to think or conceptualize is the key factor in explaining the strength of association between the CS and the CR.

64. Regarding research on the classical conditioning of taste aversions, which of the following statements is FALSE?
    a. Conditioning of taste aversions can be acquired on the basis of a single pairing of the flavor with a nausea-inducing substance.
    b. Taste aversions can be acquired when the flavor is presented hours before the nausea-inducing substance.
    c. Garcia and Koelling's work on taste aversions was no surprise to their colleagues; the research turned out as expected.
    d. Garcia has applied his research to solve real-world problems.
    e. Conditioned taste aversions have survival benefits.

65. The systematic application of learning principles to help people overcome phobias is called ______ therapy.
    a. aversion
    b. cognitive
    c. conditioning
    d. behavior
    e. reexposure

66. Your significant other gives you a compliment, and you smile at him/her. The probability that s/he will give you another compliment increases. This is an example of which type of learning?
    a. Latent learning
    b. Insight learning
    c. Observational learning
    d. Classical conditioning
    e. Instrumental learning

67. In Garcia's research on taste aversions, what was the neutral stimulus?
    a. radiation
    b. taste of the water
    c. nausea
    d. electric shocks
    e. taste of the food

Essentials of Psychology Chapter 5

68. In Pavlov's studies of classical conditioning, the unconditioned stimulus was one that caused
   a. an unexpected response.
   b. a controlled response.
   c. an unlearned response or reflex.
   d. a conditioned response or reflex.
   e. a neutral response.

69. Which of the following does NOT belong?
   a. observation
   b. modeling
   c. vicarious learning
   d. conditioned stimulus
   e. imitation

70. Which of the following is the best definition of spontaneous recovery?
   a. the weakening and disappearance of a conditioned response over time
   b. displaying a conditioned response to stimuli similar to the conditioned stimulus
   c. displaying a conditioned response to new neutral stimuli
   d. displaying a conditioned response in the absence of the conditioned stimulus
   e. return of a conditioned response following extinction

71. "Mental learning" is closest in meaning to which form of learning?
   a. operant conditioning
   b. cognitive learning
   c. classical conditioning
   d. creative learning
   e. higher-order conditioning

72. Zorba gives his dog a treat for rolling over. Zorba explains this procedure as a form of
   a. conditioned reinforcement.
   b. punishment.
   c. negative reinforcement.
   d. positive reinforcement.
   e. classical conditioning.

73. To which area of human behavior was Thorndike particularly excited about applying principles of animal learning?
   a. parenting
   b. law enforcement
   c. medicine
   d. advertising
   e. education

74. In Watson's research with Little Albert, what was the CS?
    a. a loud sound
    b. a white rat
    c. an electric shock
    d. a spanking
    e. the Santa Claus mask

75. Behaviors that result in satisfying effects are strengthened and behaviors that result in discomfort are weakened. This statement is explained by
    a. the Law of Effect.
    b. classical conditioning.
    c. latent learning.
    d. radical behaviorism.
    e. insight learning.

76. A puff of air to the eye causes a reflexive blink. If you precede the puff of air with a buzzer, eventually the buzzer will cause a blink. In this example, the buzzer begins as the _____ and eventually becomes the ______.
    a. neutral stimulus; conditioned stimulus
    b. conditioned stimulus; neutral stimulus
    c. unconditioned stimulus; conditioned stimulus
    d. neutral stimulus; unconditioned stimulus
    e. unconditioned stimulus; neutral stimulus

77. Caroline has an "Aha!" experience when solving a problem. Caroline most likely experienced which type of learning?
    a. latent learning
    b. insight learning
    c. observational learning
    d. operant conditioning
    e. classical conditioning

78. Following extinction, a conditioned response can be learned again more quickly than it was learned originally. This process is called
    a. spontaneous recovery.
    b. generalization.
    c. discrimination.
    d. reconditioning.
    e. shaping.

Essentials of Psychology Chapter 5

79. Which of the following can best be described as an example of insight learning?
    a. Deborah, who gives her 4-year-old son a hug every time he puts his toys away.
    b. Samantha, who has wandered through the downtown area a number of times without having a particular goal in mind. When she is asked to take a friend to a particular restaurant, she almost immediately picks the shortest route.
    c. Dr. Caruthers , who has been working on a particularly thorny problem in microbiology for a number of months. She then suddenly realizes the solution to her problem, seemingly without effort.
    d. Jason, who has a flat tire while driving on a country road. He remembers having seen his dad change a flat tire before, so he doesn't hesitate to attempt the task himself. He is successful in the attempt and is soon on his way again.
    e. Patrick, who is planning to spend the day at the beach. He packs sunscreen and applies it to himself every two hours while he is at the beach because he doesn't want to get a sunburn.

80. Through classical conditioning, Alyce has developed a fear of mice. She also shows a fear response to gerbils and hamsters. Alyce is demonstrating
    a. stimulus generalization.
    b. stimulus discrimination.
    c. spontaneous recovery.
    d. extinction.
    e. reconditioning.

81. Operant conditioning is also known as
    a. classical conditioning.
    b. vicarious learning.
    c. observational learning.
    d. instrumental learning.
    e. cognitive learning

82. Which of the following people is on a variable-ratio schedule of reinforcement?
    a. Phillip, who is playing a slot machine at a casino
    b. Colette, whose teacher uses pop quizzes
    c. Jim, whose professor schedules three exams for the semester, one for every five weeks
    d. Elissa, who receives a monthly performance evaluation
    e. Angela, who receives compensation for every student she recruits for her college

83. The Law of Effect was proposed by
    a. Pavlov.
    b. Skinner.
    c. Thorndike.
    d. Watson.
    e. Tolman.

Name:________________________ Class:________________________ Date:____________

Essentials of Psychology Chapter 5

84. Regarding operant conditioning, which of the following statements is FALSE?
    a. Positive reinforcement leads to strengthening of response, whereas negative reinforcement leads to weakening of response.
    b. Discriminative stimuli set the stage for reinforcement.
    c. Organisms are capable of learning complex behaviors through reinforcement of successive approximations to the desired behaviors.
    d. Some reinforcers are rewarding because they satisfy basic biological needs, whereas others acquire reward value through experience.
    e. Extinction is achieved by no longer reinforcing the desired response.

85. Thorndike is to _____ as Skinner is to _______.
    a. classical conditioning; Law of Effect
    b. classical conditioning; operant conditioning
    c. operant conditioning; classical conditioning
    d. Law of Effect; classical conditioning
    e. Law of Effect; operant conditioning

86. Regarding the timing of the CS and the US in classical conditioning, the STRONGEST conditioned response occurs when the
    a. CS and US are presented simultaneously.
    b. CS is presented first and remains on during the presentation of the US.
    c. CS is presented first and is terminated before the presentation of the US.
    d. US is presented first and is terminated before the presentation of the CS.
    e. US is presented first and remains on during the presentation of the CS.

87. Learning in which a previously neutral stimulus becomes capable of triggering a reflexive response is called
    a. operant conditioning.
    b. classical conditioning.
    c. instrumental conditioning.
    d. stimulus-response learning.
    e. spontaneous recovery.

88. When Sara misbehaves, her parents respond by not allowing her to watch TV for a certain amount of time. Her parents are using which method of discipline?
    a. escape learning
    b. avoidance learning
    c. negative reinforcement
    d. positive reinforcement
    e. punishment

Essentials of Psychology Chapter 5

89. All of the following are concerns about the use of punishment EXCEPT
   a. it suppresses rather than eliminates behavior.
   b. it may model inappropriate behavior.
   c. it is difficult to administer.
   d. it does not teach new behaviors.
   e. it can lead to strong negative emotions.

90. In an example reported in your text, a man was trapped behind a refrigerator and nearly suffocated. Subsequently, he has a phobia of tight, enclosed spaces and is afraid to ride on small, crowded elevators. However, he has no fear of large, uncrowded elevator rides. The man's fear of small elevators is an example of ______, and his lack of fear toward large elevators is an example of _______.
   a. reconditioning; extinction
   b. stimulus generalization; extinction
   c. stimulus generalization; stimulus discrimination
   d. stimulus discrimination; extinction
   e. stimulus discrimination; stimulus generalization

91. Cognitive learning involves
   a. mental processes that cannot be directly observed.
   b. higher-order conditioning.
   c. creative processes.
   d. focused attention.
   e. learning that occurs through repeated practice.

92. Which of the following can best be described as an example of latent learning?
   a. Deborah, who gives her four-year-old son a hug every time he puts his toys away.
   b. Samantha, who has wandered through the downtown area a number of times without having a particular goal in mind. When she is asked to take a friend to a particular restaurant in that neighborhood, she almost immediately picks the shortest route.
   c. Dr. Caruthers , who has been working on a particularly thorny problem in microbiology for a number of months. She then suddenly realizes the solution to her problem, seemingly without effort.
   d. Jason, who has a flat tire while driving on a country road. He remembers having seen his dad change a flat tire before, so he doesn't hesitate to attempt the task himself. He is successful in the attempt and is soon on his way again.
   e. Patrick, who is planning to spend the day at the beach. He packs sunscreen and applies it to himself every two hours while he is at the beach because he doesn't want to get a sunburn.

Essentials of Psychology Chapter 5

93. Regarding classical conditioning, which of the following statements is FALSE?
    a. Stimulus generalization helps explain the development of phobias.
    b. In extinction, conditioned responses gradually weaken and disappear.
    c. By learning to differentiate among related stimuli, animals are able to distinguish between threatening and nonthreatening situations.
    d. Stimulus generalization has survival value because it allows animals to generalize learned responses to originally threatening stimuli.
    e. Extinguished responses are forgotten if they are not reinforced.

94. Watson investigated the classical conditioning of which type of responses?
    a. anger
    b. sadness
    c. happiness
    d. fear
    e. sexual arousal

95. Which of the following pairings is correct?
    a. Garcia -- conditioned emotional response
    b. Thorndike -- schedules of reinforcement
    c. Skinner -- operant conditioning
    d. Watson -- classical conditioning of reflexes
    e. Pavlov -- classical conditioning of emotions

96. Paul has turned to alcohol in order to flee from the problems in his marriage. We can explain his behavior as a form of
    a. superstitious behavior.
    b. escape learning.
    c. latent learning.
    d. insight learning.
    e. observational learning.

97. LaGina walks into a room and feels as if she has been there before, even though she knows that she has not. LaGina's experience of deja vu may be explained by which concept from classical conditioning?
    a. Extinction
    b. Stimulus generalization
    c. Stimulus discrimination
    d. Spontaneous recovery
    e. Reconditioning

Essentials of Psychology Chapter 5

98. "When in Rome, do as the Romans do," underscores the importance of ______ in learning.
    a. modeling
    b. latency
    c. insight
    d. shaping
    e. reinforcement

99. In an application of classical conditioning principles reported in the text, how were sheep ranchers able to protect their sheep from coyotes?
    a. The sheep ranchers learned to shoot more accurately through reinforcement.
    b. Live sheep were injected with a poison that would kill coyotes.
    c. Sheep carcasses were injected with poison that would kill coyotes.
    d. Sheep carcasses were injected with a poison that would sicken but not kill coyotes.
    e. Sheep were classically conditioned to fear coyotes.

100. In applying a cognitive perspective to explaining classical conditioning, a psychologist would emphasize the extent to which the CS __________ the US.
    a. interferes with
    b. predicts
    c. follows
    d. reduces
    e. is elicited by

101. Following _____, a conditioned response may reappear. This process is known as ______.
    a. generalization; spontaneous recovery
    b. discrimination; extinction
    c. extinction; spontaneous recovery
    d. discrimination; spontaneous recovery
    e. generalization; extinction

102. In a typical classical conditioning experiment by Pavlov, a buzzer or tone serves as a(n)
    a. neutral stimulus that is paired with a conditioned response.
    b. conditioned stimulus that becomes a neutral stimulus through the process of association.
    c. unconditioned stimulus that becomes a conditioned stimulus.
    d. neutral stimulus that becomes an unconditioned stimulus.
    e. neutral stimulus that becomes a conditioned stimulus.

103. All but which of the following are primary reinforcers?
    a. money
    b. sexual stimulation
    c. novel visual stimuli
    d. air, food, and water
    e. relief from pain

Essentials of Psychology Chapter 5

104. Every time her husband pays her a compliment, Sarah looks him in the eye and smiles at him. This is an example of
   a. negative reinforcement.
   b. positive reinforcement.
   c. primary reinforcement.
   d. observational learning.
   e. latent learning.

105. In classical conditioning, a conditioned response can weaken and eventually disappear. This is referred to as
   a. spontaneous recovery.
   b. generalization.
   c. discrimination.
   d. reconditioning.
   e. extinction.

106. Who is most closely associated with the study of conditioned emotional reactions?
   a. John Watson
   b. Ivan Pavlov
   c. John Garcia
   d. B.F. Skinner
   e. Robert Rescorla

107. Pauline became ill after eating eggs contaminated with salmonella. She subsequently becomes nauseous whenever she sees eggs. This is an example of
   a. conditioned taste aversion.
   b. stimulus discrimination.
   c. spontaneous recovery.
   d. a phobia.
   e. conditioned emotional reaction.

108. Most psychologists define learning as
   a. any change in behavior.
   b. any change in behavior due to maturation.
   c. any change in behavior due to experience.
   d. a relatively permanent change in behavior due to natural development.
   e. a relatively permanent change in behavior due to experience.

109. A reflexive reaction triggered by a stimulus is a(n)
   a. conditioned response.
   b. unconditioned response.
   c. unconditioned stimulus.
   d. neutral response.
   e. operant response.

Essentials of Psychology Chapter 5

110. An "Open" sign in the window of a store that tells Ivan he can go in to purchase a beverage he finds particularly reinforcing. In this example, the sign serves as a
   a. primary reinforcer.
   b. discriminative stimulus.
   c. conditioned reinforcer.
   d. conditioned stimulus.
   e. secondary reinforcer.

111. Which of the following best describes the nature of learning?
   a. Learning is always adaptive. It involves enduring, but not necessarily permanent, changes in behavior.
   b. Learning is always adaptive. It involves permanent changes in behavior.
   c. Learning is adaptive in most cases. It involves enduring, but not necessarily permanent, changes in behavior.
   d. Learning is adaptive in most cases. It involves permanent changes in behavior.
   e. Learning is adaptive in most cases. It involves any type of change in behavior.

112. Which of the following best describes Bandura's research and subsequent general conclusions about the effects of violent television on behavior?
   a. Bandura believed that children become more aggressive after observing aggressive models on television, and his research has been supported.
   b. Bandura believed that children become more aggressive after observing aggressive models on television, and his research has been partially supported with only some groups of children.
   c. Bandura believed that children become more aggressive after observing aggressive models on television, and his research has been supported, but only with children who showed aggressive tendencies beforehand.
   d. Bandura believed that children do become more aggressive after observing aggressive models on television, and his research has not been supported.
   e. Bandura believed that children do not become more aggressive after observing aggressive models on television, and his hypothesis has been supported.

113. In the classic latent learning experiments described in your text, it appears that the rats developed a mental representation of the maze. Researchers call this mental representation a
   a. discriminative stimulus.
   b. cognitive map.
   c. mental device.
   d. secondary reinforcer.
   e. latent structure.

114. Which view holds that behavior is completely determined by environmental and genetic influences?
   a. the Law of Effect
   b. radical behaviorism
   c. behavior modification
   d. programmed instruction
   e. cognitive learning

Essentials of Psychology Chapter 5

115. Which of the following can best be described as an example of observational learning?
   a. Deborah, who gives her four-year-old son a hug every time he puts his toys away.
   b. Samantha, who has wandered through the downtown area a number of times without having a particular goal in mind. When she is asked to take a friend to a particular restaurant in that neighborhood, she almost immediately picks the shortest route.
   c. Dr. Caruthers , who has been working on a particularly thorny problem in microbiology for a number of months. She then suddenly realizes the solution to her problem, seemingly without effort.
   d. Jason, who has a flat tire while driving on a country road. He remembers having seen his dad change a flat tire before, so he doesn't hesitate to attempt the task himself. He is successful in the attempt and is soon on his way again.
   e. Patrick, who is planning to spend the day at the beach. He packs sunscreen and applies it to himself every two hours while he is at the beach because he doesn't want to get a sunburn.

116. Which of the following represents an application of a cognitive perspective on classical conditioning?
   a. The organism uses the CS to make predictions about the occurrence of events in the environment.
   b. The stronger the CS, the stronger the CR.
   c. The stronger the CS, the greater the resistance to extinction.
   d. The US holds information value that the organism uses to know how to respond.
   e. The US becomes a reliable signal for predicting the occurrence of the CS.

117. A clear connection between a behavior and a reinforcement is referred to as
   a. a continuity.
   b. a contingency.
   c. a discriminative stimulus.
   d. a reinforcement connection.
   e. a primary connection.

118. Dr. Emmanuel demonstrates a typical Pavlovian conditioning experiment for his psychology class. Emmanuel pairs a neutral stimulus with an unconditioned stimulus and then asks the class, "What is the neutral stimulus called now?" The correct answer is
   a. conditioned response.
   b. conditioned stimulus.
   c. reinforcer.
   d. conditioned reinforcer.
   e. unconditioned response.

119. Although Little Albert was classically conditioned to fear a rat, he also began to fear dogs, rabbits, and a Santa Claus mask. This is an example of
   a. spontaneous recovery.
   b. stimulus generalization.
   c. stimulus discrimination.
   d. extinction.
   e. reconditioning.

Essentials of Psychology Chapter 5

120. Advertising makes use of classical conditioning. For example, a product is presented along with some naturally appealing stimulus (e.g., a physically attractive person). In this case, the product begins as the
   a. unconditioned stimulus.
   b. neutral stimulus.
   c. conditioned stimulus.
   d. unconditioned response.
   e. conditioned response.

121. Helena has learned that she gets motion sickness easily. If Helena takes medicine before a boat ride so she doesn't get sea sick, she is demonstrating
   a. avoidance learning.
   b. a phobia.
   c. stimulus discrimination.
   d. escape learning.
   e. shaping.

122. Compared to continuous reinforcement, partial reinforcement results in _______ learning that is _______ to extinguish.
   a. faster; harder
   b. slower; harder
   c. faster; easier
   d. slower; easier
   e. faster; equally difficult

123. In the past three psychology labs, Liliya has been attempting to classically condition a lab rat. Her strategy has been to present the US and CS simultaneously. Which of the following should she do to strengthen the conditioned response of the rat?
   a. Make less frequent pairings of CS and US.
   b. Present the CS first and have it remain present during presentation of US.
   c. Present the US prior to CS.
   d. Present the CS first and withdraw it before introducing the US.
   e. Decrease the intensity of the US.

124. Karl wishes to reinforce positive behavior in his fourth-grade students. After identifying the desired behaviors, what would be Karl's next step?
   a. track the frequency of desired behaviors
   b. wean the children from the reinforcers
   c. explain contingencies
   d. select reinforcers
   e. apply reinforcers

Essentials of Psychology Chapter 5

125. Observational learning is also referred to as
    a. insight learning or latent learning.
    b. operant conditioning.
    c. vicarious learning or modeling.
    d. classical conditioning.
    e. creativity.

126. Through classical conditioning, Eduardo has developed a fear of dogs. However, he only fears large, longhaired dogs but not small, longhaired dogs or large, shorthaired dogs. Eduardo is demonstrating
    a. spontaneous recovery.
    b. stimulus discrimination.
    c. stimulus generalization.
    d. latent learning.
    e. extinction.

127. In operant conditioning, positive reinforcement ______ the likelihood of repeating a response, negative reinforcement ______ the likelihood of repeating a response, and punishment ______ the likelihood of repeating a response.
    a. strengthens; weakens; weakens
    b. strengthens; strengthens; strengthens
    c. weakens; strengthens; strengthens
    d. strengthens; weakens; strengthens
    e. strengthens; strengthens; weakens

128. A "scalloped" response pattern is typical of which type of reinforcement schedule?
    a. fixed-ratio
    b. fixed-interval
    c. variable-ratio
    d. variable-interval
    e. continuous

129. A puff of air to the eye causes a reflexive blink. If you precede the puff of air with a buzzer, eventually the buzzer will cause a blink. In this example, the puff of air is called the
    a. unconditioned stimulus.
    b. conditioned stimulus.
    c. neutral stimulus.
    d. unconditioned response.
    e. conditioned response.

130. Compared to ratio schedules, interval schedules
    a. result in faster response rates.
    b. result in slower response rates.
    c. result in similar response rates.
    d. sometimes result in faster response rates and sometimes result in slower response rates.
    e. can only be administered on a variable basis.

131. Donatello is using the guidelines for reinforcement with her son Giovanni. Donatello tells her son, "Giovanni, when you clean up all of your toys, you'll get a gold star on your chart." Which guideline is Donatello working with?
    a. using social reinforcement to maintain the behavior
    b. selecting a reinforcer
    c. applying the reinforcer
    d. tracking the frequency of desired behavior
    e. explaining the contingency

132. Omar's parents have been trying to teach him their telephone number. He appears unable to recite it correctly. One day, he overhears his father mention that he would buy Omar a new toy if he could learn the number. Omar immediately blurts out the correct number. This demonstrates
    a. latent learning.
    b. spontaneous recovery.
    c. observational learning.
    d. creativity.
    e. insight learning.

133. A schedule of reinforcement in which the first response performed after a specific amount of time has passed is reinforced is called a
    a. fixed-ratio schedule.
    b. fixed-interval schedule.
    c. variable-interval schedule.
    d. variable-ratio schedule.
    e. continuous reinforcement schedule.

134. Classical conditioning is best described as learning by
    a. trial and error.
    b. association.
    c. stimulus response.
    d. insight.
    e. observation.

Essentials of Psychology Chapter 5

135. ______ is learning that occurs without the opportunity of first performing the learned response or being reinforced for it.

a. Operant conditioning

b. Higher-order conditioning

c. Classical conditioning

d. Creative learning

e. Cognitive learning

Name:________________________ Class:________________ Date:__________

Essentials of Psychology Chapter 6

1. When it comes to retention, in general,
   a. spaced practice is superior to massed practice.
   b. massed practice is superior to spaced practice.
   c. spaced practice is superior to massed practice for short intervals only.
   d. spaced practice is superior to massed practice for long intervals only.
   e. massed practice is superior to spaced practice for short intervals only.

2. Cliff has vivid memories of burning his hand on a birthday candle at his seventh birthday party. But his mother corrects him, saying, “You never burned your hand. But I would tell you at every birthday to be careful of the candles.” Which theoretical model best accounts for Cliff’s misremembering?
   a. Levels of processing theory
   b. Decay theory
   c. Interference theory
   d. Repressed memory theory
   e. Constructionist theory

3. Regarding eidetic imagery, which of the following statements is TRUE?
   a. Eidetic images refer to intense auditory memories.
   b. Eidetic imagery usually disappears by age twenty.
   c. Eidetic imagery is more common in children than adults.
   d. About forty-five percent of children have eidetic imagery.
   e. Eidetic imagery is a very intense form of photographic memory that has greater accuracy..

4. Semantic memory is most analogous to a(n)
   a. best-selling novel.
   b. diary.
   c. journal.
   d. day planner.
   e. encyclopedia.

5. ______ occurs when eyewitnesses are given incorrect data during the retention interval of memory.
   a. The serial position effect
   b. Proactive interference
   c. The primacy effect
   d. Retroactive interference
   e. The misinformation effect

Essentials of Psychology Chapter 6

6. A group of students make a presentation on theories of forgetting. Which student was assigned retrieval theory?
   a. Apollo says, "Forgetting results from a failure to access stored memories, either from encoding failure or from a lack of access cues."
   b. Bryan says, "Forgetting happens as a result of a psychological defense mechanism trying to keep threatening material from entering consciousness."
   c. Courtney says, "Forgetting happens as a result of amnesia caused by traumatic brain injuries."
   d. Darla says, "Forgetting is a result of memory traces gradually fading out over time."
   e. Elena says, "Forgetting happens when memory is disrupted because of proactive or retroactive interference."

7. The _____ plays an important role in encoding emotional experiences, such as fear responses.
   a. hippocampus
   b. cingulate gyrus
   c. thalamus
   d. amygdala
   e. hypothalamus

8. Why do students generally perform better on multiple-choice tests than on essay tests?
   a. Multiple-choice tests provide more retrieval cues.
   b. Multiple-choice tests encourage better memory consolidation.
   c. Multiple-choice tests have higher long-term potentiation.
   d. Multiple-choice tests have less retroactive interference.
   e. Multiple-choice tests have less proactive interference.

9. Where memory is concerned, the hippocampus _____.
   a. is involved with processing procedural memories, but not dispositional information
   b. is involved with processing emotional memories, but not memories of factual information
   c. is involved with processing memories of factual information, but not emotional memories
   d. is involved with processing long-term memories, but not memories of intermediate duration
   e. is involved with processing semantic and episodic memories, but not procedural memories

10. Many psychologists think of human memory as a type of information processing system that has _____ basic processes that are called ______.
    a. 2; declarative memory and procedural memory
    b. 2; implicit memory and explicit memory
    c. 3; consolidation, elaboration, and rehearsal
    d. 3; sensory memory, short-term memory, and long-term memory
    e. 3; encoding, storage, and retrieval

Essentials of Psychology Chapter 6

11. Most people consider recognition tasks to be easier than recall tasks, possibly because _____.
    a. recall tests require us to retrieve more information than do recognition tasks.
    b. recognition tasks provide more retrieval cues than do recall tasks.
    c. serial recall tasks provide hints that can be used in recognition tasks.
    d. recognition tasks help us focus on appropriate areas of memory storage.
    e. answers for one question may be found in the choices of another question.

12. Maintenance rehearsal is
    a. synonymous with chunking.
    b. consciously repeating information over and over again.
    c. connecting to-be-remembered information with already-stored information.
    d. synonymous with whole rehearsal.
    e. picturing an object, pattern, or image in your mind.

13. Sean stopped outside his professor's office to check on the answers to a quiz. When he began to write the answers down, his pen ran out of ink. He repeated the last four answers to himself while he rushed to his dorm room to write them down. This is best explained by the concept of
    a. maintenance rehearsal.
    b. elaborative rehearsal.
    c. whole rehearsal.
    d. partial rehearsal.
    e. chunking.

14. In sensory memory, auditory stimuli are to _____ memory as visual stimuli are to ______ memory.
    a. eidetic; iconic
    b. iconic; echoic
    c. echoic; iconic
    d. iconic; eidetic
    e. eidetic; echoic

15. Regarding long-term memory, which of the following statements is FALSE?
    a. Declarative memory consists of semantic memory and episodic memory.
    b. Prospective memory is remembering to remember.
    c. Implicit memory is closely related to procedural memory and may even be a form of procedural memory.
    d. Long-term memory relies primarily on acoustic and visual encoding.
    e. The two major types of long-term memory are declarative memory and procedural memory.

16. In most cases, long-repressed memories of childhood abuse come to light during
    a. dreams.
    b. hypnosis or psychotherapy.
    c. periods of relative calm.
    d. everyday life tasks.
    e. interviews with law enforcement personnel.

Essentials of Psychology Chapter 6

17. When asked to report his social security number Ian says, "999-99-1111." Ian has taken the larger 9-digit number and broken it down into smaller pieces, which makes it easier to recall. This is best explained by the concept of
    a. maintenance rehearsal.
    b. elaborative rehearsal.
    c. flashbulb memory.
    d. the savings method.
    e. chunking.

18. Regarding eyewitness testimony, which of the following statements is FALSE?
    a. Eyewitness testimony is often flawed and full of errors.
    b. Eyewitnesses are more likely to make mistakes when identifying members of a race other than their own.
    c. The more confidently an eyewitness expresses his/her testimony, the much higher the accuracy of the person's testimony is likely to be.
    d. People who take longer to answer questions in giving testimony are less likely to be accurate than those who respond quickly.
    e. Highly attractive or highly unattractive faces are more likely to be accurately identified than faces of average attractiveness.

19. A physical trace of memory in the brain is termed a(n)
    a. flashbulb memory.
    b. schema.
    c. engram.
    d. mnemonic.
    e. neuronal network.

20. The best memory usually results from which type of encoding?
    a. verbal
    b. semantic
    c. acoustic
    d. visual
    e. echoic

21. The Ebbinghaus Forgetting Curve suggests that forgetting
    a. occurs slowly at first, then speeds up.
    b. occurs uniformly over time.
    c. occurs quickly at first, and then slows down.
    d. does not occur until at least 24 hours have passed.
    e. is complete within the first few hours.

Essentials of Psychology Chapter 6

22. Which of the following best describes memory storage?
    a. the process of retaining information in memory
    b. the recognition and storage of sensory impressions
    c. the process of accessing and bringing into consciousness information stored in memory
    d. lingering mental representations of a visual image
    e. the process of converting information into a form that can be stored in memory

23. Pedro has suffered a head injury that causes him to have no memory of the events preceding the injury. He is suffering from
    a. retrograde amnesia.
    b. anterograde amnesia.
    c. proactive interference.
    d. retroactive interference.
    e. dissociative amnesia.

24. From a biological perspective, memories are most like which of the following?
    a. an etching or trace
    b. a flashbulb
    c. a circuit
    d. a photograph
    e. computer software

25. In general, which type of memory task produces better retrieval?
    a. serial recall
    b. pair-associates recall
    c. free recall
    d. recall
    e. recognition

26. By manipulating a particular gene in mice, scientists have been able to
    a. implant memories from other flies.
    b. erase specific memories from the brain.
    c. breed a super fly that never forgets.
    d. enhance learning and memory ability.
    e. prevent flies from acquiring any new memories.

27. The process of converting unstable, short-term memory into lasting, stable memories is called
    a. eidetic engineering.
    b. maintenance rehearsal.
    c. elaborative rehearsal.
    d. consolidation.
    e. chunking.

Name:________________________ Class:__________________ Date:________

Essentials of Psychology Chapter 6

28. An organized knowledge structure reflecting one's past experience and future expectations is called a
    a. stereotype.
    b. phonological loop.
    c. memory schema.
    d. semantic network.
    e. reconstructed memory.

29. The World Wide Web's structure, which is organized in terms of a network of associated concepts, is based on which of the following?
    a. retrieval theory
    b. constructionist theory
    c. levels-of-processing theory
    d. semantic network model
    e. three-stage model of memory

30. Lionel takes an exam in his French class. He is presented a word in English and asked to list the French equivalent. What type of memory task is Lionel completing?
    a. paired-associates recall
    b. free recall
    c. serial recall
    d. recognition
    e. retrieval

31. Compared to short-term memory, long-term memory relies
    a. more on semantic coding and less on acoustic coding.
    b. more on visual coding and less on acoustic coding.
    c. about the same on acoustic coding.
    d. about the same on semantic coding.
    e. equally on acoustic, visual, and semantic coding.

32. Long-term potentiation involves _____.
    a. the creation of new neural circuits in the thalamus
    b. the encoding of a fear response in the amygdala
    c. a long-lasting increase in the strength of synaptic connections
    d. the creation of neuronal networks in the cerebellum
    e. a relatively temporary memory created in the hippocampus

33. Jeffrey crams for all of his exams. In scientific terms, Jeffrey's approach to memorization is called
    a. spaced practice.
    b. distributed practice.
    c. massed practice.
    d. delayed practice.
    e. overlearning.

Essentials of Psychology Chapter 6

34. Flashbulb memories are most likely to be associated with
    a. misinformation effects.
    b. recovered memories of early childhood abuse.
    c. emotionally charged experiences.
    d. near-death experiences.
    e. situations that are similar to the situation in which the memory was first encoded.

35. In retrograde amnesia,
    a. new memories interfere with old.
    b. old memories interfere with new.
    c. new long-term memories cannot be formed.
    d. old long-term memories are lost.
    e. all memories are kept hidden from awareness.

36. Cells that "fire together, wire together." This saying best captures the concept of
    a. memory consolidation.
    b. amnesia.
    c. repression.
    d. long-term potentiation.
    e. overlearning.

37. A retrieval cue is
    a. an experimental task in which subjects are presented with a stimulus that primes them to respond in a particular way.
    b. a process for enhancing retention of information by breaking the information into smaller, more easily recalled chunks.
    c. a lingering mental representation of a sound.
    d. a lingering mental representation of a visual image.
    e. a stimulus associated with original learning that helps jog one's memory.

38. Who invented the World Wide Web?
    a. Berners-Lee
    b. Miller
    c. Averhart and Bigler
    d. Loftus
    e. Ebbinghaus

Essentials of Psychology Chapter 6

39. According to constructionist theory, memories of life experiences may be described by all but which of the following?
    a. distorted simplifications of actual events and experiences
    b. fabrications
    c. missing important details
    d. like impressionist paintings
    e. mental snapshots of experiences

40. The "Magic 7" refers to the
    a. duration of sensory memory.
    b. capacity of short-term memory.
    c. capacity of sensory memory.
    d. duration of short-term memory.
    e. number of systems in the leading model of short-term memory.

41. To avoid interference effects on memory, your text recommends all but which of the following?
    a. Study material directly before going to sleep.
    b. Practice or rehearse fresh memories aloud.
    c. Practice new memories beyond the point necessary to reproduce them without error.
    d. Don't schedule your classes one right after another.
    e. Study material that is similar in content in back-to-back fashion.

42. All of the following are categories of declarative memory EXCEPT
    a. semantic.
    b. episodic.
    c. procedural.
    d. prospective.
    e. retrospective.

43. What is the current status of research on memory-enhancing drugs?
    a. Mixed evidence for the effectiveness of the drugs in memory enhancement among normal individuals
    b. Strong evidence that the drugs enhance memory in normal individuals
    c. Strong evidence that the drugs enhance memory in normal individuals, but only if the drugs are taken for at least two years
    d. Strong evidence that the drugs enhance memory in normal individuals, but only if combined with memory-retraining exercises
    e. No compelling scientific evidence that the drugs enhance memory in normal individuals

Name:______________________ Class:______________________ Date:______________

Essentials of Psychology Chapter 6

44. In memory processes, the primacy effect refers to
    a. inferior memory for items at the beginning of a list.
    b. inferior memory for items at the end of a list.
    c. superior memory for items at the end of a list.
    d. superior memory for items at the beginning of a list.
    e. superior memory for items at both the beginning and end of the list.

45. Procedural long-term memory might best be described as
    a. knowing when.
    b. knowing what.
    c. knowing how.
    d. knowing which.
    e. knowing that.

46. In investigative questioning, how do leading questions and open-ended questions compare?
    a. Open-ended questions lead to more accuracy but fewer details than leading questions.
    b. Open-ended questions lead to more accuracy and more details than leading questions.
    c. Leading questions lead to more accuracy but fewer details than open-ended questions.
    d. Leading questions lead to more accuracy and more details than open-ended questions.
    e. Both types of questions lead equally to many details, but little accuracy.

47. Regarding ideas about where memories are stored, the current belief is that
    a. engrams do exist in the way Lashley believed.
    b. long-term memories are stored in the amygdala.
    c. engrams exist, but modern technology is unable to identify them.
    d. memories are stored in neuronal networks rather than individual cells.
    e. the engram is housed in the brainstem.

48. Declarative memory is also known as
    a. procedural memory.
    b. demonstrative memory.
    c. semantic memory.
    d. explicit memory.
    e. implicit memory.

49. All but which of the following factors influence the reliability of eyewitness testimony?
    a. ease of recall
    b. degree of confidence
    c. the serial position effect
    d. general knowledge about a subject
    e. types of questions asked

Essentials of Psychology Chapter 6

50. ______ is the system by which we retain information and bring it to mind.
    a. Recall
    b. Cognition
    c. Learning
    d. Memory
    e. Perception

51. Which student is taking a test that is a recognition task?
    a. Elaine, who takes an exam in her Spanish class in which she is presented with a word in English and then must write the Spanish equivalent.
    b. Erin, who takes an oral exam in her astronomy class in which she must list the planets in order.
    c. Melissa, who takes a multiple-choice exam in her sociology class in which she must identify key events and founders in the history of sociology from a list of choices.
    d. Sharon, who takes an essay exam in her history class in which she must list key events and dates during the Vietnam War.
    e. Jordan, who takes an essay exam in her film studies class in which she must discuss two philosophical positions presented in *The Matrix*.

52. One of Ebbinghaus's innovations was using ______ as study material for testing memory.
    a. common words
    b. numbers
    c. foreign words
    d. nonsense syllables
    e. symbols

53. Because of an accident he suffered last month, Jason suffers from anterograde amnesia. As a result, he may have trouble remembering _____.
    a. the name of the high school from which he graduated.
    b. events that occurred just before his accident.
    c. names of people he just met.
    d. where he moved to shortly before the accident.
    e. the names of common objects.

54. Motivated forgetting is another name for
    a. repression.
    b. regression.
    c. retroactive interference.
    d. anterograde amnesia.
    e. childhood amnesia.

Essentials of Psychology Chapter 6

55. Flashbulb memories are __________ other long-term memories.
    a. less vivid and less accurate than
    b. more vivid and more accurate than
    c. more vivid and about the same level of accuracy as
    d. less vivid and about the same level of accuracy as
    e. more vivid and less accurate than

56. When children are first learning the alphabet, they tend to be accurate on the ABCD portion and the WXYZ portion while making lots of mistakes in between. This represents the
    a. primacy effect.
    b. recency effect.
    c. serial position effect.
    d. retrograde amnesia.
    e. anterograde amnesia.

57. The serial position effect occurs when people
    a. remember the first things in a list the best.
    b. remember the last things in a list the best.
    c. remember the first and last things in a list the best.
    d. have difficulty remembering the first and last things in a list.
    e. remember things they learn first better than things they learn last.

58. Regarding declarative memory, which of the following statements is FALSE?
    a. Declarative memory is a type of long-term memory.
    b. Declarative memory is memory of facts and personal information.
    c. Declarative memories are recalled without conscious effort.
    d. Declarative memory is described as explicit.
    e. The two types of declarative memory are semantic and episodic.

59. Regarding research on forgetting and decay theory, which of the following statements is FALSE?
    a. Ebbinghaus used himself as the research subject in his experiments.
    b. Decay theory does not account for memory loss that occurs due to the passage of time.
    c. Decay theory is also known as trace theory.
    d. Decay theory does not help explain why some memories endure better through time than others.
    e. If Ebbinghaus had studied the retention of meaningful information, he probably would have found different experimental results.

60. To make your studying more productive, your text suggests all but which of the following?
    a. Eat a large meal before sitting down to study in order to avoid distractions from hunger.
    b. Place yourself in an area conducive to studying and free of distractions.
    c. Space your study sessions rather than cramming lots of studying into one period.
    d. Form a mental image of yourself performing the intended action.
    e. Adopt a healthy diet, regular sleep schedule, and regular exercise regimen.

Essentials of Psychology Chapter 6

61. Herman counts the number of times it takes to rehearse a list of nonsense syllables in order to memorize it. Then he counts the number of times it takes to relearn the list after a month has passed. Herman then calculates the difference between the number of times and determines the percentage gain he made between the two efforts at memorization. Herman uses this figure as a measure of memory retention. Which technique is Herman using?
   a. Savings method
   b. Mnemonics technique
   c. Long-term potentiation
   d. Massed practice
   e. Free recall technique

62. Many people cannot say whether the doorknob is on the left or right side of their front door. This is most likely due to
   a. proactive interference.
   b. retroactive interference.
   c. retrograde amnesia.
   d. encoding failure.
   e. the serial position effect.

63. Keiko knows that Salt Lake City is the capital of Utah and that George Washington was the first president of the United States. These are examples of
   a. procedural memory.
   b. declarative memory.
   c. historical memory.
   d. working memory.
   e. prospective memory.

64. Regarding implicit and explicit memory, which of the following statements is TRUE?
   a. Implicit memory requires a conscious effort to recall, while explicit memory does not.
   b. Explicit memory requires a conscious effort to recall, while implicit memory does not.
   c. Both implicit and explicit memory require a conscious effort to recall.
   d. Neither implicit nor explicit memory requires a conscious effort to recall.
   e. Implicit memory requires a conscious effort to recall, while explicit memory does not, but only for procedural memories.

65. Dr. Ohno conducts research on retrospective memory. Which type of memory will Ohno's research participants be recalling?
   a. past experiences or events and previously acquired information
   b. repressed experiences
   c. past personal experiences only
   d. things they plan to do in the future
   e. sensory memories of current experiences

Essentials of Psychology Chapter 6

66. Regarding the role of the hippocampus in memory, which of the following statements is FALSE?
    a. The hippocampus serves as a temporary storage bin for holding new memories before they are transferred to other parts of the brain for long-term storage.
    b. The hippocampus plays a role in converting newly learned facts into long-term memory.
    c. The hippocampus plays a role in converting daily experiences into long-term memory.
    d. The hippocampus does not play a role in procedural memory.
    e. The hippocampus is the final destination for new memories.

67. Eric Kandel studied the formation of memories in the
    a. garden slug.
    b. sea snail.
    c. tree frog.
    d. white rat.
    e. smart fly.

68. Which statement best describes the current state of opinion on recovered memories of childhood abuse?
    a. Most recovered memories of childhood abuse are genuine, and these memories are credible sources of testimony in legal cases.
    b. Most recovered memories of childhood abuse are genuine, but they are still not credible sources of testimony in legal cases.
    c. Most recovered memories of childhood abuse are false, and they should not be considered a credible source of testimony in legal cases.
    d. Some recovered memories are genuine, whereas others are false, and psychologists lack the tools to differentiate between them.
    e. Some recovered memories are genuine, whereas others are false, and psychologists have now developed techniques that can reliably distinguish between them.

69. Sleep is important for which memory process?
    a. Perception of sensory information in the sensory register
    b. Formation of flashbulb memories
    c. Maintenance rehearsal
    d. Consolidation of short-term memories into long-term memories
    e. Holding material in the eidetic engine

70. The levels-of-processing theory explains the
    a. interaction among the components of working memory.
    b. organization of the semantic network model.
    c. superiority of elaborative rehearsal over maintenance rehearsal.
    d. direction of spreading activation.
    e. process of consolidating memories during sleep.

Name:____ Class:_________________________ Date:_____________

Essentials of Psychology Chapter 6

71. Advances in genetic engineering show that it is possible to
    a. enhance learning and memory ability in nonhuman organisms.
    b. erase specific memories from the brain.
    c. graft parts of the brain from one organism into another to share memories.
    d. breed animals that perform as well as humans on memory tests.
    e. increase memory functioning in humans.

72. A memory storage system that contains memory of impressions for a very brief time (a few seconds or less) is called
    a. short-term memory.
    b. limited memory.
    c. sensory memory.
    d. temporary memory.
    e. echoic memory.

73. Jessica is participating in an experiment on memory. She has been asked to memorize a long list of word pairs. Once she has mastered the list, she will be asked a series of questions about which words were paired with each other. This is an example of a _____ test of memory.
    a. free recall
    b. serial recall task
    c. paired-associates recall
    d. recognition task
    e. time savings task

74. Which of the following statements best describes the benefits of research on the genetic bases of memory?
    a. Presently available drugs show benefits in boosting human memory.
    b. Understanding the genetic bases of memory has led to development of drugs to boost memory in both Alzheimer's patients and normal individuals.
    c. Scientists can prevent Alzheimer's disease in some cases through genetic manipulation of particular genes.
    d. Scientists have identified specific proteins regulated by so-called memory genes that can be synthesized to improve human memory.
    e. No drugs or supplements are yet available that have been shown to enhance memory in normal individuals.

75. Proactive inference occurs when
    a. older memories interfere with newer memories.
    b. newer memories interfere with older memories.
    c. more frequently experienced events interfere with less frequently experienced events.
    d. less frequently experienced events interfere with more frequently experienced events.
    e. items in the middle of a list interfere with memorizing the first and last items.

Essentials of Psychology Chapter 6

76. Maintenance rehearsal involves practice based on __________, whereas elaborative rehearsal involves practice based on _________.
   a. repetition; rehearsing meaningful associations.
   b. strengthening neural connections; strengthening neural nets.
   c. repeating information as a whole; breaking the information into smaller pieces.
   d. chunking; partial rehearsal.
   e. partial rehearsal; chunking.

77. The view that memory is based on recreating representations of the past rather than recalled verbatim images of the past is called
   a. the semantic network model.
   b. the three-stage model of memory.
   c. retrieval theory.
   d. constructionist theory.
   e. levels-of-processing theory.

78. Neville is memorizing parts of the brain for his psychology exam. Neville rehearses the information over and over, past the point of practice needed to recognize and list all of the parts of the brain. Which memory technique is Neville utilizing?
   a. eidetic imagery
   b. mnemonics
   c. distributed practice
   d. spaced practice
   e. overlearning

79. In memory, as time passes between learning and recall,
   a. both the primacy and recency effects weaken.
   b. neither the primacy nor the recency effects weaken.
   c. the primacy but not the recency effect weakens.
   d. the recency but not the primacy effect weakens.
   e. the recency effect becomes stronger and the primacy effect weakens.

80. In his research on memory, Kandel demonstrated that
   a. memory power can be boosted through the use of mnemonics.
   b. damage to the hippocampus can prevent the formation of new memories.
   c. memories are stored in complex networks of interconnected brain cells called neuronal networks.
   d. manipulation of particular genes can enhance learning and memory, producing “smart” organisms.
   e. memory formation involves biochemical changes occurring at the synaptic level.

Essentials of Psychology Chapter 6

81. During the war in Iraq, Max saw his best friend killed during an enemy attack. Max felt that he was partially responsible for his friend's death, and he has a great deal of guilt. Subsequently, Max has perfect recall of his war experience, except for his friend's death. Max's psychologically caused amnesia is referred to as
    a. dissociative amnesia.
    b. retrograde amnesia.
    c. reactive amnesia.
    d. anterograde amnesia.
    e. repressive amnesia.

82. The overall outcome of Lashley's search for the engram was the
    a. discovery of different engrams for different sorts of memories.
    b. realization that memories are not stored in any specific brain structure.
    c. discovery of a single engram for various sorts of memories.
    d. localization of engrams in the hippocampus.
    e. confirmation that memories are housed in the cerebral cortex.

83. To learn the EGBDF musical scale, Rybeccah uses the saying "Every Good Boy Deserves Fudge." Which mnemonic technique is Rybeccah using?
    a. Acrostic
    b. Acronym
    c. Elaborative rehearsal
    d. Overlearning
    e. Chunking

84. The conversion of short-term memory into long-term declarative memory most likely involves the
    a. hypothalamus.
    b. hippocampus.
    c. thalamus.
    d. medulla.
    e. brainstem.

85. Which of the following psychologists is a leading expert on eyewitness testimony?
    a. Baddeley
    b. Loftus
    c. Lashley
    d. Kandel
    e. Miller

Essentials of Psychology Chapter 6

86. Ella has suffered a head injury. She is no longer able to form new long-term memories. She is suffering from
    a. retrograde amnesia.
    b. anterograde amnesia.
    c. proactive interference.
    d. retroactive interference.
    e. dissociative amnesia.

87. Regarding procedural memory, which of the following statements is FALSE?
    a. Procedural memory is used when we need to consciously recall a set of procedures to be followed in completing a task.
    b. Procedural memories are hard to verbalize.
    c. Procedural memory is engaged without conscious effort.
    d. Procedural memory involves motor or performance skills.
    e. Athletes' use of the term "muscle memory" captures the nature of procedural memory.

88. In anterograde amnesia, there is
    a. an inability to form new long-term memories.
    b. an inability to retrieve old long-term memories.
    c. a problem where new information interferes with old.
    d. a problem where old information interferes with new.
    e. a problem where all memories are kept hidden from awareness.

89. While Althea was filling out a job application, memory of her current address prevented her from accurately remembering her previous address. This is an example of
    a. retrograde amnesia.
    b. anterograde amnesia.
    c. retroactive interference.
    d. proactive interference.
    e. the serial position effect.

90. The major role of genes in memory may be their ability to control
    a. development of new neurons.
    b. which neurons die.
    c. production of proteins.
    d. which experiences are encoded.
    e. synaptic connections.

Essentials of Psychology Chapter 6

91. The "Try This Out" Feature in your text, "What's in the Photograph?" applies which concept from the unit on memory?
    a. People are better able to recall information that is consistent with their existing schemas.
    b. People can better recall data that they have "chunked" into smaller bits.
    c. Emotionally arousing events can leave vivid, flashbulb memories permanently etched into the brain.
    d. False memories of events that never took place can be induced experimentally.
    e. Memory retrieval is impaired by a lack of retrieval cues, as well as by failure to encode information.

92. Of the following mnemonics, which involves forming a word composed of the first letters of a series of words?
    a. acrostics
    b. acronyms
    c. overlearning
    d. elaborative rehearsal
    e. chunking

93. In her yoga teacher training, Reissa uses "Roy G. Biv" to memorize the colors associated with the seven chakras. Which memory technique is Reissa utilizing?
    a. first-letter system
    b. overlearning
    c. acrostic
    d. chunking
    e. acronym

94. Strengthening synaptic connections between neurons by repeated stimulation is known as
    a. long-term potentiation.
    b. short-term potentiation.
    c. electroshock therapy.
    d. neuronal networking.
    e. long-term consolidation.

95. _____ are memory circuits in the brain that consist of complicated networks of nerve cells.
    a. Engrams
    b. Retrieval cues
    c. Memory schemas
    d. Semantic networks
    e. Neuronal networks

96. Procedural memory is to ______ as declarative memory is to ______.
    a. knowing how; knowing that
    b. knowing that; knowing when
    c. knowing when; knowing who
    d. knowing that; knowing who
    e. knowing how; knowing who

Essentials of Psychology Chapter 6

97. The capacity of short-term memory was investigated by
    a. Loftus.
    b. Sperling.
    c. Baddeley.
    d. Miller.
    e. Tulving.

98. When Louise told her friend about a book she had just read, she was able to provide a lot of details about the last several pages. This demonstrates the
    a. spaced practice effect.
    b. distributed practice effect.
    c. primacy effect.
    d. recency effect.
    e. massed versus spaced practice effect.

99. Kandel found that the amount of neurotransmitters released into synapses involved in the gill withdrawal reflex _____ as the animal learned the conditioned response.
    a. increased
    b. decreased
    c. increased at first, and then decreased
    d. decreased at first, and then increased
    e. stayed the same

100. Phillip's doctor has recommended that Phillip take his medication early in the mornings. Phillip is having trouble remembering to take his blood pressure medication in the mornings when he wakes up. Sometimes he doesn't remember to take his medication all day, and thus misses a dose. One approach Phillip might take to improving his memory for this task is to _____.
    a. develop a mental image that represents him taking the medication
    b. create an acronym to help him remember the medication
    c. pay more attention to his daily activities
    d. devise a rhyme that reminds him to take the medication in the morning
    e. link this task to an external time-based cue, such as having breakfast

101. Regarding episodic memory, which of the following statements is FALSE?
    a. Episodic memory is like a diary, holding memories of things that have happened to the individual.
    b. Episodic memories are better remembered when regularly retrieved and rehearsed.
    c. Episodic memory is a type of declarative memory.
    d. Episodic memory is also known as autobiographical memory.
    e. Episodic memory is found in humans, as well as other species.

Essentials of Psychology Chapter 6

102. When Jacques wants to learn a new concept, he attempts to connect it with previously existing knowledge. This is an example of

a. elaborative rehearsal.

b. maintenance rehearsal.

c. spaced practice.

d. overlearning.

e. massed practice.

103. In a free recall task, an individual is asked _____.

a. to recall as much information as possible about a particular topic in any order

b. to recall a series of items or numbers in a particular order

c. to recall pairs of items that had been previously memorized

d. to select the correct answer from a range of alternatives

e. to reproduce information that has been previously committed to memory

104. What is the order of processing in memory?

a. storage, retrieval, encoding

b. storage, encoding, retrieval

c. encoding, storage, retrieval

d. encoding, retrieval, storage

e. retrieval, storage, encoding

105. Even though she was only a toddler at the time, 45-year-old Jean has a vivid picture in her mind of her mother weeping when the television announced that President Kennedy had been assassinated. Jean's experience is an example of which of the following?

a. retrograde amnesia

b. tip-of-the-tongue phenomenon

c. overlearning

d. misinformation effect

e. flashbulb memory

106. Mark's friends say he has a "photographic memory." In scientific terms, Mark's memory ability is described as

a. iconic memory.

b. eidetic imagery.

c. immediate imagery.

d. semantic memory.

e. echoic memory.

Essentials of Psychology Chapter 6

107. The idea that memory gradually disintegrates over time is the basis of
a. decay theory.
b. interference theory.
c. the semantic network model.
d. retrieval theory.
e. constructionist theory.

108. When questioning eyewitnesses, open-ended questions tend to ________ but tend to elicit _________.
a. lead to misidentification of perpetrators; more information
b. greater confidence in eyewitness testimony; less information
c. fewer misidentifications than leading questions; more information
d. increase accuracy, fewer details
e. decrease accuracy, more details

109. Loraine is planning to spend most of her time studying for a physiology class this semester. As a result, she knows that she will have little time to study for her psychology class. She is planning to make up for her limited study time by cramming all night for her psychology exams. Loraine should be told that _____.
a. spaced practice is more effective at boosting retention than massed practice.
b. she should choose an interesting playlist for her iPod while she studies psychology.
c. chunking may be an effective approach to learning large amounts of information.
d. she should rely heavily on visual cues and visual imagery to make learning occur faster.
e. she needs to embed the psychological information in easily remembered rhymes.

110. Your general world information (e.g., state capitals, U.S. presidents) is stored in
a. episodic memory.
b. semantic memory.
c. prospective memory.
d. retrospective memory.
e. short-term memory.

111. The semantic network model proposes a process called ______ in which thinking of a concept leads to a rippling effect that triggers other related concepts.
a. consolidation
b. spreading activation
c. neuronal networking
d. long-term potentiation
e. eidetic engineering

Essentials of Psychology Chapter 6

X 112. Which of the following suggests that long-term memory is organized in terms of an elaborate arrangement of associated concepts?
a. Semantic network model
b. Constructionist theory
c. Three-stage model
d. Levels-of-processing theory
e. Retrieval theory

113. Many researchers believe that memory conversion of short-term memory into long-term memory requires
a. the creation of new neurons.
b. the creation of new synapses.
c. the development of new neurotransmitters.
d. long-term potentiation.
e. weakening neuronal networks.

114. In his studies of memory, Ebbinghaus found that ______ of the information was lost by the end of the first day after studying, and that ______ of the information was lost after a month had passed.
a. 22%; 66%
b. 33%; 66%
c. 33%; 80%
d. 66%; 80%
e. 66%; 99%

115. In a study reported in the text, African-American children were told stories in which light- and dark-complexioned African-American characters were associated with either positive or negative attributes. When the children were asked to recall the stories, what happened?
a. The children remembered more stories in which the light-complexioned characters had positive attributes and the dark-complexioned characters had negative attributes.
b. The children remembered more stories in which the light-complexioned characters had negative attributes and the dark-complexioned characters had positive attributes.
c. The children preferred stories in which the light-complexioned characters had positive attributes and the dark-complexioned characters had negative attributes.
d. The children preferred stories in which the light-complexioned characters had negative attributes and the dark-complexioned characters had positive attributes.
e. The children were able to remember all stories equally well, regardless of the attributes assigned to the characters.

Essentials of Psychology Chapter 6

116. While taking her psychology exam, Edith is certain that she knows who developed the forgetting curve. She remembers studying it, and she can get a vague picture of where the material is in her textbook. Edith's certainty that she knows something, but inability to recall it is called
  a. dissociative amnesia.
  b. proactive interference.
  c. retroactive interference.
  d. the serial position effect.
  e. the tip-of-the-tongue phenomenon.

117. In memory encoding, mental picture is to _____ as meaning is to _____.
  a. auditory; semantic
  b. auditory; visual
  c. visual; auditory
  d. visual; semantic
  e. semantic; auditory

118. Experts suggest that college students distribute their study sessions throughout the semester rather than preparing for exams by cramming. This means that college students should use which approach to memorization?
  a. spaced practice
  b. massed practice
  c. distributed learning
  d. delayed practice
  e. overlearning

119. In contrast to maintenance rehearsal, elaborative rehearsal involves
  a. repetition of information to strengthen new learning.
  b. strengthening neural connections.
  c. breaking down complex material into smaller pieces.
  d. chunking information.
  e. focusing on the meaning of the material..

120. Regarding short-term memory, which of the following statements is FALSE?
  a. Short-term memory is also called working memory.
  b. People vary in their short-term memory capacities, but people can increase their capacity by using chunking or other techniques.
  c. Short-term memory allows a person to process and retain newly acquired information for about 30 seconds.
  d. Use of maintenance rehearsal can extend short-term memory.
  e. Short-term memory relies more on visual coding than acoustic coding.

Essentials of Psychology Chapter 6

121. After receiving a cute boy's cell phone number, Tammie mentally repeats the number over and over in her head. This process converts auditory signals into strings of recognizable sounds, and it is called __________ encoding.
   a. vocal
   b. internal
   c. acoustic
   d. sub-auditory
   e. semantic

122. Grace knows how to tie a square knot and how to drive an automobile with a standard transmission. These are examples of
   a. declarative memory.
   b. semantic memory.
   c. procedural memory.
   d. prospective memory.
   e. episodic memory.

123. All but which of the following are difficulties with the concept of repression, as presented by Freud?
   a. Freud's concept of repression does not account for ordinary forgetting.
   b. Many people who have been traumatized retain vivid, fragmented memories of their experiences.
   c. Many victims of trauma have difficulty putting the events out of their minds.
   d. Since repression operates unconsciously, it is almost impossible to test scientifically.
   e. Today, most experts believe that repression does not occur.

124. The storage device of sensory memory is called the
   a. eidetic engine.
   b. consolidation register.
   c. temporary storage center.
   d. sensory register.
   e. semantic network.

125. Which theory of forgetting suggests that forgetting is the result of a failure to access stored memories?
   a. interference theory
   b. constructionist theory
   c. three-stage theory
   d. decay theory
   e. retrieval theory

126. Which brain structure plays an important role in encoding fear and anger?
   a. amygdala
   b. hippocampus
   c. hypothalamus
   d. cortex
   e. brainstem

Essentials of Psychology Chapter 6

127. According to constructionist theory, Gwendolyn's negative stereotype of how Asians behave is an example of a(n)
   a. prospective memory.
   b. retrospective memory.
   c. schema.
   d. engram.
   e. misinformation effect.

128. Which question is most likely to be associated with episodic memory?
   a. Who wrote *A Catcher in the Rye*?
   b. Where did I go on my first date?
   c. What time is my dentist's appointment next week?
   d. Who was the first astronaut to walk on the moon?
   e. Which courses will I take in my next semester of college?

Name:________________________Class:__________________Date:____________

Essentials of Psychology Chapter 7

Indicate the answer choice that best completes the statement or answers the question.

1. Gardner describes intelligence as being composed of
   a. a general factor alone.
   b. a general factor and several specific abilities.
   c. seven primary mental abilities.
   d. eight distinct intelligences.
   e. three aspects.

2. The fact that Rosa has very good "people skills" but is not particularly adept at linguistic skills is best accounted for by _____.
   a. Wechler's theory of verbal/nonverbal intelligences
   b. Sternberg's triarchic theory of intelligence
   c. Spearman's 'g' theory
   d. Thurstone's theory of primary mental abilities
   e. Gardner's model of multiple intelligences

4. In research reported in the text, African American children adopted by upper middle-class White American families
   a. scored the same on IQ tests as African American children raised by their biological parents.
   b. scored the same on IQ tests as African American children adopted by African American families.
   c. scored 15 points higher on IQ tests than would be expected of African American children in general.
   d. scored 15 points higher on IQ tests than White children adopted by African American families.
   e. failed to maintain childhood gains on IQ test scores during adulthood.

X

9. Regarding intellectual disability, which of the following statements is FALSE?
   a. Low IQ scores are sufficient to determine intellectual disability.
   b. Most individuals with intellectual disability fall in a mild range of severity.
   c. Many children with intellectual disability are placed in regular classrooms.
   d. The causes of intellectual disability can be biological, environmental, or both.
   e. About 1 to 2 percent of those with intellectual disability have severe delays in all areas of development.

14. In intelligence testing, norms are
   a. control questions on IQ tests.
   b. trial questions on IQ tests.
   c. criteria for comparing an individual's IQ score with those of the general population.
   d. minimum standards for performance on an IQ test.
   e. the average scores achieved on IQ tests.

17. Chalanda is described as suffering from a moderate intellectual disability. She likely has an IQ in the range of
   a. 81 to 90.
   b. 71 to 80.
   c. 50 to 70.
   d. 35 to 49.
   e. 20 to 34.

Name:____Class:______________________Date:____________

Essentials of Psychology Chapter 7

19. In the normal distribution of IQ scores, approximately what percentage of scores falls between 85 and 115?
    a. 95%
    b. 2%
    c. 34%
    d. 68%
    e. 14%

X

21. Regarding Wechsler's tests of intelligence, which of the following statements is FALSE?
    a. Wechsler's tests are the most widely used intelligence tests in the United States and Canada.
    b. There are separate Wechsler tests for preschool children, school-age children, and adults.
    c. Wechsler scales are standardized so that an average score is set at 100.
    d. Wechsler developed the first measure of a mental quotient.
    e. The Wechsler scales introduced the concept of the deviation IQ.

22. Whose theory of intelligence has had a particularly strong influence on the field of education?
    a. Thurstone's
    b. Gardner's
    c. Sternberg's
    d. Spearman's
    e. Terman's

X

23. In its original conception, intelligence quotient was defined as
    a. mental age multiplied by chronological age and multiplied by 100.
    b. mental age divided by chronological age and multiplied by 100.
    c. mental age subtracted from chronological age and multiplied by 100.
    d. chronological age subtracted from mental age and multiplied by 100.
    e. mental age divided by chronological age and divided by 100.

24. Helena takes the subtests of the Wechsler Intelligence Scale for Adults (WAIS). She will take all but which of the following?
    a. letter-number sequencing
    b. vocabulary
    c. comprehension
    d. similarities
    e. name memory

X

27. Spearman proposed that intelligence is composed of
    a. seven primary mental abilities.
    b. a general factor he termed "g."
    c. a general factor he termed "g" and other specific abilities.
    d. eight different factors.
    e. three aspects – analytic, reactive, and practical.

Name:______________________________Class:____________________Date:__________

Essentials of Psychology Chapter 7

28. Kelly is a 12-year-old with intellectual disability. Even though she has difficulty with math and reading, Kelly is placed in a regular classroom for her entire school day. Which educational practice for students with intellectual disability is Kelly's school using?
    a. brainstorming
    b. enrichment
    c. standardization
    d. culture-fair testing
    e. mainstreaming

29. According to the text, which of the following definitions best describes intelligence?
    a. the process of mentally representing and manipulating information
    b. a form of problem solving in which a person selects a course of action from the available alternatives
    c. originality of thought associated with the development of new, workable products or solutions
    d. the ability to conceive of new ways of viewing situations and new uses for familiar objects
    e. the capacity to think and reason clearly and to act purposefully and effectively in adapting to the environment

30. Guilford was a pioneer in the development of tests that measured
    a. functional fixedness.
    b. divergent thinking.
    c. confirmation bias.
    d. convergent thinking.
    e. heuristics.

31. Tom's parents have just been told that Tom has dyslexia. What does this mean?
    a. He has impaired ability in mathematics.
    b. He has an intellectual disability.
    c. Tom is hyperactive.
    d. He has impaired ability in reading.
    e. He is intellectually or artistically gifted.

35. In studies of the correlation of IQ scores among twins, the correlation of scores of monozygotic twins raised apart is
    a. higher than for monozygotic twins raised together.
    b. lower than for dizygotic twins raised apart.
    c. higher than for dizygotic twins raised together.
    d. the same as for monozygotic twins raised together.
    e. the same as for dyzygotic twins raised together.

39. Your best friend takes an IQ test and tells you that s/he scored "average." Generalizing from the normal distribution of IQ scores, you know that your friend's score
    a. was below 100.
    b. was above 100.
    c. was 100.
    d. fell somewhere between 85 and 115.
    e. fell somewhere between 115 and 130.

Essentials of Psychology Chapter 7

43. Among these individuals, who would be considered the earliest pioneer in the field of intelligence testing?
    a. Lewis Terman
    b. Alfred Binet
    c. Charles Spearman
    d. Robert Sternberg
    e. Howard Gardner

44. What percentage of people with intellectual disability can be described as having a profound level of intellectual disability?
    a. almost all, more than 90%
    b. the majority, 85%
    c. about half, 49%
    d. about 10% to 20%
    e. very few, 2% or less

45. In his work on the measurement of intelligence, Binet was initially attempting to
    a. identify intellectually gifted children.
    b. identify children who would benefit from special education.
    c. determine grade placement for school children.
    d. determine which children had enough schooling to go to work.
    e. identify intellectually superior individuals.

46. Concerns with intelligence tests include all of the following EXCEPT
    a. they may be culturally biased.
    b. they may encourage self-fulfilling prophecies.
    c. they may be overemphasized.
    d. there is a lack of access to them.
    e. they can lead to lower expectations.

47. A deviation IQ is an IQ score based on
    a. an average score after taking the test repeatedly.
    b. typical IQ divided by grade in school.
    c. typical IQ divided by age.
    d. the difference of a person's test score from the norms for that person's age group.
    e. the ratio of mental age to chronological age.

Essentials of Psychology Chapter 7

52. Dr. Fabiano wishes to assess the reliability of an intelligence test he recently developed. Fabiano chooses the test- retest method of assessing reliability. What will Dr. Fabiano have to do?
   a. Compare subjects' scores on the tests to their performance in academic arenas.
   b. Give one version of the test to a group of subjects and then re-administer a parallel version of the test to the same subjects.
   c. Make certain that he follows uniform procedures in administering the test to different subjects.
   d. Give the test once to a group of subjects and then re-administer the test to a different group of subjects after a short time interval.
   e. Give the test to a group of subjects and then re-administer it to the same subjects after a short time interval.

53. Esther scores 130 on a test of intelligence. Esther's score corresponds to the________percentile of the population.
   a. 50th
   b. 60th
   c. 72nd
   d. 80th
   e. 98th

54. In Gardner's model, an architect would likely have high levels of which type of intelligence?
   a. Logical-mathematical
   b. Spatial
   c. Bodily-kinesthetic
   d. Intrapersonal
   e. Naturalist

55. Samuel faces the challenge of intellectual disability. He has been working as a cashier in a convenience store for several years. He has learned to do relatively simple arithmetic as it applies to his job, and he can read well enough to understand the daily newspaper, but he cannot easily go beyond these tasks. Samuel is best described as having ______.
   a. profound disability
   b. severe disability
   c. moderate disability
   d. mild disability
   e. non-functional disability

57. Tara has experienced severe delays in all areas of development, though she has learned some basic speech skills. Her doctors think she may be able to learn some simple tasks, but she will require fairly close supervision in everything she does. Tara is best described as having______.
   a. profound disability
   b. severe disability
   c. moderate disability
   d. mild disability
   e. non-functional disability

Essentials of Psychology Chapter 7

59. Regarding general trends in IQ scores in the United States, which of the following is TRUE?
    a. IQ scores have been rising steadily, at about 15 points per decade, for several generations.
    b. IQ scores have been falling steadily, at about 3 points per decade, for several generations.
    c. IQ scores have been rising steadily, at about 3 points per decade, for several generations.
    d. IQ scores have remained about the same over the past several decades.
    e. IQ scores have been falling steadily, at about 15 points per decade, for several generations.

60. The Binet-Simon test of intelligence was brought to the U.S. and translated into English by
    a. Terman.
    b. Spearman.
    c. Stanford.
    d. Goddard.
    e. Galton.

62. Francesca has very high levels of linguistic intelligence. The model of multiple intelligences suggests that Francesca might be best suited to be a(n)
    a. poet.
    b. dancer.
    c. musician.
    d. painter.
    e. engineer.

65. In testing,________is to consistency of results as________is to accuracy of results.
    a. norm; validity
    b. norm; reliability
    c. reliability; norm
    d. validity; norm
    e. reliability; validity

70. In Gardner's model, interpersonal intelligence is defined as the ability to
    a. understand one's own feelings and behavior.
    b. understand and use words.
    c. analyze, compose, or perform music.
    d. relate effectively to others and to understand others' moods and motives.
    e. recognize objects and patterns in nature.

73. Louise is a 35-year-old woman with intellectual disability. She has the reading and math skills of a normal sixth grader. She can function fairly independently and has a productive job. Her level of intellectual disability is most likely described as_____.
    a. mild
    b. moderate
    c. severe
    d. profound
    e. serious

Essentials of Psychology Chapter 7

74. Regarding the effects of nature and nurture in intelligence, which of the following statements is FALSE?
    a. Heritability estimates of intelligence range from 50 to 75 percent.
    b. Home environments emphasizing verbal interaction and reading can influence children's intellectual development.
    c. Twin and adoptee studies provide strong evidence for the influence of genetics on intelligence.
    d. Genetic and environmental factors interact in complex ways in shaping intelligence.
    e. Heredity influences intelligence in infancy and childhood, but not during adolescence and adulthood.

75. Regarding intelligence, psychologists have long argued about all but which of the following?
    a. how to define it
    b. what factors govern it
    c. whether different racial and ethnic groups have different levels of intelligence and what accounts for these differences
    d. how to measure it
    e. whether it varies among members of a population

79. Other factors being equal, which of the following is predicted for Roxanne and her brother Reginald?
    a. Roxanne will outperform Reginald in terms of reading, writing, and spelling.
    b. Reginald will have poorer visual-spatial abilities than Roxanne.
    c. Roxanne will have higher general intelligence than Reginald.
    d. Roxanne is more likely to have dyslexia than Reginald.
    e. Roxanne will be better at playing chess and solving geometry problems.

81. Marvin is a 25-year-old man with intellectual disability. He has very simple communication and manual skills, but has great difficulty in reading and math. Based on this description, Marvin's IQ score most likely falls between
    a. 0 and 20.
    b. 20 and 34.
    c. 35 and 49.
    d. 50 and 70.
    e. 71 and 90.

82. According to the text, which of the following definitions best describes intelligence?
    a. the ability to hold and manipulate information in mind
    b. the ability to perform well on achievement tests in school
    c. the ability to think clearly in challenging situations
    d. the ability to conceive of new ways of viewing situations and new uses for familiar objects
    e. the capacity to think and reason clearly and to act purposefully and effectively in adapting to the environment

Essentials of Psychology Chapter 7

89. Eric was tested at school for entry into the gifted program. It is likely that Eric scored at least_______on his intelligence test.
    a. 100
    b. 115
    c. 130
    d. 150
    e. 175

94. Anna has the ability to apply what she knows to her everyday life. Her friends say that Anna is "street smart." The triarchic theory of intelligence would label Anna as having________intelligence.
    a. multiple
    b. analytic
    c. emotional
    d. creative
    e. practical

97. Third-grade teacher Victor serves as a proctor for administration of group IQ tests to children at his school. Victor has been instructed to make sure that he follows the uniform procedures for administering the test in order to make sure the test is used correctly. With which criteria of test administration is Victor concerned?
    a. Standardization
    b. Norming
    c. Validity
    d. Accuracy
    e. Reliability

101. Compared to White Americans of European descent, African Americans score, on average,
    a. about 5 points lower on IQ tests.
    b. about 5 points higher on IQ tests.
    c. about 10 points lower on IQ tests.
    d. about 15 points lower on IQ tests.
    e. about the same on IQ tests.

102. In the history of intelligence tests, which event is the most recent?
    a. development of the deviation IQ
    b. use of group-administered intelligence tests in the U.S. Army
    c. development of a mental quotient
    d. development of norms for the Stanford-Binet Intelligence Scale
    e. development of the intelligence quotient

Essentials of Psychology Chapter 7

105. Irene has a mental age of 10 and a chronological age of 8. Using the IQ formula from your text, Irene's IQ would be
a. 200.
b. 125.
c. 80.
d. 18.
e. 12.5.

106. Intelligence consisting of seven different primary mental abilities was proposed by
a. Charles Spearman.
b. Louis Thurstone.
c. Howard Gardner.
d. Alfred Binet.
e. Robert Sternberg.

110. Culture-fair IQ tests are not widely used because they
a. are generally unavailable.
b. do not predict academic performance as well as standard tests.
c. are too expensive.
d. are invalid.
e. rely too heavily on verbal tasks.

111. Which group is predicted to have the most highly correlated IQ scores?
a. Monozygotic twins reared together
b. Dizygotic twins reared together
c. Monozygotic twins reared apart
d. Dizygotic twins reared apart
e. Siblings

112. Which of Sternberg's types of intelligence is typically measured in traditional tests of intelligence?
a. all of them—analytic, creative, and practical
b. analytic only
c. practical only
d. creative and analytic only
e. practical and creative only

114. Among a large group of adopted children, the IQ scores of the children are predicted to be
a. more similar to those of their biological parents than their adoptive parents.
b. more similar to those of their adoptive parents than their biological parents.
c. as similar to those of their adoptive parents as to their biological parents.
d. unrelated to those of their adoptive parents.
e. unrelated to those of their biological parents.

Name:________________ Class:____________ Date:________

Essentials of Psychology Chapter 7

116. In Binet's method of intelligence testing, the age at which a child's performance peaked was considered his or her
   a. chronological age.
   b. intelligence quotient.
   c. mental age.
   d. intellectual age.
   e. deviation IQ.

119. A given trait has a heritability of 75 percent. This means
   a. 75 percent of people show a genetic inheritance for the trait.
   b. 75 percent of the genes associated with the trait have been identified.
   c. 75 percent of the trait is genetically controlled.
   d. 75 percent of the variability among people on the trait can be explained by genetic factors.
   e. people have a 75 percent chance of inheriting the trait when the gene is present.

122. Regarding theories of intelligence, which of the following statements is FALSE?
   a. Spearman believed that intelligence consisted of a general factor and other specific abilities.
   b. Thurstone felt that a general factor of intelligence is sufficient to assess intelligence.
   c. Thurstone and his wife, Thelma, developed the *Primary Mental Abilities Test*.
   d. Gardner rejects the view that there is a single entity called "intelligence."
   e. Most standard IQ tests were developed to measure "g."

124. School psychologist Miguel Blackstone sometimes is called upon to administer the Alternate Uses Test. Which of the following is Blackstone measuring?
   a. intelligence
   b. convergent thinking
   c. multiple intelligence
   d. language skills
   e. divergent thinking

127. Kristina scored below average on an intelligence test in 5th grade. As a result, she was held back a year. Her parents and teachers developed low expectations for her. Ultimately, Kristina quit high school and took a low-paying job at a convenience store. This is an example of
   a. self-fulfilling prophecy.
   b. culturally biased testing.
   c. lack of standardization.
   d. an unreliable intelligence test.
   e. mainstreaming.

133. Who adapted the Binet-Simon Intelligence Test for American use and established norms for the test?
   a. Alfred Binet
   b. Henry Goddard
   c. Theodore Simon
   d. Lewis Terman
   e. Ira Stanford

136. Pascal has a mental age of 15 and a chronological age of 20. Using the IQ formula from the text, Pascal's IQ would be described as
   a. below average.
   b. average.
   c. slightly above average.
   d. significantly above average.
   e. none of these; it cannot be determined with the information provided.

140. In Sternberg's model of intelligence, creative intelligence includes
   a. applying and using.
   b. using and doing.
   c. analyzing and evaluating.
   d. evaluating and doing.
   e. inventing and designing.

X 141. The most widely used intelligence tests in America today were developed by
   a. Sir Francis Galton.
   b. Alfred Binet.
   c. Lewis Terman.
   d. David Wechsler.
   e. Howard Gardner.

143. Taking an overview of the theories of intelligence, all but which of the following are fair conclusions?
   a. We should broaden our thoughts about what intelligence is and how it should be measured.
   b. Human intelligence consists of multiple aspects.
   c. It is important to take cultural context into consideration when assessing human intelligence.
   d. Gardner and Sternberg's theories can be characterized as "theory rich, but data poor."
   e. Since there is strong evidence for the existence of separate types of intelligence, we should replace existing intelligence tests with tests that measure these types of intelligence.

Name:_________________________ Class:_________________________ Date:_____________

Essentials of Psychology Chapter 9

1. As discussed in the text, in which culture do fathers engage in more physical play than mothers with their children?
   a. American
   b. Chinese
   c. Malaysian
   d. Indian
   e. Hmong

2. Instead of focusing on what she is no longer able to do, 80-year-old Pauline uses her time and money to make up for the shortcomings associated with aging, focusing on activities that are meaningful and important to her. Pauline demonstrates which characteristic associated with successful aging?
   a. self-challenge
   b. pessimism
   c. realistic expectations
   d. optimism
   e. selective optimization and compensation

3. In a cross-cultural study of moral reasoning in Americans and Indians reported in the text, which of the following was found?
   a. Neither Indians nor Americans placed much emphasis on justice or interpersonal responsibility; instead, they emphasized care and nurturing.
   b. Americans placed more emphasis on interpersonal responsibilities, while Indians placed more emphasis on justice.
   c. Indians placed more emphasis on interpersonal responsibilities, while Americans placed more emphasis on justice.
   d. Indians and Americans both placed less emphasis on justice and more emphasis on interpersonal responsibilities.
   e. Americans and Indians both placed more emphasis on justice and less emphasis on interpersonal responsibilities.

4. Sharon is in the fourth week of her pregnancy. At which stage of prenatal development is her offspring?
   a. conception
   b. fetal
   c. germinal
   d. amniotic
   e. embryonic

5. Regarding physical and cognitive changes in late adulthood, which of the following statements is FALSE?
   a. Age-related declines in memory are generally not at a level significant enough to impair daily functioning.
   b. Aging brings loss of bone density and muscle mass, as well as reduced sharpness or acuity of the senses.
   c. Reaction times slow, which may have an impact on driving abilities.
   d. Immune system functioning declines, making older people more susceptible to illness.
   e. Fluid intelligence increases across much of the life span, only beginning to decline around age 70.

Essentials of Psychology Chapter 9

6. Regarding infant sensory abilities, which of the following statements is FALSE?
   a. Infants develop the ability to detect their mother's odor after three months of age.
   b. Newborns can discriminate among different tastes and show a preference for sweetness.
   c. Newborns can recognize a scrambled picture of their mother's face just as well as a properly arranged picture.
   d. By about 4 to 6 months of age, infants show a preference for faces reflecting their own racial characteristics.
   e. By about 2 months of age, infants have developed basic color vision.

7. According to Piaget, a(n) ______ is an organized system of mental representations used to understand the world.
   a. schema
   b. reflex
   c. instinct
   d. operation
   e. hierarchy

8. Regarding the development of identity, which of the following statements is FALSE?
   a. Everyone eventually grapples with an identity crisis, whether in adolescence or in adulthood.
   b. Some adolescents develop ego identity by modeling themselves after others, without soul-searching or self-examination.
   c. Some contemporary scholars prefer to use the term exploration, rather than crisis, to describe the period of soul-searching and self-examination associated with identity development.
   d. People may experience many identity crises throughout life.
   e. The development of ethnic identity is an important part of identity formation, especially for adolescents of color.

9. An influential theory of death and dying was developed by
   a. Erikson.
   b. Kübler-Ross.
   c. Arnett.
   d. Levinson.
   e. Gilligan.

10. A fertilized egg cell is called a(n)
    a. teratogen.
    b. zygote.
    c. fetus.
    d. embryo.
    e. placenta.

Essentials of Psychology Chapter 9

11. Vygotsky's concept of the zone of proximal development is best described
    a. by the principle of scaffolding.
    b. as the range between children's present level of skills and knowledge and their potential level with appropriate guidance
    c. as the range between the child's current level of intelligence and potential intelligence if provided with an enriched environment.
    d. as the child's zone of equilibrium or range of potential development based on current level of intelligence.
    e. as the range between the child's proximal and distal level of abilities.

12. Which of the following is the leading cause of dementia?
    a. brain infections, tumors, and injuries
    b. Parkinson's disease
    c. strokes
    d. chronic alcoholism
    e. Alzheimer's disease

13. What is the fastest-growing segment of the U.S. population?
    a. children under age 5
    b. children aged 6 to 12
    c. young adults aged 18 to 30
    d. adults aged 40 to 60
    e. adults aged 65 and older

14. Eight-month-old Finnegan is playful and responds positively to changes. He generally has a happy mood, and he quickly developed a regular sleeping and feeding schedule. Based on this description from the New York Longitudinal Study, Finnegan would be categorized as a(n) ______ child.
    a. pleasant
    b. secure
    c. positive
    d. easy
    e. slow-to-warm-up

15. Regarding physical changes in adulthood, which of the following statements is FALSE?
    a. Significant weight gain is an inevitable consequence of aging.
    b. After their twenties, most people lose about seven pounds of lean body mass every decade.
    c. Between ages twenty to seventy, people are likely to lose as much as 30 percent of their muscle cells.
    d. Gradual losses of muscle strength throughout adulthood can be offset by following a weight-bearing exercise program.
    e. People begin to start losing lean body tissue in their late twenties.

Essentials of Psychology Chapter 9

16. What is the correct sequencing of Piaget's stages of cognitive development?
    a. Concrete operational, sensorimotor, preoperational, formal operational
    b. Preoperational, concrete operational, formal operational, sensorimotor
    c. Sensorimotor, preoperational, formal operational, concrete operational
    d. Sensorimotor, concrete operational, preoperational, formal operational
    e. Sensorimotor, preoperational, concrete operational, formal operational

17. All of the following are stages in Kohlberg's theory EXCEPT
    a. social contract orientation.
    b. care and justice orientation.
    c. universal ethical principle orientation.
    d. obedience and punishment orientation.
    e. authority or law-and-order orientation.

18. Twenty-five-year-old Allison is predicted to be in which stage of psychosocial development?
    a. industry vs. inferiority
    b. identity vs. role diffusion
    c. generativity vs. stagnation
    d. integrity vs. despair
    e. intimacy vs. isolation

19. If Felicity's development is average, she can be expected to discriminate among happy, angry, and neutral facial expressions at what age?
    a. at birth
    b. 2 to 4 weeks
    c. 1 to 2 months
    d. 4 to 6 months
    e. 10 to 12 months

20. The New York Longitudinal Study identified ______ types of temperament, and they are called ______.
    a. 4; secure, insecure-avoidant, disorganized, and insecure-resistant
    b. 3; easy, difficult, and slow-to-warm-up
    c. 3; Types A, B, and C
    d. 3; permissive, authoritarian, and authoritative
    e. 2; assimilating and accommodating

21. Impaired hearing and vision, deformed teeth and bones, and liver damage may occur as a result of which teratogen?
    a. Congenital syphilis
    b. Rubella
    c. Spina bifida
    d. Alcohol
    e. Nicotine

Name:______________________ Class:______________ Date:________

Essentials of Psychology Chapter 9

22. A medical doctor believes that terminally ill people have the right to control the time and circumstances of their death. Despite the fact that assisting a suicide is illegal, the doctor provides the means for many terminally ill people to end their lives. The doctor's actions best fit which level of moral reasoning?
    a. postconventional
    b. preconventional
    c. conventional
    d. unconventional
    e. formal operational

23. Fourth-grade teacher Julie Farraday finds that her students are very eager to be helpful. They seem to care about being productive and involved in the class, as well as in their school. Farraday's students are best described at which stage of psychosocial development?
    a. Autonomy vs. shame and doubt
    b. Trust vs. mistrust
    c. Initiative vs. guilt
    d. Identity vs. role diffusion
    e. Industry vs. inferiority

24. Who studied the process of imprinting in geese and other species?
    a. John Bowlby
    b. Harry Harlow
    c. Diana Baumrind
    d. Konrad Lorenz
    e. Mary Ainsworth

25. According to the stages of development presented in the text, Carlotta's daughter Bella is considered in middle childhood when she is between ages
    a. 2 and 3.
    b. 3 and 6.
    c. 6 and 12.
    d. 3 and 12.
    e. 6 and 9.

26. Paula has recently dropped out of high school. She is not sure where she is headed in life, but school does not seem to be a part of it. She has started drinking and hanging around whoever has some alcohol. It sounds like Paula is in a state of
    a. menarche.
    b. inferiority.
    c. role diffusion.
    d. imaginary audience.
    e. ego despair.

Essentials of Psychology Chapter 9

27. Regarding the effects of teratogens on prenatal development, it appears that
    a. the embryonic stage is the one most susceptible to major damage to arms and legs from teratogens.
    b. the fetal stage is the one most susceptible to major structural abnormalities from teratogens.
    c. the germinal stage is the one most susceptible to major structural abnormalities from teratogens.
    d. the amniotic stage is the one most susceptible to major structural abnormalities from teratogens.
    e. all of the stages have an equal risk of major structural abnormalities from teratogens.

28. Disbelief that one is really dying is characteristic of which stage of death and dying?
    a. depression
    b. acceptance
    c. denial
    d. bargaining
    e. anger

29. In the film "*Fly Away Home*," a group of abandoned goslings develop a strong bond with a young girl. Since their mother is not there, the girl teaches the geese to fly using an ultralite airplane. This film is a good example of which concept from development psychology?
    a. Attachment
    b. Parenting styles
    c. Conservation
    d. Temperament
    e. Imprinting

30. The typical order of the stages in death and dying is
    a. anger, denial, depression, bargaining, acceptance.
    b. denial, anger, bargaining, depression, acceptance.
    c. anger, depression, denial, bargaining, acceptance.
    d. denial, depression, anger, bargaining, acceptance.
    e. depression, denial, bargaining, anger, acceptance.

31. Sharleen believes she is unlike anyone else and is invulnerable. When she is having a crisis and her parents try to talk to her, Sharleen says, "You can't possibly understand what I'm going through!" This reflects which aspect of adolescent cognitive development?
    a. imaginary audience
    b. formal operations
    c. deductive reasoning
    d. personal fable
    e. role diffusion

Essentials of Psychology Chapter 9

32. Six-month-old Charlotte fits the characteristics of a slow-to-warm-up temperament. Charlotte would be expected to exhibit all but which of the following?
    a. low activity level
    b. interest in novel stimuli
    c. need for more time in adjusting to new situations
    d. mild distress in new situations
    e. withdrawal in unfamiliar settings

33. Fifteen-year-old Mareek believes that other people are as interested in him as he is. This reflects which aspect of adolescent cognitive development?
    a. imaginary audience
    b. personal fable
    c. animistic thinking
    d. formal operations
    e. centration

34. An unlearned response to a particular stimulus is a(n)
    a. teratogen.
    b. habit.
    c. reflex.
    d. ability.
    e. skill.

35. Research on parenting styles suggests that the most effective parenting style is
    a. authoritative.
    b. authoritarian.
    c. permissive.
    d. secure.
    e. assertive.

36. What general term does Piaget use for the process of changing to function more effectively in responding to environmental challenges?
    a. equilibrium
    b. adaptation
    c. diffusion
    d. conservation
    e. habituation

Essentials of Psychology Chapter 9

37. Piaget's primary research technique involved
    a. rigorous experimental methodology.
    b. long questionnaires.
    c. extensive surveys.
    d. careful observation.
    e. twin studies.

38. Xan's offspring is in the embryonic stage of development. All but which of the following are occurring for Xan's offspring?
    a. The neural tube is forming.
    b. The head and blood vessels are forming.
    c. A primitive heart has taken shape and begins beating.
    d. The major organs are beginning to take shape.
    e. The offspring has grown from one ounce to two pounds.

39. In Piaget's theory, the tendency to view the world only from one's own perspective is
    a. centration.
    b. authoritarianism.
    c. conservation.
    d. egocentrism.
    e. irreversibility.

40. All but which of the following are characteristic of the preoperational stage of cognitive development?
    a. egocentrism
    b. conservation
    c. irreversibility
    d. centration
    e. animistic thinking

41. Lawrence Kohlberg was interested in which aspect of development?
    a. physical
    b. social
    c. intellectual
    d. moral
    e. emotional

42. Nine-year-old Dakoda realizes that the quantity of water in a glass remains the same, even when the water is poured into a different shaped glass and appears to look like more or less. In Piaget's terms, Dakoda has developed
    a. conservation.
    b. assimilation.
    c. accommodation.
    d. object permanence.
    e. centration.

Essentials of Psychology Chapter 9

43. Children who react negatively to change and are generally irritable are classified as having what kind of temperament?
   a. resistant
   b. insecure
   c. avoidant
   d. difficult
   e. slow-to-warm-up

44. Vygotsky saw cognitive development through the lens of children's
   a. egocentrism.
   b. culture and social worlds.
   c. biological programming.
   d. parental controls.
   e. schemas.

45. Which hormones fuel a woman's sex drive?
   a. androgens
   b. estrogens
   c. progesterone
   d. corticosteroids
   e. endorphins

46. Eleven-year-old Jorge looks forward to "becoming a man." What is the first sign of puberty that Jorge will experience?
   a. appearance of facial hair
   b. deepening of his voice
   c. appearance of pubic hair
   d. enlarged testes
   e. his first ejaculation

47. Regarding peer relationships in childhood, which of the following statements is FALSE?
   a. Peer relationships give children the opportunity to develop skills in relating to others.
   b. Peer relationships can have negative consequences on a child's development.
   c. The acceptance of peer group members can help shape a child's self-esteem.
   d. Peer groups can influence a child's developing sense of competence.
   e. Children and teens with a strong need for peer acceptance are less likely to engage in deviant activities.

Essentials of Psychology Chapter 9

48. If 6-month-old Mikhail's development is normal, he can be expected to do all but which of the following?
    a. Grasp a stationary object
    b. Sit without support
    c. Roll over
    d. Catch a moving object
    e. Bring an object into his field of view

49. Which activity might allow Gwyneth to help her six-month-old granddaughter develop object permanence?
    a. playing peek-a-boo with her
    b. singing the alphabet song with her
    c. singing songs like "Itsy Bitsy Spider"
    d. playing patty-cake with her
    e. reading children's books to her

50. If 60-year-old Evelyn wants to increase her chances of preserving mental sharpness, which activity might she consider taking up?
    a. mentally challenging games like chess
    b. crossword or jigsaw puzzles
    c. writing, painting, or sculpting
    d. reading
    e. Any of the above may help Evelyn preserve mental sharpness.

51. Shawn was born with fetal alcohol syndrome. Shawn's symptoms may include all of the following EXCEPT
    a. flattened nose.
    b. missing extremities.
    c. underdeveloped upper jaw.
    d. widely spaced eyes.
    e. mental retardation.

52. The ability to solve abstract problems best describes someone at which of Piaget's stages of cognitive development?
    a. abstract operations
    b. formal operations
    c. concrete operations
    d. preoperational
    e. sensorimotor

Essentials of Psychology Chapter 9

53. Wilfred was diagnosed with a terminal illness. He is beginning to feel a sense of loss and hopelessness. This is characteristic of which stage of death and dying?
    a. anger
    b. depression
    c. denial
    d. acceptance
    e. bargaining

54. Pierre's second-grade teacher is very critical of all his work. She rarely praises him and frequently ridicules even his best efforts. As a result, Pierre is reluctant to attempt new tasks. Erikson's theory predicts that Pierre is likely to end up with a sense of
    a. mistrust.
    b. guilt.
    c. inferiority.
    d. shame and doubt.
    e. insecurity.

55. The Strange Situation was developed to study
    a. imprinting in birds.
    b. attachment in monkeys.
    c. attachment in human infants.
    d. bonding with surrogate mothers.
    e. temperament of human infants.

56. All of the following are examples of teratogens EXCEPT
    a. folic acid.
    b. lead.
    c. X-rays.
    d. mercury.
    e. infectious organisms.

57. Which theorist identified stages of psychosocial development?
    a. Lev Vygotsky
    b. Mary Ainsworth
    c. Jean Piaget
    d. Lawrence Kohlberg
    e. Erik Erikson

Essentials of Psychology Chapter 9

58. Carol Gilligan suggested that, when making moral decisions,
    a. women rely more on a care orientation and men rely more on a justice orientation.
    b. men rely more on a care orientation and women rely more on a justice orientation.
    c. women rely exclusively on a care orientation and men rely exclusively on a justice orientation.
    d. women and men both rely more on a care orientation than a justice orientation.
    e. men and women both rely more on a justice orientation than a care orientation.

59. Imaginary audience and personal fable are components of which aspect of adolescent thinking?
    a. formal operations
    b. deductive reasoning
    c. egocentrism
    d. concrete operations
    e. role diffusion

60. Compared to the other temperament groups, difficult infants are more likely to experience all but which of the following in childhood?
    a. develop acting-out behaviors
    b. develop mental health problems
    c. be highly spirited
    d. not be a "pushover"
    e. anxiety or depression

61. What is the correct sequence of psychosocial stages in child development?
    a. industry, autonomy, trust, initiative
    b. autonomy, initiative, trust, industry
    c. autonomy, trust, initiative, industry
    d. trust, initiative, autonomy, industry
    e. trust, autonomy, initiative, industry

X 62. Psychologists use the term _____ to describe a characteristic style of behavior or disposition.
    a. habit
    b. temperament
    c. reflex
    d. instinct
    e. personality

63. According to Erik Erikson, people who forge a strong sense of ego identity earlier in development are more likely to achieve what in early adulthood?
    a. inferiority
    b. intimacy
    c. industry
    d. initiative
    e. generativity

Essentials of Psychology Chapter 9

64. Murray has a condition that has caused him to experience a major deterioration of his mental abilities. He has lost much of his reasoning and judgment abilities, and he has great difficulty carrying out purposeful behavior. Based on this description, what is Murray's condition most likely to be?
    a. centration
    b. cognitive dissonance
    c. osteoporosis
    d. dementia
    e. role diffusion

65. Research examining the effects of full-time day care on infant attachment has found
    a. strong evidence that day care interferes with attachment.
    b. strong evidence that day care interferes with attachment, but only in high-quality day-care settings.
    c. mixed evidence regarding the effects of day care on attachment.
    d. no strong evidence that day care interferes with attachment.
    e. compelling evidence that day care enhances attachment.

66. According to the text, all but which of the following factors are associated with adolescent risk-taking?
    a. hormonal influences
    b. the personal fable
    c. having close friends who engage in risky behavior
    d. impulsivity
    e. family problems

67. A child who explains that putting his toys away is good because he will get a treat is at what level of moral development?
    a. unconventional
    b. conventional
    c. preconventional
    d. postconventional
    e. preoperational

68. Which is the first sign of puberty in a female?
    a. breast buds
    b. pubic hair
    c. underarm hair
    d. first menstruation
    e. ovulation

Name:______________________ Class:______________________ Date:______________

Essentials of Psychology Chapter 9

69. Tara contracts Rubella during the early part of her pregnancy. Her offspring is at increased risk for developing
   a. heart disease, deafness, and mental retardation.
   b. lung disease and kidney damage.
   c. liver disease and kidney damage.
   d. facial deformities.
   e. asthma.

70. Nolan was born with a hole in the tube surrounding his spinal cord. Which disorder does Nolan have?
   a. German measles
   b. Teratogenitis
   c. Spina bifida
   d. Rubella
   e. Congenital syphilis

71. Sixty-five-year-old Pablo is terminally ill with cancer. In terms of the stages of death and dying, how can his family and health care providers best help him?
   a. Do everything possible to help Pablo avoid the acceptance stage, since this stage represents giving up hope.
   b. Ignore Pablo's depressive state, and make efforts to cheer him up.
   c. Respond back to Pablo's expressions of anger.
   d. Understand the stages, and help Pablo attain a state of final acceptance.
   e. Help Pablo think of ways to bargain, since this will keep his mind off of his pending death.

72. When are newborn infants typically capable of imitating their parents' facial expressions?
   a. within minutes of their birth
   b. about 1 week of age
   c. about 2 weeks of age
   d. about 4 weeks of age
   e. about 2 months of age

73. All but which of the following people are using compensation to successfully respond to challenges of aging?
   a. Arsenio, who uses a cane to get around
   b. Bobbie, who responds to hearing loss by using a hearing aid
   c. Craig, who writes notes to remember things he has to do each day
   d. DeeDee, who gives herself extra time when she has to learn something new
   e. Eduardo, who maintains an optimistic mindset and seeks out new challenges

74. If Gertrude is like the average woman, she can expect to experience menopause in her
   a. late thirties or early forties.
   b. mid-forties.
   c. late forties or early fifties.
   d. mid-fifties.
   e. late fifties or early sixties.

Essentials of Psychology Chapter 9

75. According to Erikson, middle adulthood is to ______ as early adulthood is to _______.
    a. ego identity vs. despair; intimacy vs. isolation
    b. intimacy vs. isolation; generativity vs. stagnation
    c. generativity vs. stagnation; intimacy vs. isolation
    d. ego integrity vs. despair; identity vs. role diffusion
    e. generativity vs. stagnation; identity vs. role diffusion

76. An average child in the concrete operational stage of cognitive development can be expected to do all but which of the following?
    a. recognize that other people's thoughts and feelings may differ from his/her own
    b. perform simple logical operations tied to tangible examples
    c. be less egocentric than her/his younger siblings
    d. understand that quantity or amount of an object remains constant despite superficial changes in outward appearance
    e. generate hypotheses and think deductively

X 77. Toma is almost five years old. As he was struggling to learn to tie his shoes, his parents became exasperated with him and bought him shoes with Velcro closures. When he had trouble learning to ride a two-wheeler with training wheels, his parents made him go back to a tricycle. According to Erikson's theory, Toma may end up with a feeling of
    a. shame.
    b. guilt.
    c. mistrust.
    d. inferiority.
    e. doubt.

78. What type of infant temperament is generally associated with better adjustment in adulthood?
    a. inhibited
    b. slow-to-warm-up
    c. difficult
    d. easy
    e. secure

79. Of the following characteristics Fiona experienced during puberty, which is a primary sex characteristic?
    a. breast development
    b. enlarged uterus
    c. pubic hair and underarm hair
    d. breast development and enlarged uterus
    e. breast development, pubic hair, and underarm hair

Name:______________________ Class:______________________ Date:______________

Essentials of Psychology Chapter 9

80. The protective environment inside the mother's uterus is called the ______, and nutrients and waste materials are exchanged between the mother and embryo via the ______.
   a. amniotic sac; placenta
   b. placenta; amniotic sac
   c. placenta; neural tube
   d. umbilical cord; placenta
   e. amniotic sac; neural tube

81. Kohlberg's theory of moral development has _____ levels, and they are called ______.
   a. 4; sensorimotor, preoperational, concrete operational, and formal operational
   b. 4; identity, intimacy, generativity, and integrity
   c. 3; preconventional, conventional, and postconventional
   d. 3; selective optimization, optimism, and self-challenge
   e. 2; care orientation and justice orientation

82. Preserved intellectual ability in later life is associated with which factor(s)?
   a. engagement in stimulating activities
   b. general physical health
   c. gender
   d. gender and general physical health
   e. engagement in stimulating activities, general physical health, and openness to new experiences

83. Regarding adult crystallized intelligence and fluid intelligence, which of the following statements is TRUE?
   a. Both types of intelligence generally increase throughout the adult life span.
   b. Both types of intelligence generally decrease throughout the adult life span.
   c. After early adulthood, fluid intelligence generally decreases, while crystallized intelligence stays about the same or increases.
   d. After early adulthood, crystallized intelligence generally decreases, while fluid intelligence stays about the same or increases.
   e. Both types of intelligence decrease, but only in late adulthood.

84. Nurse Ross Millhouse works in an assisted living facility where he cares for residents over the age of 85. Assuming the residents are typical of people of their age, about what percentage of the residents under Millhouse's care would be expected to suffer from Alzheimer's disease?
   a. around one in a hundred
   b. just under one in fifty
   c. about one in ten
   d. more than one in three
   e. it is impossible to assess since Alzheimer's disease can not be diagnosed until after death.

Name:______________________ Class:______________ Date:________

Essentials of Psychology Chapter 9

85. Regarding infants' learning abilities, which of the following statements is FALSE?
    a. Research evidence shows that learning begins prenatally.
    b. Infants can learn simple responses at young ages.
    c. Infants can remember learned responses for days or weeks.
    d. Infants as young as six months old can retain memories for faces.
    e. Infants are active perceivers and passive learners in their environment.

86. In her research on attachment, Ainsworth noted ______ different styles of attachment, and they are called _______.
    a. 2; imprinting and bonding
    b. 3; easy, difficult, and slow-to-warm-up
    c. 3; authoritative, authoritarian, and permissive
    d. 3; secure, insecure-avoidant, and insecure-resistant
    e. 4; secure, insecure-avoidant, insecure-resistant, and slow-to-warm-up

87. At the beginning of the twentieth century, the average American girl began to show signs of puberty by around age
    a. 6.
    b. 8.
    c. 10.
    d. 13.
    e. 15.

88. Which of the following answers to the "Heinz dilemma" best reflects postconventional moral reasoning?
    a. Heinz should steal the drug because he needs his wife and she might die without it.
    b. Heinz should steal the drug to avoid being blamed if his wife dies.
    c. People would lose respect for Heinz if he didn't at least try to save his wife by stealing the drug.
    d. Heinz must steal the drug because he has a duty to protect his wife.
    e. Heinz would be morally wrong not to steal the drug because it would violate his belief in the absolute value of human life.

89. The ability to think abstractly and flexibly in solving problems is referred to as
    a. practical intelligence.
    b. fluid intelligence.
    c. applied intelligence.
    d. crystallized intelligence.
    e. emotional intelligence.

90. Which pioneer of psychology characterized adolescence as a period of "storm and stress?"
    a. G. Stanley Hall
    b. Jean Piaget
    c. Lawrence Kohlberg
    d. Sigmund Freud
    e. Erik Erikson

Essentials of Psychology Chapter 9

91. Harold says that hitting his sister is wrong because he will be punished if he does. Harold's reasoning reflects which level of moral development?
    a. conventional
    b. preconventional
    c. postconventional
    d. unconventional
    e. preoperational

92. What is the correct order of stages in prenatal development?
    a. germinal, embryonic, fetal
    b. germinal, fetal, embryonic
    c. embryonic, germinal, fetal
    d. embryonic, fetal, germinal
    e. fetal, germinal, embryonic

93. Louisa is pregnant with her first child. By which week of prenatal development are all of her offspring's major organ systems likely to have formed?
    a. week six
    b. week nine
    c. week twelve
    d. week twenty
    e. week thirty

94. Among parenting styles, rigid is to ______ as lax is to ______.
    a. authoritative; permissive
    b. authoritarian; authoritative
    c. permissive; authoritarian
    d. permissive; authoritative
    e. authoritarian; permissive

95. Elvin is 75 years old. He is rather sad because he regrets the wasted opportunities in life and feels he has made a lot of mistakes. From Erikson's perspective, this reflects a sense of
    a. despair.
    b. ego integrity.
    c. isolation.
    d. stagnation.
    e. generativity.

Name:________________________ Class:________________ Date:__________

Essentials of Psychology Chapter 9

96. How are bonding and attachment different?
    a. Bonding happens in animals, and attachment happens in humans.
    b. Bonding happens with mothers, while attachment happens with mothers or fathers.
    c. Bonding is the parent's tie to the infant, whereas attachment is the infant's tie to the caregiver.
    d. The environment primarily influences bonding, while attachment is influenced primarily by genetics.
    e. They are not different; they are alternate terms for the same concept.

97. Fluid intelligence is to _____ as crystallized intelligence is to ________,
    a. speed of problem solving, acquired information
    b. practical intelligence, analytic intelligence
    c. emotional intelligence, practical intelligence
    d. applying knowledge, perceiving relationships among patterns

98. Psychologist Jeffrey Arnett describes the transition from adolescence to adulthood with the term
    a. selective optimization.
    b. intimacy versus isolation.
    c. emerging adulthood.
    d. midlife crisis.
    e. moratorium.

99. Joshua is a normal, six-day-old baby. He can be expected to do which of the following?
    a. distinguish components of music, such as pitch and tempo
    b. retain memory for faces
    c. discriminate among happy, angry, and neutral facial expressions
    d. detect the mother's odor
    e. differentiate between various speech sounds, such as "ba" and "ma"

100. Twenty-three-year-old Venetia is thinking about getting pregnant. Her doctor recommends that Venetia begin taking folic acid supplements in order to reduce the risk of ______ in her offspring.
    a. miscarriage
    b. fetal alcohol syndrome
    c. spina bifida
    d. rubella
    e. sudden infant death syndrome

101. Kohlberg's model of moral development has been criticized as culturally biased because
    a. the stages have only been found in people from Western cultures.
    b. research has found that people from different cultures vary in how they proceed through the stages.
    c. there is little evidence that people reach the level of postconventional reasoning.
    d. it emphasizes moral standards that appeal to males rather than females.
    e. it emphasizes ideals found primarily in Western cultures.

Essentials of Psychology Chapter 9

102. Dontarius was born at thirty-one weeks of gestation with a birth weight of four pounds and twelve ounces. Dontarius is classified as
   a. premature.
   b. low birth weight.
   c. both premature and low birth weight.
   d. lacking the age of viability.
   e. having FAS.

103. ______ was the most influential theorist on cognitive development and may be considered the most important developmental theorist of all time.
   a. Lawrence Kohlberg
   b. Carol Gilligan
   c. Erik Erikson
   d. Lev Vygotsky
   e. Jean Piaget

104. Chris and Pat set limits for their children without being overcontrolling. Which style of parenting are they using?
   a. authoritative
   b. authoritarian
   c. permissive
   d. assertive
   e. assimilation

105. According to Vygotsky, the optimal relationship between adult and child is
   a. follower and leader.
   b. supervisor and employee.
   c. peer and peer.
   d. parent and student.
   e. tutor and student.

106. When Fernando babysits his niece, the infant grabs his long hair and won't let go until Fernando uncurls her fingers. Instead of getting mad at his niece for pulling his hair, Fernando understands that her actions are being driven by which reflex?
   a. Moro
   b. palmar grasp
   c. Babinski
   d. rooting
   e. eyeblink

Name:__________ Class:__________ Date:__________

Essentials of Psychology Chapter 9

107. Regarding Alzheimer's disease, which of the following statements is FALSE?
   a. Scientists have confirmed that a defect on one particular gene accounts for the disease.
   b. The number of Alzheimer's patients is expected to significantly increase over the next fifty years.
   c. The available drugs provide only modest benefits in boosting memory functioning in AD patients.
   d. There currently is no cure for Alzheimer's disease.
   e. Alzheimer's disease can affect younger people.

108. In prenatal development, the umbilical cord connects the
   a. neural tube to the placenta.
   b. placenta to the amniotic sac.
   c. amniotic sac to the embryo.
   d. embryo and fetus to the placenta.
   e. embryo and fetus to the amniotic sac.

109. The stage at which people become physically capable of reproducing is called
   a. menarche.
   b. moratorium.
   c. menopause.
   d. early adulthood.
   e. puberty.

110. The stressful time of soul searching and self-examination that many adolescents experience is the
   a. identity crisis.
   b. inferiority complex.
   c. industry struggle.
   d. initiative crisis.
   e. personal fable.

111. Which of the following best describes Erikson's concept of stagnation?
   a. ambition
   b. wisdom
   c. insecurity
   d. active
   e. self-absorption

112. Which of the following structures acts as a sort of shock absorber for the developing embryo or fetus?
   a. amniotic sac
   b. umbilical cord
   c. neural tube
   d. fallopian tube
   e. placenta

Essentials of Psychology Chapter 9

113. Pedro just began lifting his chin and bringing objects to his mouth. What age would you guess Pedro to be?
    a. less than 2 weeks old
    b. 2 to 4 weeks old
    c. 4 to 8 weeks old
    d. 2 to 3 months old
    e. 4 to 6 months old

114. The formation of a strong bond of a newborn animal to the first moving object seen after birth is called
    a. bonding.
    b. attachment.
    c. assimilation.
    d. accommodation.
    e. imprinting.

115. Teratogens that damage the arms and legs are most likely to have an effect during which weeks of pregnancy?
    a. weeks 1 and 2
    b. weeks 4 to 8
    c. weeks 10 to 12
    d. weeks 20 to 25
    e. weeks 30 to 32

116. Which of the following parental actions is associated with children having more behavior problems?
    a. excessive use of criticism, use of harsh punishment, and inconsistent discipline
    b. excessive use of criticism and inconsistent discipline only
    c. excessive use of criticism only
    d. inconsistent discipline only
    e. use of harsh punishment only

117. Ten-month-old Kazik's parents are very sensitive to her needs. Whenever she cries, someone tries to comfort her. Based on this description, she will probably effectively resolve which psychosocial crisis?
    a. autonomy vs. shame and doubt
    b. initiative vs. guilt
    c. trust vs. mistrust
    d. industry vs. inferiority
    e. identity vs. role diffusion

Essentials of Psychology Chapter 9

118. When 11-month-old Ethan is in a new environment, he feels free to explore. However, he periodically "checks in" with his caregiver during exploration. If his caregiver leaves the room, Ethan sometimes cries and limits his exploration. Upon his caregiver's return, Ethan gives a warm greeting; then he begins his exploration again. Generalizing from research on attachment, Ethan's attachment would be described as
    a. easy.
    b. secure.
    c. disorganized.
    d. insecure-avoidant.
    e. insecure-resistant.

119. Celia smokes heavily throughout her pregnancy. Celia is increasing the risk of ______ in her offspring.
    a. deformed arms and legs
    b. spina bifida
    c. sudden infant death syndrome
    d. liver damage
    e. teeth and bone deformities

120. In prenatal development, the time between conception and about week two is called the
    a. germinal stage.
    b. fetal stage.
    c. embryonic stage.
    d. first trimester.
    e. fertilization stage.

121. Third-grade teacher Ben Stallworth can expect that the majority of his eight- and nine -year-old students are in which stage of cognitive development?
    a. concrete operational
    b. initiative vs. guilt
    c. preoperational
    d. formal operational
    e. industry vs. inferiority

122. By the end of the first year of life, Evana has mastered the most difficult balancing problem ever to be encountered in her life. What skill has she mastered?
    a. walking
    b. crawling
    c. creeping
    d. balancing on one foot
    e. standing without support

Essentials of Psychology Chapter 9

123. If Maury's son's development is normal, Maury can expect that his son will develop depth perception by about what age?
   a. 3 months
   b. 6 months
   c. 9 months
   d. 12 months
   e. 18 months

124. The age of viability refers to the
   a. youngest age at which it is safe for a female to be pregnant.
   b. youngest age at which an embryo is likely to survive if born prematurely.
   c. youngest age at which a fetus is capable of sustaining life on its own.
   d. optimal age for women to become pregnant.
   e. the point of pregnancy in which the mother should reduce her normal activities.

125. Of the five senses, which is the slowest to develop?
   a. vision
   b. hearing
   c. touch
   d. taste
   e. smell

126. Which reflex may have had the survival value in ancestral times of preventing infants from falling as their mothers carried them around all day?
   a. the eyeblink reflex
   b. the palmar grasp reflex
   c. the Babinski reflex
   d. the rooting reflex
   e. the sucking reflex

127. Kohlberg studied moral development by
   a. observing people's behavior.
   b. asking people to respond to moral dilemmas.
   c. administering large-scale surveys.
   d. using extensive questionnaires.
   e. conducting extensive interviews with women and men.

128. Andrew took the family car without permission. He seriously damaged it while joyriding. Afterwards, his parents bought him a car of his own. This is an example of which parenting style?
   a. authoritarian
   b. authoritative
   c. permissive
   d. restrictive
   e. inconsistent

129. Other factors being equal, which child is at highest risk for negative outcomes in adolescence like poor school performance and low self-confidence?
   a. a boy raised by permissive parents
   b. a girl raised by permissive parents
   c. a boy raised by authoritarian parents
   d. a girl raised by authoritarian parents
   e. a boy or girl raised by authoritative parents

130. According to Piaget, full cognitive maturity occurs in which stage of cognitive development?
   a. concrete operational
   b. sensorimotor
   c. preoperational
   d. accommodational
   e. formal operational

131. Gloria's family has a large minivan she calls a car. Her grandmother buys a small hybrid that Gloria also calls a car. This is a demonstration of
   a. object permanence.
   b. conservation.
   c. assimilation.
   d. accommodation.
   e. irreversibility.

132. Maria suffers from a bone disease characterized by loss of bone density in which the bones become porous, brittle, and more prone to fracture. Which disease is she likely to have?
   a. osteoporosis
   b. menopause
   c. menarche
   d. dementia
   e. spina bifida

Essentials of Psychology Chapter 9

133. According to Erikson, psychosocial development in late adulthood centers on the crisis of
    a. identity vs. role diffusion.
    b. industry vs. inferiority.
    c. intimacy vs. isolation.
    d. ego integrity vs. despair.
    e. generativity vs. stagnation.

134. In the Moro reflex, a newborn infant
    a. blinks for protection against light or foreign objects.
    b. extends its arms and arches its back when its head falls backward or in response to loud noise.
    c. turns its head towards a cheek that has been touched.
    d. fans out and curls its toes when the sole of its foot is stroked.
    e. curls its fingers around an object that touches the palm.

135. If Aretha is like the typical older adult, the psychological problem she is most likely to face is
    a. phobia.
    b. ego disintegration.
    c. alienation.
    d. depression.
    e. anger.

136. If his development is normal, newborn baby Moses can be expected to do all but which of the following within his first week of life?
    a. Hear a variety of sounds and be particularly sensitive to sounds falling within the frequency of the human voice.
    b. Discriminate among different tastes.
    c. Detect his mother's odor.
    d. Discern his mother's voice from other female voices.
    e. Differentiate various speech sounds.

137. Gregor weighed 7 pounds at birth. About how much is he likely to weigh on his first birthday?
    a. 14 or 15 pounds
    b. 21 or 22 pounds
    c. 28 or 29 pounds
    d. 32 or 33 pounds
    e. unable to determine with information provided

Essentials of Psychology Chapter 9

138. Twenty-month-old Hannah realizes that her mother still exists even when Hannah cannot see her. What cognitive achievement has Hannah mastered?
    a. egocentrism
    b. object permanence
    c. conservation
    d. animistic thinking
    e. centration

139. Marietta, who is terminally ill, promises to go to church every Sunday if God will let her live to see the birth of her first grandchild. Marietta reflects which stage of death and dying?
    a. anger
    b. depression
    c. denial
    d. bargaining
    e. acceptance

140. Harriet is working on building a sense of independence and self-control. Generalizing from the theory of psychosocial development, Harriet is probably in which age group?
    a. infancy
    b. toddlerhood
    c. preschool
    d. middle childhood
    e. adolescence

141. If you are like the average person, you can expect to reach the peak of your physical performance in your
    a. late teens.
    b. twenties.
    c. early thirties.
    d. late thirties.
    e. early forties.

142. Developmental psychologists describe prenatal development as occurring in
    a. three stages: first, second, and third trimesters.
    b. three stages: germinal, embryonic, and fetal.
    c. nine stages corresponding to each month of pregnancy.
    d. two stages: fertilization and pregnancy.
    e. three stages: fertilization, pregnancy, and birth.

Essentials of Psychology Chapter 9

143. Maternal smoking is associated with increased risk in the offspring with all of the following EXCEPT
   a. reduced attention span.
   b. deformed extremities.
   c. learning problems.
   d. behavioral problems.
   e. childhood asthma.

144. Between birth and adulthood the brain ______ in volume.
   a. doubles
   b. triples
   c. quadruples
   d. quintuples
   e. sextuples

145. Forty-two-year-old Jon is experiencing a psychological challenge. He is grappling with the loss of his youth and feels "trapped," perceiving a lack of future options. Based on this discrimination, what is Jon most likely experiencing?
   a. Menarche
   b. Erikson's concept of middle age isolation
   c. Generativity
   d. Male menopause
   e. Midlife crisis

146. The biological unfolding of an organism according to its underlying genetic code is called
   a. imprinting.
   b. germination.
   c. development.
   d. puberty.
   e. maturation.

147. Aimee was late coming home from school. Even though she had a reasonable excuse, her parents grounded her for a month and suspended her allowance. This sounds like which style of parenting?
   a. authoritarian
   b. authoritative
   c. permissive
   d. inhibited
   e. assertive

Essentials of Psychology Chapter 9

148. Amy teaches four-year-old preschool. After taking her college developmental psychology class, Amy determines that the majority of her students will be dealing with which psychosocial crisis?
   a. autonomy vs. shame and doubt
   b. trust vs. mistrust
   c. initiative vs. guilt
   d. industry vs. inferiority
   e. identity vs. role diffusion

149. Elisabeth Kübler-Ross's model of death and dying is based on
   a. observations of terminally ill people and their families.
   b. case studies of the journals of terminally ill people.
   c. case studies of people with infamous deaths.
   d. interviews with people who work with the terminally ill – hospice workers, nurses, doctors, and chaplains.
   e. interviews with terminally ill people.

150. Regarding puberty, which of the following statements is FALSE?
   a. Girls enter puberty today at a much earlier age than in previous generations.
   b. On average, puberty lasts about three to four years.
   c. On average, African American girls begin showing signs of puberty earlier than European American girls.
   d. On average, girls begin puberty before boys.
   e. Puberty begins with appearance of primary sex characteristics.

151. Regarding the normal declines in memory functioning that occur during midlife, which of the following statements is FALSE?
   a. They often are not noticeable.
   b. They do not typically interfere with social functioning.
   c. They do not typically interfere with occupational functioning.
   d. They may be offset by the increased knowledge and experience gained through aging.
   e. They seem to appear suddenly.

152. When two-week-old Carson's father strokes the baby's left cheek, Carson turns his head to the left. Carson's response is called the _______ reflex.
   a. sucking
   b. eyeblink
   c. Moro
   d. rooting
   e. Babinski

153. If Derek is like the average American father, he is more likely than the mother to engage in which of the following activities with his infant daughter?
   a. feeding her
   b. changing her diaper
   c. playing physically with her
   d. bathing her
   e. burping her

154. In descriptions of temperament, another term for "slow-to-warm-up" is
   a. resistant.
   b. detached.
   c. inhibited.
   d. insecure.
   e. avoidant.

155. Which of the following is a secondary sex characteristic?
   a. enlarged penis
   b. enlarged testes
   c. enlarged uterus
   d. breast development
   e. menarche

156. When the sole of her foot is stroked, three-week-old Pam curls and fans her toes. Pam is demonstrating which reflex?
   a. Babinski
   b. Moro
   c. rooting
   d. palmar grasp
   e. sucking

157. In Vygotsky's terms, the range between a child's present level of skills and knowledge and their potential level of skills and knowledge with appropriate guidance is called the child's
   a. space of scaffolding.
   b. region of growth.
   c. zone of proximal development.
   d. zone of equilibrium.
   e. schema space.

Essentials of Psychology Chapter 9

158. The fetal stage of prenatal development lasts from
   a. conception to week two.
   b. conception to week eight.
   c. implantation to week eight.
   d. week nine through delivery.
   e. week twelve through delivery.

159. Suzette drives the speed limit because it's the law. Suzette's reasoning best demonstrates which level of moral reasoning?
   a. unconventional
   b. postconventional
   c. conventional
   d. preconventional
   e. concrete operational

160. Psychologist Carol Gilligan argued that Lawrence Kohlberg's theory is biased against
   a. younger people.
   b. women.
   c. minorities.
   d. people from non-Western cultures.
   e. the elderly.

161. If Paige is like the average American girl, she will have her first period at about what age?
   a. 9 to 10
   b. 10 to 11
   c. 11 to 12
   d. 12 to 13
   e. 13 to 14

162. Generalizing from the Greek word on which it is based, "teras," which of the following words best describes the nature of a teratogen?
   a. abnormal
   b. risk
   c. bad
   d. monster
   e. problem

Name:________________________________ Class:____________________ Date:__________

Essentials of Psychology Chapter 9

163. The visual cliff apparatus tests infants' sensory abilities. What, specific aspect of the infant's sensory abilities does the device allow us to study?
 a. Depth perception
 b. Color vision
 c. Sound discrimination
 d. Visual discrimination
 e. Visual tracking

164. In their research with baby rhesus monkeys, the Harlows demonstrated that ______ was a strong determinant of attachment.
 a. contact comfort
 b. a secure base
 c. food
 d. quality of care
 e. temperament

165. All but which of the following cognitive abilities generally decline after early adulthood?
 a. rapid problem solving
 b. memory for newly acquired information
 c. perception of relationships among patterns
 d. rapid abstract reasoning
 e. application of acquired knowledge

166. Regarding research on pubertal timing, which of the following statements is TRUE?
 a. Both boys and girls seem to benefit from early maturation.
 b. Both girls and boys seem to benefit from late maturation.
 c. Boys tend to benefit from early maturation, while girls tend to benefit from late maturation.
 d. Girls tend to benefit from early maturation, while boys tend to benefit from late maturation.
 e. Neither boys nor girls benefit from early maturation.

167. Research on attachment suggests that children who showed more secure attachments as infants are more likely than their less securely attached peers to show all but which of the following?
 a. Better self-esteem
 b. Better physical health
 c. Fewer behavior problems
 d. Better relationships with peers
 e. Better overall psychological adjustment

Name:________________________ Class:________________ Date:__________

Essentials of Psychology Chapter 9

168. All but which of the following have been put forth as criticisms of Piaget's theory?
    a. He observed far too many children to be able to draw any reasonable conclusions.
    b. He underestimated abilities of younger children.
    c. Development is variable from child to child and does not always progress identically.
    d. He did not take cultural differences into account.
    e. He failed to account for changes in cognitive development that occur across different stages.

169. The time in a woman's life when menstruation ends is called
    a. menarche.
    b. role diffusion.
    c. ovulation.
    d. midlife crisis.
    e. menopause.

170. Moral reasoning based on conformity with social rules is characteristic of which level of moral development?
    a. conventional
    b. preconventional
    c. postconventional
    d. unconventional
    e. formal operational

171. Regarding the New York Longitudinal Study of temperament, which of the following statements is FALSE?
    a. Investigators found that about 65 percent of children could be classified into one of the temperament groups.
    b. The majority of children, 40 percent, were classified as easy children.
    c. The least common classification assigned to children was "difficult," with 10 percent of children falling in this category.
    d. The distinct types of temperament observed in infancy predict later differences in adjustment, with easy infants showing better adjustment.
    e. The study demonstrated that basic temperament cannot be changed.

172. Regular exercise is associated with all but which of the following benefits?
    a. increased life expectancy
    b. decreased late-life depression
    c. lower risk of heart disease and stroke
    d. preservation of cognitive functioning
    e. lower risk of all types of cancer

173. All of the following are stages in Kübler-Ross's model of death and dying EXCEPT
    a. depression.
    b. compensation.
    c. anger.
    d. denial.
    e. bargaining.

Essentials of Psychology Chapter 9

174. Petra is able to imagine what would happen if parents were held legally responsible for the crimes of their children. She is capable of making an argument for or against this, regardless of her opinion. Petra is probably in which stage of cognitive development?
a. abstract operations
b. moral operations
c. concrete operations
d. formal operations
e. preoperations

175. The period of life beginning at puberty and ending with early adulthood is called
a. moratorium.
b. the teenage years.
c. the pubertal period.
d. menarche.
e. adolescence.

Name:______________________ Class:______________________ Date:______________

Essentials of Psychology Chapter 11

1. Shawn is more likely to smoke marijuana in situations where he believes it will make him relaxed than in situations where he feels he will make a fool of himself. Shawn's ideas about smoking marijuana reflect his
   a. efficacy expectations.
   b. locus of control.
   c. self-esteem.
   d. individualism.
   (e) outcome expectations.

2. Which of the following has NOT been voiced as a criticism of trait theories?
   a. They merely label rather than explain personality.
   b. They assume behavior is relatively stable.
   (c) They cannot be measured by psychological inventories.
   d. They ignore situational influences and fail to capture the uniqueness of individuals.
   e. They use circular reasoning.

3. Which of the following is most likely in Freud's latency stage of development?
   a. Jason is 16 months old and tends to bite everything (and everyone) he touches.
   b. Shana is 19 months old, and her mother has noticed that she gets a particular facial expression during the act of elimination.
   c. Shawn is now 4 years old and can often be seen walking around with his hand inside his pants.
   (d) Linda is 12 years old and, unlike some of her friends, seems to have no interest in boys.
   e. William is 14 years old and has developed a strong attraction to Sarah, who resembles his mother.

4. According to Allport, secondary traits
   (a) reflect superficial differences between people.
   b. compete with primary traits for dominance.
   c. are the most pervasive components of personality.
   d. are the basic building blocks of personality.
   e. have a widespread influence across many situations.

5. Which of the following is the best definition of archetype?
   a. the self-aware part of the personality that organizes goal-seeking efforts
   b. a constellation of personality traits characteristic of a particular stage of psychosexual development
   c. a relatively enduring personal characteristic
   d. a deep-seated form of anxiety associated with feelings of being helpless in a threatening and hostile world
   (e) a primitive image that reflects ancestral or universal human experiences

6. Social-cognitive theorists believe that personality is
   a. an unscientific term that has outlived its usefulness.
   b. composed of learned behavior only.
   c. composed of the ways that individuals think about themselves and the world only.
   (d) composed of learned behavior and the ways that individuals think about themselves and the world.
   e. based on the belief that the environment determines how genetic predispositions influence behavior.

Essentials of Psychology Chapter 11

7. Which of the following is NOT cited in the text as true of people with an internal locus of control as compared to those with an external locus of control?
   a. They cope with pain better.
   b. They are better able to start exercising when overweight.
   c. They are better able to make changes in diet when overweight.
   d. They are more likely to succeed in school.
   e. They believe they can obtain reinforcements.

8. Darius scores high on psychoticism. In which way is Darius likely to be perceived by others?
   a. Warm and concerned about others
   b. Tense, anxious, and moody
   c. Solitary, reserved, and unsociable
   d. Relaxed, calm, and even-tempered
   e. Antisocial, hostile, and insensitive

9. Who developed the Thematic Apperception Test?
   a. Hermann Rorschach
   b. Carl Jung
   c. Sigmund Freud
   d. Henry Murray
   e. Karen Horney

10. Cybill takes a personality test based on Eysenck's theory and finds that her "type" is extraverted-stable. Which description most likely fits Cybill?
   a. reliable, even-tempered, and calm
   b. passive, careful, and thoughtful
   c. moody, anxious, and rigid
   d. impulsive, optimistic, and active
   e. lively, carefree, and sociable

11. Using an iceberg analogy, the tip of the iceberg is most like which level of consciousness in Freud's theory?
   a. preconscious
   b. unconscious
   c. ego
   d. conscious
   e. superego

12. A major contribution of Jung to the psychodynamic approach was his belief in
    a. castration anxiety.
    b. womb envy.
    c. an Electra complex.
    d. a collective unconscious.
    e. the creative self.

13. Emma's sense of who or what she should be is her
    a. self-ideal.
    b. self-concept.
    c. self.
    d. self-esteem.
    e. self-efficacy.

14. Cathleen takes the 16PF test of personality. This test will measure Cathleen's _____ traits.
    a. source
    b. surface
    c. central
    d. primary
    e. cardinal

15. The Minnesota Multiphasic Personality Inventory was designed to
    a. measure intelligence.
    b. help clinicians diagnose mental disorders.
    c. find appropriate placement for military personnel.
    d. supplement the 16PF.
    e. measure a single dimension of personality.

16. Stable and enduring personal characteristics are called
    a. habits.
    b. tendencies.
    c. traits.
    d. types.
    e. genes.

17. In applying the concept of building self-esteem in our personal lives, most of the skills valued in our society are
    a. irrelevant to the concept of self-esteem.
    b. capable of being achieved by most people.
    c. out of the reach of all but the most talented.
    d. not clearly defined.
    e. academic and athletic.

Essentials of Psychology Chapter 11

18. ______ are the most widely used method for learning about personality today.
    a. Formal personality tests
    b. Case studies
    c. Observational techniques
    d. Experimental studies
    e. Phrenological studies

19. The psychoanalytic perspective suggests that too much or too little gratification at a psychosexual stage may result in
    a. an inferiority complex.
    b. repression.
    c. reaction formation.
    d. fixation.
    e. regression.

20. Francis is passive, clingy, and dependent, with a pessimistic outlook on life. In which psychosexual stage might Francis be fixated?
    a. genital
    b. oral
    c. latency
    d. phallic
    e. anal

21. Hans Eysenck thought that personality differences result from ______.
    a. pervasive characteristics that influence a person's behavior in most situations
    b. characteristics that influence behavior in some situations, but not others
    c. characteristics that can be inferred from observable behavior
    d. general traits that are composed of, or give rise to, surface traits
    e. biological differences that create variations in personality traits from person to person

22. Of the following suggestions for how we can build our self-esteem, which is most likely to have been made by Albert Ellis?
    a. create a sense of meaningfulness in your life
    b. acquire competencies
    c. set realistic, achievable goals
    d. enhance self-efficacy expectations
    e. challenge the need for constant approval

Essentials of Psychology Chapter 11

23. After six-year-old Samantha's baby brother was born, she started to have temper tantrums the way she had when she was two. This may be a case of
    a. repression.
    b. regression.
    c. projection.
    d. displacement.
    e. sublimation.

24. Alfred Adler's individual psychology emphasized the importance of the creative self, which is _____.
    a. a repository of accumulated ideas and images that is shared among all humans
    b. the part of the personality that is aware of itself and organizes goal-seeking behavior
    c. our feelings of "being isolated and helpless in a potentially hostile world"
    d. a deep form of resentment toward their parents that is ultimately repressed
    e. the banishment to the unconscious of unacceptable wishes, fantasies, urges, and impulses

25. Regarding the definition of personality, all but which of the following belong?
    a. relatively unstable
    b. psychological characteristics
    c. behavioral patterns
    d. accounting for individuality and consistency
    e. environmental adaptation

26. Carl Jung's analytical psychology emphasized the importance of the collective unconscious, which is _____.
    a. a repository of accumulated ideas and images that is shared among all humans
    b. the part of the personality that is aware of itself and organizes goal-seeking behavior
    c. our feelings of "being isolated and helpless in a potentially hostile world"
    d. a deep form of resentment toward their parents that is ultimately repressed
    e. the banishment to the unconscious of unacceptable wishes, fantasies, urges, and impulses

27. In personality testing, self-report personality inventories are also known as
    a. objective tests.
    b. subjective tests.
    c. projective tests.
    d. intelligence tests.
    e. predictive tests.

Name:________________________ Class:________________ Date:__________

Essentials of Psychology Chapter 11

28. Your textbook defines personality as _____.
    a. the relatively stable set of psychological characteristics and behavior patterns that make individuals unique and account for the consistency of their behavior over time
    b. the complex of characteristics that distinguishes an individual or a nation or group
    c. the complex of all the attributes—behavioral, temperament, emotional and mental—that characterize a unique individual
    d. an assumed role or manner of behavior that makes a person or thing distinct from another
    e. enduring patterns of perceiving, relating to, and thinking about the environment and oneself

29. Mahatma Gandhi's lifelong commitment to non-violent solutions to social problems would likely be considered an example of a(n) ______ trait.
    a. ordinal
    b. central
    c. secondary
    d. cardinal
    e. primary

30. Albert Bandura's theory emphasizes the importance of an individual's efficacy expectations, by which is meant ______.
    a. our expectations about whether our efforts can achieve desired outcomes or whether outcomes are influenced by factors outside our control
    b. our predictions regarding the outcomes of behaviors
    c. our beliefs about our own abilities to perform tasks we set out to accomplish
    d. our ability to plan courses of action to achieve our goals and to reward ourselves for accomplishing our goals
    e. our idealized sense of who and what we should be

31. In Freudian theory, the failure to acknowledge a threatening impulse or desire is called
    a. rationalization.
    b. regression.
    c. projection.
    d. denial.
    e. reaction formation.

32. Federico is a perfectionist with a strong need for self-control, order, and cleanliness. Freud would describe Federico as having a(n)
    a. orally fixated personality.
    b. anal-retentive personality.
    c. anal-expulsive personality.
    d. inferiority complex.
    e. drive for superiority.

Essentials of Psychology Chapter 11

33. Watson and Skinner believed that
    a. unconscious forces had a major influence on personality.
    b. personality is shaped by rewards and punishments.
    c. the environment played little role in influencing personality.
    d. trait theories were the best description of personality.
    e. personality consists of the individual's behavior and ways of thinking about themselves and the world.

34. Ingmar's boss ridiculed him in front of the whole office. When Ingmar returns home, he yells at his wife and children and kicks his dog. This is an example of
    a. projection.
    b. reaction formation.
    c. regression.
    d. displacement.
    e. sublimation.

35. Regarding self-esteem, which of the following statements is FALSE?
    a. Low self-esteem is often related to one's perception of falling short of some ideal.
    b. High self-esteem in adolescence is related to better emotional and physical health in adulthood.
    c. Self-esteem is primarily a fixed quality.
    d. High self-esteem in adolescence is related to greater financial success in adulthood.
    e. High self-esteem in adolescence is linked to lower levels of criminal behavior in adulthood.

36. Which neo-Freudian raised the idea that men may experience "womb envy"?
    a. Allport
    b. Adler
    c. Jung
    d. Erikson
    e. Horney

37. Gordon Allport thought that cardinal traits are ______.
    a. pervasive characteristics that influence a person's behavior in most situations
    b. characteristics that influence behavior in some situations, but not others
    c. characteristics that can be inferred from observable behavior
    d. general traits that are composed of, or give rise to, surface traits
    e. biological differences that create variations in personality traits from person to person

Essentials of Psychology Chapter 11

38. According to the text, the most important influence of the social-cognitive theorists was the
   a. development of cognitive-behavioral therapy.
   b. design of programs to help parents learn better parenting skills.
   c. introduction of the idea that unconscious influences and genetically based traits can explain much of human behavior.
   d. identification of concepts like locus of control and self-efficacy.
   e. presentation of the view that people are active seekers and interpreters of information, not just responders to environmental influences.

39. Psychodynamic theory has been criticized on all but which of the following grounds?
   a. It places too much emphasis on sexual and aggressive drives.
   b. There is a general lack of evidence supporting many of the principles on which the theory is based.
   c. The theory was based on evidence gathered from a small number of cases studies.
   d. It is difficult to test using the scientific method.
   e. It places too much emphasis on social influences.

40. Social-cognitive theorist Mischel's most recent work focuses on
   a. the influence of childhood positive regard on adult development.
   b. the role of locus of control in academic success.
   c. the influence of outcome expectancies on efficacy expectations.
   d. the interaction of emotions and situation variables.
   e. the interaction of emotions and person variables.

41. Current research on the "factors" of personality suggests that there are _____ major personality factors that best describe human personality.
   a. thousands of
   b. hundreds of
   c. twenty-four
   d. sixteen
   e. five

42. From a psychoanalytic perspective, someone with a very strong sense of morality might be described as having a very strong
   a. id.
   b. superego.
   c. ego.
   d. preconscious.
   e. conscious.

Essentials of Psychology Chapter 11

43. Which type of learning did Bandura emphasize in his social-cognitive theory?
    a. operant conditioning
    b. classical conditioning
    c. latent learning
    d. observational learning
    e. operant and classical conditioning

44. According to Freud, the purpose of defense mechanisms is to
    a. satisfy the id.
    b. destroy the id.
    c. prevent threatening thoughts from attaining awareness.
    d. unite the id and superego.
    e. protect the superego from troubling impulses.

45. The idea of reciprocal determinism was developed by
    a. Bandura.
    b. Rotter.
    c. Skinner.
    d. Cattell.
    e. Mischel.

46. In Cattell's model, characteristics of personality that can be inferred from behavior are called
    a. archetypes.
    b. source traits.
    c. central traits.
    d. surface traits.
    e. factors.

47. Freud's psychoanalytic theory posits that the superego consists of _____.
    a. information that we have in mind at any given moment in time.
    b. the demand for instant gratification without regard to social rules or customs.
    c. primitive sexual and aggressive impulses, memories of troubling emotional experiences, and unacceptable wishes or ideas.
    d. information that can be retrieved from memory and brought into awareness at any time.
    e. the internalized moral teachings of parents or other significant others that may be partially conscious and partially unconscious.

48. Freud might say that someone who was displaying excessive aggression was acting according to his or her
    a. id.
    b. ego.
    c. superego.
    d. conscience.
    e. reality principle.

Essentials of Psychology Chapter 11

49. According to Adler, because of their small size and limited abilities, all children harbor feelings of
    a. eroticism.
    b. inferiority.
    c. hostility.
    d. penis envy or castration anxiety.
    e. anxiety.

50. Rorschach test is to ______ as Thematic Apperception Test is to ______.
    a. ambiguous; clear
    b. ambiguous; unambiguous
    c. picture; objective statements
    d. inkblot; objective statements
    e. inkblot; picture

51. Which of the following best describes Bandura's ideas about the relationship between behavior, cognition, and environment?
    a. Cognitions, behaviors, and the environment mutually influence each other.
    b. Cognitions influence behaviors that, in turn, influence the environment.
    c. Behaviors influence cognitions that, in turn, influence the environment.
    d. The environment and cognitions jointly influence behavior.
    e. The environment influences cognitions and behavior.

52. In Freudian theory, different parts of the body associated with sexual pleasure are referred to as
    a. erogenous zones.
    b. fixations.
    c. archetypes.
    d. defense mechanisms.
    e. psychosexual.

53. Objective (self-report) personality tests are generally considered to be _____.
    a. unreliable indicators of personality factors
    b. valid indicators of personality factors
    c. useful for predicting criminal behavior
    d. too expensive for widespread use
    e. limited in usefulness because of stimulus pull

Essentials of Psychology Chapter 11

54. You meet a psychologist who explains behavior in terms of ego, defense mechanisms, and psychosexual stages. This psychologist represents which view of personality?
    a. trait
    b. social-cognitive
    c. humanist
    d. psychoanalytic
    e. levels-of-consciousness

55. Which of the following is most likely in Freud's phallic stage of development?
    a. Jason is 16 months old and tends to bite everything (and everyone) he touches.
    b. Shana is 19 months old, and her mother has noticed that she gets a particular facial expression during the act of elimination.
    c. Shawn is now 4 years old and can often be seen walking around with his hand inside his pants.
    d. Linda is 12 years old and, unlike some of her friends, seems to have no interest in boys.
    e. William is 14 years old and has developed a strong attraction to Sarah, who resembles his mother.

56. All but which of the following are premises of Adler's individual psychology?
    a. All children have feelings of inferiority.
    b. The creative self is a mostly unconscious part of the personality.
    c. Humans have a drive for superiority that can lead to positive or negative behaviors.
    d. There is a part of the personality that organizes goal-seeking behavior.
    e. Feelings of inferiority lead to a desire to compensate.

57. Frank says, "My conscience is bothering me." Using Freud's terminology, Frank is referring to his
    a. superego.
    b. ego.
    c. id.
    d. conscious.
    e. unconscious.

58. In humanistic theory of Rogers and Maslow, personality is best described as
    a. genetically based.
    b. a final destination.
    c. an outcome.
    d. a process, rather than an outcome.
    e. a process and an outcome.

Name:______________________________________ Class:________________________ Date:_____________

Essentials of Psychology Chapter 11

59. Psychologist Walter Mischel emphasizes the importance of self-regulatory systems and plans, by which is meant ______.
    a. our expectations about whether our efforts can achieve desired outcomes or whether outcomes are influenced by factors outside our control
    b. our predictions regarding the outcomes of behaviors
    c. our beliefs about our own abilities to perform tasks we set out to accomplish
    d. our ability to plan courses of action to achieve our goals and to reward ourselves for accomplishing our goals
    e. our idealized sense of who and what we should be

60. Abraham Maslow emphasized the importance of self-actualization, by which he meant ______.
    a. our expectations about whether our efforts can achieve desired outcomes or whether outcomes are influenced by factors outside our control
    b. our innate drive to become all that we are capable of being
    c. our beliefs about our own abilities to perform tasks we set out to accomplish
    d. our ability to plan courses of action to achieve our goals and to reward ourselves for accomplishing our goals
    e. our idealized sense of who and what we should be

61. Raymond Cattell thought that surface traits are ______.
    a. pervasive characteristics that influence a person's behavior in most situations
    b. characteristics that influence behavior in some situations, but not others
    c. characteristics that can be inferred from observable behavior
    d. general traits that are composed of, or give rise to, surface traits
    e. biological differences that create variations in personality traits from person to person

62. In psychoanalytic theory, ______ is to reality principle as ______ is to pleasure principle.
    a. ego; superego
    b. superego; id
    c. id; ego
    d. superego; ego
    e. ego; id

63. Regarding self-efficacy, which of the following statements is FALSE?
    a. People with higher levels of self-efficacy are more likely to succeed in the tasks that they undertake.
    b. Self-efficacy can play a role in the success of dieting and smoking cessation.
    c. Successful experiences boost self-efficacy in children but not in adults.
    d. Compared to people with low self-efficacy, people with high self-efficacy are more likely to persevere when facing challenges.
    e. People with low self-efficacy are easily convinced of the futility of effort in the face of difficulties.

Essentials of Psychology Chapter 11

64. Regarding the phallic stage of personality development, which of the following does NOT belong?
   a. anal-expulsive personality
   b. Oedipus complex
   c. castration anxiety
   d. penis envy
   e. Electra complex

65. Emmanuel teaches fourth graders. At which stage of psychosexual development can Emmanuel expect the majority of his students to be?
   a. phallic
   b. anal
   c. oral
   d. genital
   e. latency

66. Abraham Maslow believed all but which of the following?
   a. Self-actualization shapes our personality through motivation.
   b. The human drive toward self-actualization is innate.
   c. Humans are motivated to develop their unique potentials as human beings.
   d. The majority of humans become fully self-actualized by the time they reach old age.
   e. If given the opportunity, people will strive toward self-actualization.

67. From Freud's perspective, a boy resolves his Oedipus complex by
   a. forsaking incestuous desires for his mother and taking on an identification with her.
   b. unconsciously blaming his mother for bringing him into the world "ill-equipped" to deal with life's problems, then forgiving her.
   c. unconsciously blaming his mother for bringing him into the world "ill-equipped" to deal with life's problems, then identifying with his father.
   d. developing the ability to control elimination.
   e. forsaking incestuous desires for his mother and identifying with his father.

68. It is often said of substance abusers that the first step in recovery is admitting they have a problem. In Freudian terms, we might say they need to overcome
   a. projection.
   b. denial.
   c. reaction formation.
   d. rationalization.
   e. displacement.

Essentials of Psychology Chapter 11

69. Wanda takes a personality test in which she is required to tell stories in response to a series of ambiguous pictures? Which test is Wanda taking?
    a. Rorschach test
    b. Minnesota Multiphasic Personality Inventory
    c. Eysenck Personality Inventory
    d. Thematic Apperception Test
    e. 16PF

70. Freud's psychoanalytic theory posits that the preconscious consists of _____.
    a. information that we have in mind at any given moment in time.
    b. the demand for instant gratification without regard to social rules or customs.
    c. primitive sexual and aggressive impulses, memories of troubling emotional experiences, and unacceptable wishes or ideas.
    d. information that can be retrieved from memory and brought into awareness at any time.
    e. the internalized moral teachings of parents or other significant others that may be partially conscious and partially unconscious.

71. Which of the following is not one of the four basic personality types derived from the Eysenck Personality Inventory?
    a. introverted-stable
    b. extraverted-psychotic
    c. extraverted-stable
    d. introverted-neurotic
    e. extraverted-neurotic

72. Rationalization is
    a. using self-justifications to explain away unacceptable behavior.
    b. directing unacceptable impulses into socially constructive pursuits.
    c. imposing one's own impulses or wishes onto another.
    d. refusal to recognize a threatening impulse or desire.
    e. transferring unacceptable impulses away from threatening persons toward safer or less threatening objects.

73. The U.S. Army's slogan, "Be all that you can be" is most consistent with which concept from personality theory?
    a. self-actualization
    b. locus of control
    c. projection
    d. sublimation
    e. openness

Name:________________________ Class:________________________ Date:____________

Essentials of Psychology Chapter 11

74. Paul forgets to call his mother-in-law on her birthday. He says it just slipped his mind. In the Freudian view, this type of forgetting may represent the defense mechanism of
    a. repression.
    b. sublimation.
    c. rationalization.
    d. reaction formation.
    e. displacement.

75. The primary contributors to social-cognitive theory are
    a. Bandura, Rotter, and Mischel.
    b. Skinner, Watson, and Adler.
    c. Jung, Adler, and Horney.
    d. Allport, Eysenck, and Cattell.
    e. Maslow, Rogers, and Murray.

76. Herschel believes that he will be able to perform the behaviors necessary for him to succeed at college. Bandura used the term ______ to describe Herschel's beliefs.
    a. locus of control
    b. outcome expectations
    c. efficacy expectations
    d. reciprocal determinism
    e. positive regard

77. Regression is
    a. keeping unacceptable thoughts from awareness.
    b. refusing to recognize a threatening thought.
    c. the use of self-justifications to explain unacceptable behavior.
    d. the return of behavior that is typical of earlier stages of development.
    e. channeling unacceptable impulses into acceptable behaviors.

78. ________ consists of 567 true-false items that produce scores on 10 clinical scales and additional scales measuring other personality dimensions and response tendencies.
    a. The NEO-PI
    b. The Thematic Apperception Test
    c. The 16-PF test
    d. The Rorschach test
    e. The MMPI-2

Essentials of Psychology Chapter 11

79. According to the text, Parvati can enhance her self-esteem by doing all but which of the following?
   a. developing skills that allow her to achieve her goals
   b. developing abilities that help enhance her self-worth
   c. challenging her perfectionistic expectations
   d. learning to accept herself when she falls short of her ideals
   e. developing a strong need for social approval

80. _____'s model of personality describes personality in terms of three major traits: introversion-extraversion, neuroticism, and psychoticism.
   a. Cattell
   b. Eysenck
   c. Allport
   d. Freud
   e. Jung

81. In psychoanalytic theory, the personality structure that organizes ways to handle delays of gratification and represents "reason and good sense" is the
   a. ego.
   b. id.
   c. superego.
   d. conscience.
   e. unconscious.

82. The construct of ______represents the belief that behavior involves an interrelationship between personality traits and situational factors.
   a. eclecticism
   b. interactive associationism
   c. reciprocal determinism
   d. self-efficacy expectations
   e. interactionism

83. Regarding psychological tests, which of the following statements is FALSE?
   a. A large body of evidence supports the validity of self-report personality inventories.
   b. One problem with projective tests is that scoring of test responses is largely based on the examiner's subjective impressions.
   c. One problem with objective tests is their stimulus pull.
   d. The validity of the Rorschach test continues to be debated in the psychological community.
   e. Standardized scoring has been introduced for the Rorschach test.

Name:____________________ Class:________________ Date:__________

Essentials of Psychology Chapter 11

84. According to humanists, personality is
    a. consistency of behavior.
    b. the interaction between genes and environment.
    c. the expression of conscious experience of directing ourselves towards achieving our own unique potentials.
    d. determined by reinforcement and punishment.
    e. based on a hierarchy of pervasive characteristics.

85. Ruth has conflicting feelings about getting married that she has not allowed to enter her consciousness. On the night before her wedding, Ruth says, "Tomorrow I'm going to my funeral." Ruth's comment is an example of a(n)
    a. displacement.
    b. projection.
    c. rationalization.
    d. inferiority complex.
    e. Freudian slip.

86. An extension of behaviorism that includes roles for internal mental processes and the influences of other people on our behavior is called
    a. social-cognitive theory.
    b. phrenology theory.
    c. humanistic theory.
    d. psychodynamic theory.
    e. expectancy theory.

87. According to Freud, the Oedipus complex arises during which stage of psychosexual development?
    a. anal
    b. phallic
    c. latency
    d. genital
    e. oral

88. Rorschach developed a famous personality test that uses __________ as stimuli.
    a. inkblots
    b. geometric patterns
    c. ambiguous photographs
    d. stick figures
    e. artwork

Name:______________________________ Class:____________________ Date:__________

Essentials of Psychology Chapter 11

89. From the psychoanalytic perspective, it is possible for a person to unconsciously banish unacceptable wishes, urges, and impulses. This type of motivated forgetting, thought by Freud to be a primary defense mechanism, is called
    a. sublimation.
    b. repression.
    c. regression.
    d. reaction formation.
    e. projection.

90. Which part of the personality might be described as "the great compromiser"?
    a. self-concept
    b. self-esteem
    c. superego
    d. ego
    e. id

91. In Mischel's theory, which person variable concerns the ability to plan courses of action to achieve goals and obtain rewards?
    a. subjective values
    b. self-regulatory systems and plans
    c. expectancies
    d. competencies
    e. encoding strategies

92. A strategy that prevents awareness of unacceptable desires is a ______, and the ______ makes use of such strategies.
    a. defense mechanism; ego
    b. defense mechanism; id
    c. defense mechanism; superego
    d. fixation; ego
    e. fixation; superego

93. In comparison to psychodynamic and behaviorist explanations of human behavior and thought processes, humanistic theory
    a. is more positive and endorses the idea of personal freedom.
    b. is more negative, but endorses the idea of personal freedom.
    c. is more positive, but discounts the idea of personal freedom.
    d. is more negative and discounts the idea of personal freedom.
    e. is neutral and unconcerned with issues of personal freedom.

Essentials of Psychology Chapter 11

94. In the five-factor model of personality, the extent to which a person is sensitive, warm, and tolerant versus callous, cold, and hostile is captured in which personality factor?
   a. extraversion
   b. neuroticism
   c. openness
   d. conscientiousness
   e. agreeableness

95. A(n) ______ culture is one that emphasizes social roles and obligations.
   a. archetypal
   b. self-actualized
   c. individualistic
   d. humanistic
   e. collectivistic

96. Who developed the 16PF personality test?
   a. Eysenck
   b. Cattell
   c. Allport
   d. Jung
   e. Bandura

97. The most widely adopted trait model of personality today is the
   a. self-actualization model.
   b. Cattell sixteen-trait model.
   c. Allport hierarchical model.
   d. five-factor model.
   e. Eysenck three-trait model.

98. Regarding Eysenck's model of personality, which of the following statements is FALSE?
   a. According to Eysenck, there are four basic personality types.
   b. Eysenck's trait model is more complicated than Cattell's.
   c. Eysenck found that mountain climbers tended to be extraverted and emotionally stable.
   d. Eysenck believed that introverts inherit a nervous system that operates at a higher level of arousal than that of extraverts.
   e. Eysenck believed that biological differences are responsible for variations in personality traits.

99. Who are the two main contributors to the humanistic perspective?
   a. Jung and Adler
   b. Bandura and Rotter
   c. Cattell and Allport
   d. Murray and Rorschach
   e. Maslow and Rogers

Essentials of Psychology Chapter 11

100. According to Freud, most of the human mind resides in the ______, and primitive sexual and aggressive instincts lie in the ______.
    a. preconscious; unconscious
    b. unconscious; unconscious
    c. conscious; preconscious
    d. unconscious; preconscious
    e. conscious; unconscious

101. The belief that people's character and mental abilities could be judged by the patterns of bumps on their skull is called
    a. psychometrics.
    b. psychophysics.
    c. phrenology.
    d. psychokinesis.
    e. projective testing.

102. Which of the following is NOT true of the Rorschach test?
    a. Certain test responses may predict success in psychotherapy.
    b. It can distinguish between different types of mental disorders.
    c. It can rule out biological causes for various psychological problems.
    d. It can identify underlying needs for dependency.
    e. Its value is debated in the psychological community.

103. Jacob and his friends like to lie around on summer days, stare up at the clouds, and tell each other what they see in the clouds. Their activity is most like which test of personality?
    a. The Thematic Apperception Test
    b. The Minnesota Multiphasic Personality Inventory
    c. The Rorschach test
    d. The 16PF
    e. The Eysenck Personality Inventory

104. Imposing one's own impulses or wishes onto another is called
    a. projection.
    b. sublimation.
    c. displacement.
    d. rationalization.
    e. reaction formation.

Name:______________________________________ Class:________________________ Date:______________

Essentials of Psychology Chapter 11

105. In Karen Horney's theory of personality development, children may develop a deep form of resentment toward their parents. Horney labeled this
    a. basic anxiety.
    b. basic hostility.
    c. infantile regression.
    d. drive for superiority.
    e. inferiority complex.

106. What is the correct ordering of Freud's psychosexual stages of development?
    a. anal, oral, latency, phallic, genital
    b. oral, anal, phallic, latency, genital
    c. oral, anal, latency, phallic, genital
    d. oral, phallic, anal, latency, genital
    e. anal, oral, phallic, latency, genital

107. Emilio's therapist says that Emilio's personality is fixated at the earliest stage of development. In layman's terms, the therapist means that Emilio's personality is ______ at the earlier stage.
    a. defended
    b. mapped
    c. comfortable
    d. malfunctioning
    e. stuck

108. All but which of the following are considered strengths of self-report personality inventories?
    a. They are inexpensive to administer and score.
    b. People may be more willing to disclose personal information on these inventories than in face-to-face situations.
    c. They can be used as stand-alone diagnostic tools.
    d. The results of these tests can be used to predict a wide range of behaviors.
    e. Their validity is well-established.

109. When taken to extremes, individualistic values might lead to undesirable consequences, such as _____.
    a. an incomplete awareness of all parts of ourselves, which prevents self-actualization
    b. excessive feelings of intrinsic worth and unrealistic expectations of success
    c. excessive dependence on others' approval to maintain self-esteem
    d. needlessly encouraging unrestrained greed and the exploitation of others
    e. needlessly limiting creativity, innovation, and personal initiative

Name:________________________ Class:________________ Date:__________

Essentials of Psychology Chapter 11

110. The impressions you have of yourself compose your _____, while the degree of liking you have for yourself is your _____.
   a. self-theory; self-esteem
   b. self-awareness; self-esteem
   c. self-awareness; self-efficacy
   d. self-concept; self-esteem
   e. self-concept; self-evaluation

111. On the Minnesota Multiphasic Personality Inventory, the number of items scored in the same direction as the diagnostic group are converted into
   a. raw scores.
   b. reliability scales.
   c. five factors.
   d. standard scores.
   e. validity scales.

112. In Freudian theory, the level of consciousness that corresponds to our current level of awareness is the
   a. unconscious.
   b. conscious.
   c. preconscious.
   d. superego.
   e. ego.

113. An individual's general belief about his or her ability to obtain reinforcements is referred to as
   a. subjective value.
   b. objective value.
   c. locus of control.
   d. reciprocal determinism.
   e. self-efficacy.

114. Tifara takes a personality test measuring the "Big Five" factors of personality. Results from one of the test's subscales suggest that Tifara is conforming, practical, and conventional. Which factor is being measured with this subscale?
   a. openness
   b. neuroticism
   c. conscientiousness
   d. agreeableness
   e. extraversion

Name:_______________ Class:_______________ Date:_______________

Essentials of Psychology Chapter 11

115. Id, ego, and superego refer to which component of psychoanalytic theory?
    a. They describe the levels of consciousness.
    b. They are types of defense mechanisms.
    c. They describe the stages of psychosexual development.
    d. They are methods of psychoanalytic therapy.
    e. They describe the structure of personality.

116. A culture in which the sense of self is tied to personal accomplishments s best described as
    a. archetypal.
    b. self-actualized.
    c. individualistic.
    d. humanistic.
    e. collectivistic.

117. William's self-esteem is relatively low. According to social-cognitive theorists, William might improve his self-esteem by _____.
    a. setting difficult goals for himself
    b. thinking about how fortunate he is, compared to others
    c. improving a particular skill, such as playing a piano
    d. searching out those others who will approve of him as he is
    e. critically examining each task he completes, searching for ways to improve his performance

118. Which social-cognitive theorist argues that behavior is influenced by situation variables and person variables?
    a. Walter Mischel
    b. Carl Jung
    c. Abraham Maslow
    d. Carl Rogers
    e. Alfred Adler

119. The use of projective tests in measuring personality is most consistent with which perspective on personality?
    a. humanist
    b. psychodynamic
    c. behaviorist
    d. social-cognitive
    e. trait

120. Dr. Provost lectures to her Psychology of Personality class on the "Big Five." What is the topic of Provost's lecture?
    a. Freud's five psychosexual stages of personality development
    b. The five levels of Maslow's hierarchy
    c. The five pioneers of personality theory
    d. Five ways of measuring personality
    e. The five-factor model of personality

121. Regarding Freud's view on personality development, which of the following statements is FALSE?
    a. Freud believed that physical activities connected to basic life functions are basically sexual in nature.
    b. Freud believed that personality formed through five stages of development.
    c. Freud believed that the stages of personality development involve a shift in the focus of erogenous zones.
    d. Freud believed that the stages of personality development are related to the ways in which children seek pleasure from sexually sensitive parts of the body.
    e. Freud believed that boys develop womb envy and girls develop penis envy.

122. Freud believed that personality consists of _____ structures, and they are called _____.
    a. 3; self-concept, self-esteem, and self-efficacy
    b. 5; neuroticism, extraversion, openness, agreeableness, and conscientiousness
    c. 5; oral, anal, phallic, latency, and genital
    d. 3; unconscious, preconscious, and conscious
    e. 3; id, ego, and superego

123. Amy is from a collectivistic culture. Compared to her cousin Andre, who is from an individualistic culture, Amy is MORE likely to value which of the following?
    a. Personal accomplishments
    b. Respect for elders
    c. Her career's potential for status
    d. Accrual of wealth
    e. Self-sufficiency

124. The most widely held view in contemporary psychology is that _____.
    a. genetic factors determine our personalities
    b. environmental factors determine our personalities
    c. neither genetics nor environmental factors ultimately determine our personalities
    d. genetic factors interact with environmental factors to determine our personalities
    e. genetic factors are somewhat more important than environmental factors in determining our personalities

125. Karen Horney's feminine psychology emphasized the importance of our basic anxiety, which is _____.
    a. a repository of accumulated ideas and images that is shared among all humans
    b. the part of the personality that is aware of itself and organizes goal-seeking behavior
    c. our feelings of "being isolated and helpless in a potentially hostile world"
    d. a deep form of resentment toward their parents that is ultimately repressed
    e. the banishment to the unconscious of unacceptable wishes, fantasies, urges, and impulses

Name:______________________ Class:______________________ Date:______________

Essentials of Psychology Chapter 11

126. Freud developed an approach to personality called ______ theory.
   a. psychoanalytic
   b. trait
   c. social-cognitive
   d. humanistic
   e. levels of consciousness

127. In Rotter's theory, a subjective value is
   a. a measure of the importance of a trait.
   b. the worth one places on a desired outcome.
   c. other people's evaluation of one's personality.
   d. one's own evaluation of one's personality.
   e. the likelihood that a person will perform a behavior that s/he sets out to accomplish.

128. In social-cognitive theory, expectancies are
   a. personal predictions about the outcome of behavior.
   b. a defense mechanism in which one's expectancies keep one from recognizing one's true motives.
   c. stable patterns of behavior across time and situations.
   d. how other people predict one's own behavior.
   e. values placed on desired outcomes.

129. Using the iceberg analogy, which personality structure(s) lies completely below the water?
   a. superego and ego
   b. ego and id
   c. superego and id
   d. superego only
   e. id only

130. The social-cognitive perspective of personality development is associated with which approach to therapy?
   a. phrenology
   b. client-centered therapy
   c. psychodynamic therapy
   d. behavior therapy
   e. cognitive-behavioral therapy

131. Projective personality tests have been criticized on the basis of each of the following EXCEPT _____.
   a. scoring of responses is objective
   b. questions about interpretation of responses
   c. some test stimuli may elicit certain types of responses over others
   d. there is limited evidence for the overall validity of these tests
   e. questionable usefulness

Name:______________________ Class:______________ Date:________

Essentials of Psychology Chapter 11

132. Carl Rogers' theory suggests that self-esteem is a function of how closely we come to matching our self-ideals, which are _____.
   a. our expectations about whether our efforts can achieve desired outcomes or whether outcomes are influenced by factors outside our control
   b. our efforts to realize our own unique potential
   c. our beliefs about our own abilities to perform tasks we set out to accomplish
   d. our ability to plan courses of action to achieve our goals and to reward ourselves for accomplishing our goals
   e. our idealized sense of who and what we should be

133. Which of the following is FALSE regarding objective personality tests?
   a. They use truly objective measures of personality.
   b. They can be scored objectively because the response options are limited.
   c. They rely on people's opinions and judgments.
   d. They are derived from evidence gathered in research studies.
   e. They are used to measure both single and multiple dimensions of personality.

134. In Allport's view, cardinal traits are
   a. the most pervasive characteristics of one's personality.
   b. basic building blocks of personality.
   c. specific preferences.
   d. fluctuating patterns of behavior.
   e. superficial traits inferred from observation.

135. Comparing self-esteem among young African Americans with that of young White Americans, which of the following has been found?
   a. On average, White Americans have higher levels of self-esteem than African Americans.
   b. On average, White American children and adolescents have higher self-esteem than African American children and adolescents, but African American adults have higher self-esteem than White American adults.
   c. On average, African American children and adolescents have higher self-esteem than White American children and adolescents, but White American adults have higher self-esteem than African-American adults.
   d. On average, African Americans have higher levels of self-esteem than White Americans.
   e. On average, there are no differences in the level of self-esteem of African Americans and White Americans.

136. In social-cognitive theory, all but which of the following play a role in explaining personality?
   a. a person's rewards and punishments
   b. expectancies a person holds about the outcomes of her/his behavior
   c. the value a person places on rewards
   d. the ways in which a person thinks about him/herself
   e. a person's unconscious impulses

Name:______________________________ Class:____________________ Date:____________

Essentials of Psychology Chapter 11

137. All but which of the following countries would be classified as individualistic?
   a. England
   b. France
   c. Canada
   d. United States
   e. Mexico

138. William has set a series of goals for himself that are practically unachievable, and his self-esteem drops each time he fails to meet one of his goals. William needs to know that _____.
   a. setting realistic, achievable goals will enhance his self-esteem
   b. being or becoming competent at something will not affect his self-esteem
   c. meeting smaller, clearly achievable goals will have no effect on self-esteem
   d. his perfectionist expectations will ultimately lead to a boost in self-esteem if he is successful
   e. a need for the approval of others will help to boost his self-esteem

139. Kathie is reserved and unsociable, and she prefers solitude. According to Eysenck's model, Kathie would be described as
   a. shy.
   b. emotionally stable.
   c. introverted.
   d. extraverted.
   e. emotionally unstable.

140. When taken to extremes, collectivistic values might lead to undesirable consequences, such as _____.
   a. an incomplete awareness of all parts of ourselves, which prevents self-actualization
   b. excessive feelings of intrinsic worth and unrealistic expectations of success
   c. excessive dependence on others' approval to maintain self-esteem
   d. needlessly encouraging unrestrained greed and the exploitation of others
   e. needlessly limiting creativity, innovation, and personal initiative

141. Regarding Freud's psychoanalytic theory, which of the following statements is FALSE?
   a. Freud suggested that animal drives and instinctual pleasures are contained in the id.
   b. Freud uses the reality principle and the pleasure principle to explain the governing principles of the ego and the id.
   c. Freud believed that the id, ego, and superego were structures in the brain that would eventually be located.
   d. The id is proposed to be the only psychic structure that is present at birth.
   e. Freud felt that the superego develops between ages three and five.

Essentials of Psychology Chapter 11

142. In _____, people are presented with a set of ambiguous stimuli that produce responses that must be interpreted by the examiner.
    a. self-report personality inventories
    b. multiphasic personality inventories
    c. projective personality measures
    d. humanistic personality measures
    e. true-false personality indicators

143. For extra credit in her psychology class, Lucretia just took a 567-item self-report personality inventory administered by a graduate student in training. The graduate student told Lucretia that the test measures 10 clinical scales. Which test did Lucretia take?
    a. MMPI-2
    b. Rorschach
    c. TAT
    d. WAIS
    e. 16PF

144. Reciprocal determinism
    a. refers to a people's personal predictions of the outcomes of their behavior.
    b. refers to people's belief that they can obtain reinforcements through work and effort.
    c. refers to people's belief that reinforcements are largely controlled by external forces beyond their control.
    d. is the idea that cognitions, behaviors, and environmental factors influence each other.
    e. maintains that people determine the value of a behavior based on the desired outcome of that behavior.

145. Generalizing from Roger's ideas about positive regard, which tactic should parents take with their children?
    a. Prize their children regardless of their behavior at any particular time.
    b. Accept all of their children's behavior.
    c. Bestow approval on their children only when they behave properly.
    d. Teach their children to judge their behavior based on whether or not they meet other people's expectations.
    e. Reward their children for appropriate behavior and ignore their inappropriate behavior.

146. Rodina has suffered from substance abuse for many years. She stopped using and now competes in extreme sports. She may be demonstrating
    a. projection.
    b. displacement.
    c. rationalization.
    d. regression.
    e. sublimation.

Essentials of Psychology Chapter 11

147. Angela unconsciously despises old people. Yet, she volunteers two days each week at a retirement home. This is a classic case of
a. regression.
b. displacement.
c. reaction formation.
d. sublimation.
e. projection.

148. Freud's psychoanalytic theory posits that the pleasure principle is _____.
a. information that we have in mind at any given moment in time
b. the demand for instant gratification without regard to social rules or customs
c. primitive sexual and aggressive impulses, memories of troubling emotional experiences, and unacceptable wishes or ideas
d. information that can be retrieved from memory and brought into awareness at any time
e. the internalized moral teachings of parents or other significant others that may be partially conscious and partially unconscious.

149. Allport proposed ______ types of traits in the personality, and they are called _____.
a. 2; internal and external locus of control
b. 5; neuroticism, extraversion, openness, agreeableness, and conscientiousness
c. 3; introversion-extraversion, neuroticism, and psychoticism
d. 2; surface and source traits
e. 3; cardinal, central, and secondary traits

150. William feels a strong need for social approval, and his self-esteem drops each time he encounters even relatively mild criticism from others. William needs to consider whether _____.
a. setting realistic, achievable goals will not enhance his self-esteem
b. being or becoming competent at something will not affect his self-esteem
c. experiencing disapproval is really as terrible as he may think it is
d. his perfectionist expectations will ultimately lead to a boost in self-esteem if he is successful
e. a need for the approval of others will help to boost his self-esteem

151. Rebecca is learning to play cello and is highly motivated. She is confident that she can learn cello easily and with great ability because she already knows how to play violin. From Mischel's perspective, Rebecca's attitude is best explained by which variable?
a. encoding strategies
b. expectancies
c. subjective values
d. self-regulatory systems
e. competencies

Name:________________________ Class:________________ Date:__________

Essentials of Psychology Chapter 12

1. Which of the following definitions best describes out-group negativism?
   a. The belief that members of other groups hold prejudiced attitudes toward members of one's own group
   b. The perception that members of out-groups are more alike than members of in-groups
   c. A predisposition to attribute more positive characteristics to members of in-groups than to members of out-groups
   d. A sense of threat evoked in members of stereotyped out-groups
   e. A predisposition to attribute more negative characteristics to members of out-groups than to those of in-groups

2. In Milgram's study, ______ percent of the original subjects obeyed every order. In subsequent studies, when the subjects instructed others to administer the shock, the obedience rate ______.
   a. 25; rose to about half
   b. 33; rose to more than half
   c. 65; rose to more than 90%
   d. 33; fell to about 20%
   e. 25; fell to about 10%

3. Explanations formed about causes of behavior or events are called
   a. stereotypes.
   b. attributions.
   c. social schemas.
   d. attitudes.
   e. self-fulfilling prophecies.

4. A salesperson used a persuasive technique that was not based on the principle of compliance. Which technique was used?
   a. low-ball
   b. foot-in-the-door
   c. switch-and-pay
   d. door-in-the-face
   e. bait-and-switch

5. A researcher compares cross-cultural differences in the fundamental attribution error by showing a film of someone stealing and then asking participants to explain why the person stole. Participants from East Asian cultures are most likely to make which attribution?
   a. The thief is too lazy and not motivated to earn money to support his family.
   b. The thief is not intelligent.
   c. The thief was born evil.
   d. The thief lacks morality.
   e. The thief was raised in a family that condoned stealing when money was not available for basic needs.

Name:__________ Class:__________ Date:__________

Essentials of Psychology Chapter 12

6. Dana and Fox have a relationship in which they have intense sexual desires for each other. Their relationship can be described by which component of love in the triangular model?
   a. Romance
   b. Intimacy
   c. Decision
   d. Commitment
   e. Passion

7. In which condition is a person most likely to carefully evaluate a persuasive message?
   a. When the message is consistent with what they already believe
   b. When the message is inconsistent with what they already believe
   c. When the message is irrelevant to what they already believe
   d. When they are distracted and the message is not particularly meaningful
   e. When they are highly motivated and they have the skills to evaluate the message

8. A person's individual identity is best described as her/his
   a. social identity.
   b. self-concept.
   c. self-esteem.
   d. self-schema.
   e. personal identity.

9. From the perspective of the field of psychology, love is
   a. a motive, but not an emotion.
   b. an emotion, but not a motive.
   c. both an emotion and a motive.
   d. impossible to study.
   e. a topic not worthy of study.

10. Janice leads a team of 20 employees. If Janice wants to reduce the chances of social loafing in her team, she should do all but which of the following?
    a. increase the appeal of the team's task
    b. give public feedback on each team member's good performance
    c. give public feedback on each team member's poor performance
    d. evaluate performance for the group only
    e. increase the visibility of each individual's contribution in the group

Name:______________________ Class:______________________ Date:______________

Essentials of Psychology Chapter 12

11. The triangular model of love is described by each of the following components the triangular theory of love EXCEPT
    a. passion.
    b. intimacy.
    c. commitment.
    d. trust.
    e. decision.

12. When social psychologists discuss impression formation, what are they talking about?
    a. A person's efforts to make a good impression on someone else
    b. The process by which people form opinions of others
    c. The tendency to form impressions of other people's behavior after a period of time of getting to know them.
    d. The tendency to ignore first impressions
    e. The expectation that someone will behave the way you predict

13. Regarding impression formation, which of the following statements is FALSE?
    a. People tend to form first impressions quickly.
    b. Our impressions of others are influenced by the amount of information they choose to disclose.
    c. First impressions are relatively easy to change once we get to know the person.
    d. First impressions tend to be long-lasting.
    e. Preconceived ideas influence the impressions we form of people before we even meet them.

14. A group of psychologists discuss the causes of aggression. Which psychologist speaks from a sociocultural perspective?
    a. Dr. Sherry says, "Violent behavior is perpetuated through generations as children observe the adults in their lives use violence to solve their problems."
    b. Dr. Wendrowski says, "Men have higher levels of testosterone than women, and research evidence shows that males are more aggressive than females across many cultures."
    c. Dr. Reeves says, "Interpersonal violence takes place in the context of poverty, unemployment, and violent communities."
    d. Dr. Bowen says, "High temperatures cause people to be aggressive by increasing their hostile thoughts and feelings."
    e. Dr. Richards says, "People act aggressively when they are frustrated."

15. Angela believes that people from Stovenia are basically dishonest. Angela is demonstrating
    a. self-fulfilling prophecy.
    b. fundamental attribution error.
    c. cognitive dissonance.
    d. stereotyping.
    e. a dispositional cause.

16. According to the elaboration likelihood model, when elaboration likelihood is low, people
    a. use a peripheral route of processing information.
    b. use a central route of processing information.
    c. ignore persuasive messages.
    d. focus on aspects of the persuasive message that are consistent with prior beliefs.
    e. focus on the content of the message.

17. Recent research on the actor-observer effect suggests that
    a. the tendency to make this error has a genetic component.
    b. males are more likely than females to make this error.
    c. with globalization, cross-cultural differences in the effect have disappeared.
    d. it may be weaker than originally suspected and limited to certain situations.
    e. it is difficult to demonstrate in an experimental setting.

18. Which of the following statements regarding prejudice is FALSE?
    a. Social psychologists have found a disparity between what people say about their racial attitudes and their response to racial cues.
    b. Prejudice and discrimination usually increase during times of high unemployment.
    c. Prejudice consists of cognitive, emotional, and behavioral components.
    d. Stereotypes and prejudice are equally likely to be negative or positive.
    e. Prejudice is acquired in the same way that other attitudes are learned.

19. Paul and Joanna have a love relationship characterized by high levels of intimacy, passion, and commitment. Using the triangular model, their love would be described as
    a. romantic love.
    b. infatuation.
    c. fatuous love.
    d. consummate love.
    e. companionate love.

20. Asch is to ______ as Milgram is to ______.
    a. conformity; obedience
    b. compliance; obedience
    c. conformity; bystander intervention
    d. obedience; bystander intervention
    e. obedience; compliance

21. Using models to sell automobiles most directly addresses which aspect of the source?
    a. credibility
    b. likeability
    c. authenticity
    d. similarity
    e. trustworthiness

Essentials of Psychology Chapter 12

22. Which of the following concepts from social psychology are concerned with the effect of the presence of others on the quality of a person's performance?
    a. groupthink and group polarization
    b. conformity, compliance, and obedience
    c. dispositional and situational attributions
    d. prejudice and discrimination
    e. social facilitation and social loafing

23. The famous case of Kitty Genovese best represents which concept from social psychology?
    a. diffusion of responsibility
    b. conformity
    c. obedience
    d. groupthink
    e. prejudice

24. Research on attraction suggests that you will be most attracted to someone who is
    a. similar to you.
    b. different from you.
    c. more attractive than you.
    d. less attractive than you.
    e. uninterested in you.

25. ______ play(s) a role in explaining why people obey immoral commands.
    a. Social validation, but not legitimization of authority,
    b. Social comparison, but not legitimization of authority,
    c. Legitimization of authority, but not social validation,
    d. Legitimization of authority, but not social comparison,
    e. Social comparison and legitimization of authority

26. A judgment of either liking or disliking something or someone is a(n)
    a. attitude.
    b. attribution.
    c. stereotype.
    d. prejudice.
    e. bias.

27. Which personality type has been found to be associated with the development of prejudice?
    a. authoritarian
    b. authoritative
    c. obsessive-compulsive
    d. antisocial
    e. universalist

28. Edwin happens upon a crime in progress but does nothing to assist the victims or even summon the police. Later, he says he was afraid for his personal safety. This type of explanation, which may help explain the inaction of witnesses in the case of Kitty Genovese, is best described by the principle of _________.
    a. perceived cost.
    b. situational ambiguity.
    c. diffusion of responsibility.
    d. attributions of the cause of need.
    e. cognitive dissonance.

29. The matching hypothesis predicts that Sandra will look for a partner who
    a. lives near her apartment.
    b. is similar to her in physical attractiveness.
    c. regularly compliments her.
    d. comes from the same town or city.
    e. is interested in her.

30. Compared to a person from a collectivist culture, a person from an individualistic culture
    a. is less prone to make the fundamental attribution error.
    b. has a greater tendency to make situational attributions for the behavior of others.
    c. is more likely to commit the fundamental attribution error.
    d. emphasizes external causes of behavior to explain the behavior of others.
    e. relies little on dispositional causes in making attributions.

31. Marcel protests in front of stores that sell animal furs. This reflects which component of his attitude toward animal furs?
    a. attribution
    b. expectation
    c. emotion
    d. cognition
    e. behavior

32. When people explain their own behavior by making a situational attribution and the behavior of others by making a dispositional attribution it is called
    a. stereotyping.
    b. the fundamental attribution error.
    c. self-serving bias.
    d. self-fulfilling prophecy.
    e. the actor-observer effect.

Essentials of Psychology Chapter 12

33. Making friends with neighbors supports which influence on attraction?
    a. matching
    b. reciprocity
    c. attractiveness
    d. similarity
    e. proximity

34. The fundamental attribution error, which helps explain how cognitive biases affect attributions, involves
    a. taking credit for your own good behavior.
    b. taking the blame for your own bad behavior.
    c. overemphasizing internal factors when explaining the behavior of others.
    d. overemphasizing situational factors when explaining the behavior of others.
    e. overemphasizing internal factors when explaining personal successes and situational factors when explaining personal failures.

35. Dr. Vanchella suspects that one of her college students does not have any money for food. She arranges for money to be put on the student's meal card without telling the student. Which term best describes Vanchella's motive?
    a. self-centered
    b. communal
    c. reciprocal
    d. conformist
    e. altruistic

36. Charlie is most likely to experience cognitive dissonance if he decides to buy the car that
    a. is black inside and outside, which might mean less maintenance, a good thing since he hates fussing with cars.
    b. is advertised as quick to accelerate up to 80 miles per hour, a feature that he looked for because he likes to pass slow drivers.
    c. received a high rating in customer satisfaction, which is important to him because his last car was a lemon.
    d. uses alternative fuel and is therefore environmentally friendly, something Charlie cares deeply about.
    e. is sleek and so much sexier than all the other cars but is also a gas guzzler and costs much more than he wants to spend.

37. Compared to people of higher intelligence, people of lower intelligence are generally
    a. incapable of processing persuasive messages.
    b. very difficult to persuade.
    c. just as easy to persuade.
    d. difficult to persuade if the message is complicated.
    e. easier to persuade.

Essentials of Psychology Chapter 12

38. A social psychological explanation of the poor decisions of President Kennedy's administration in the Bay of Pigs incident is best described by which principle?
    a. obedience
    b. social facilitation
    c. social loafing
    d. cognitive dissonance
    e. groupthink

39. Of the following people with attitudes toward hybrid vehicles, which one best describes the behavioral component of attitudes?
    a. Tony says, "Hybrid vehicles cost more than gas vehicles, so they don't save you any money."
    b. A.J. purchases a Honda hybrid car with his graduation money.
    c. Jennifer gets angry every time she sees someone driving a big SUV.
    d. Carmella says, "I think the government should give bigger tax credits to people who purchase hybrid vehicles."
    e. After looking at a hybrid on a car lot, Paulie says, "It's nice, but I worry about its acceleration."

40. JoAnne goes to the local electronics store to purchase a $30 DVD player that was advertised in the paper. Upon arriving, the salesperson tells her that they have just run out and offers to show JoAnne some other models. JoAnne ends up purchasing a $150 DVD player. JoAnne has been the victim of which technique of persuasion?
    a. bait-and-switch
    b. foot-in-the-door
    c. switch-and-pay
    d. high-ball
    e. low-ball

41. Sven believes that his co-worker was promoted to manager because of her hard effort and winning personality. What type of attribution has Sven made?
    a. external
    b. situational
    c. contextual
    d. dispositional
    e. environmental

42. Erika is not registered to vote and lives with her parents. Her friend takes her to a debate between two people running for City Council regarding property taxes. She would probably use which form of processing?
    a. dissonance
    b. central
    c. peripheral
    d. attributional
    e. reciprocal

Essentials of Psychology Chapter 12

43. All but which of the following is cited in the text as a factor explaining human aggression?
    a. neural circuitry in the brain that regulates anger
    b. emotional states
    c. alcohol use
    d. the role of GABA
    e. learning influences

44. Shiloh canvasses for her favorite politicians. She has discovered that asking someone to do a small favor makes it easier to convince that person to do a larger favor that supports her candidate. Which technique of persuasion has Shiloh discovered?
    a. low-ball
    b. switch-and-pay
    c. door-in-the-face
    d. foot-in-the-door
    e. bait-and-switch

45. Which of the following is the best definition of obedience?
    a. the tendency to work harder in the presence of others than when alone
    b. the tendency to use other people's behavior as a standard for judging the appropriateness of one's own behavior
    c. granting legitimacy to the orders of people in authority
    d. the tendency to adjust one's behaviors to perceived social pressures
    e. compliance with the commands of authority figures

46. When Anne first met Jules, he had been suffering from insomnia and was a little short-tempered. Subsequently, when she was around Jules, she interpreted a lot of what he did as reflecting his hostile personality. This reflects the power of
    a. social schemas.
    b. stereotyping.
    c. discrimination.
    d. cognitive dissonance.
    e. self-fulfilling prophecy.

47. Regarding influences on helping, which of the following statements is FALSE?
    a. A person is more likely to help a victim if they make an external attribution about the cause of the victim's circumstances.
    b. The presence of others increases the likelihood that someone will choose to help.
    c. In ambiguous situations, people are less likely to offer help than in clear-cut situations.
    d. Factors of similarity, mood, and gender have effects on helping behavior.
    e. People with baby-faced features are more likely to receive help than people with more mature features.

Essentials of Psychology Chapter 12

48. The failure of witnesses to help Kitty Genovese when she was viciously attacked may have been due to the tendency to believe that others would act and so they wouldn't need to. This explanation is based on the principle of __________.
    a. perceived cost.
    b. situational ambiguity.
    c. diffusion of responsibility.
    d. attributions of the cause of need.
    e. self-interest.

49. In the famous study on conformity presented in the text, approximately what percentage of college students sided with the incorrect majority at least once?
    a. 35%
    b. 90%
    c. 75%
    d. 50%
    e. 66%

50. According to the text, one of the most common ways to reduce cognitive dissonance is to
    a. change beliefs.
    b. change behaviors.
    c. change beliefs and behaviors.
    d. use rationalizations.
    e. ignore the inconsistencies until they fade away.

51. In persuasion, presenting both sides of an argument is
    a. ineffective because it tends to confuse people.
    b. ineffective because it seems ambivalent.
    c. always ineffective.
    d. almost always effective.
    e. effective when the counter-argument is refuted.

52. One possible biological explanation for aggression involves the neurotransmitter ______, which acts like a "behavioral seat belt."
    a. dopamine
    b. serotonin
    c. acetylcholine
    d. GABA
    e. melatonin

Essentials of Psychology Chapter 12

53. Cognitive dissonance results when
    a. a person makes the fundamental attribution error.
    b. one's attitudes and behaviors are inconsistent.
    c. stereotypes are confirmed through experience.
    d. attraction is high between two people.
    e. elaboration likelihood is high.

54. A community organization sponsors a talk arguing against increased military spending. Who should they contract to give the talk?
    a. an avowed pacifist
    b. a civilian
    c. a person who actively avoided military service
    d. a military officer
    e. a person with mixed views on the subject

55. Regarding attributions, which of the following statements is FALSE?
    a. The actor-observer effect is strong across a wide variety of situations.
    b. The tendency to attribute others' behavior to internal causes, while attributing our own behavior to situational demands is explained by the actor-observer effect.
    c. Attributions are influenced by cognitive biases like the fundamental attribution error, the actor-observer effect, and the self-serving bias.
    d. The self-serving bias is widespread in Western cultures.
    e. In the fundamental attribution error, people overemphasize internal causes when explaining others' behavior.

56. Billy Ray is from an individualistic culture and Diego is from a collectivistic culture. Other factors being equal, compared to Billy Ray, Diego is
    a. much less likely to conform.
    b. slightly less likely to conform.
    c. equally likely to conform.
    d. more likely to conform.
    e. more likely to conform, but only if it is in private.

57. The stated task in the Asch study of conformity involved
    a. rating pictures of people in terms of physical attractiveness.
    b. administering electric shocks to people.
    c. judging the length of lines.
    d. arguing against one's own belief.
    e. performing easy and difficult tasks in front of others.

Essentials of Psychology Chapter 12

58. Contemporary theorists are least likely to choose which factor to explain human aggression?
    a. biological influences
    b. sociocultural influences
    c. alcohol and other drugs
    d. environmental factors, like heat
    e. instinct

59. All of the following make attitudes more likely to influence behavior EXCEPT
    a. stability.
    b. situational attributions.
    c. certainty.
    d. specificity.
    e. easy recall.

60. Dr. Longstocking is a research psychologist who studies attitudes, cognitive dissonance, and first impressions. Which type of psychologist is Dr. Longstocking?
    a. social psychologist
    b. health psychologist
    c. counseling psychologist
    d. educational psychologist
    e. developmental psychologist

61. Compared to people from collectivist cultures, people from individualistic cultures are
    a. less likely to make the fundamental attribution error.
    b. more likely to make situational attributions when explaining the behavior of others.
    c. less likely to show a self-serving bias.
    d. more likely to show a self-serving bias.
    e. more likely to attribute success to luck.

62. The argument that "everyone's doing it" may help explain why people obey immoral commands. This argument may be explained by the principle of
    a. legitimization of authority.
    b. cognitive dissonance.
    c. social facilitation.
    d. social validation.
    e. groupthink.

63. In the elaboration likelihood model, peripheral is to ______ as central is to ______.
    a. fatigued; alert
    b. alert; fatigued
    c. cognition; behavior
    d. behavior; cognition
    e. skilled; unskilled

Essentials of Psychology Chapter 12

64. The self-defense explanation of a crime essentially involves convincing the jury to make what sort of attribution about the defendant's actions?
    a. situational
    b. dispositional
    c. personal
    d. cognitive
    e. internal

65. Results of attitude research with twins has revealed
    a. significant shared attitudes that cannot be explained by common environments.
    b. almost no similarities in attitudes.
    c. similarities in attitudes that reflect shared environments.
    d. completely identical attitudes.
    e. that people inherit genes for particular attitudes.

66. Regarding cross-cultural differences in cognitive biases, which of the following statements is TRUE?
    a. People from individualistic cultures are more prone to make the fundamental attribution error and less prone to demonstrate a self-serving bias.
    b. People from collectivist cultures are more prone to make the fundamental attribution error and less prone to demonstrate a self-serving bias.
    c. People from individualistic cultures are less prone to make the fundamental attribution error and more prone to demonstrate a self-serving bias.
    d. People from collectivist cultures are less prone to make the fundamental attribution error and more prone to demonstrate a self-serving bias.
    e. People from individualistic cultures are more prone to self-serving bias and the fundamental attribution error than are people from collectivist cultures.

67. In group decision-making, the tendency for group discussion to be limited to a single point of view is best described by which psychological principle?
    a. diffusion of responsibility
    b. social loafing
    c. groupthink
    d. legitimization of authority
    e. consensus-building

68. Joylin assumes her husband smacked the dog because the dog had just bitten him. Joylin is making what sort of attribution?
    a. dispositional
    b. personal
    c. internal
    d. situational
    e. cognitive

Essentials of Psychology Chapter 12

69. Experiments on conformity suggest that conformity decreases under all but which of the following conditions?
    a. when people give their responses in private rather than in public
    b. when the size of the group increases
    c. when the task is less ambiguous
    d. when there is another person who does not conform
    e. when people have higher self-esteem

70. The tendency to adjust one's behavior to actual or perceived social pressures is called
    a. obedience.
    b. conformity.
    c. groupthink.
    d. prejudice.
    e. compliance.

71. Barbara, an American, believes that all French people hate Americans, are rude, and love to drink wine. Barbara's beliefs are an example of
    a. in-group favoritism.
    b. discrimination.
    c. out-group homogeneity.
    d. out-group heterogeneity.
    e. out-group favoritism.

72. Regarding research on attraction, which of the following statements is FALSE?
    a. Men, but not women, tend to emphasize physical attractiveness when assessing partners for casual sexual relationships.
    b. Compared to less attractive people, more attractive people are generally judged as more socially competent, intelligent, and psychologically adjusted; they are also judged as less modest and more vain.
    c. On average, people are more likely to marry others whose first or last names resemble their own.
    d. The saying "Birds of a feather flock together" is supported by research on interpersonal attraction.
    e. In considering the personality traits of an ideal partner, people tend to be interested in partners who match up with their own personality traits.

73. All but which of the following are predicted to help an individual reduce prejudice and stereotypical thinking?
    a. telling oneself not to think in stereotypical terms
    b. participating in diversity education
    c. rehearsing positive images of out-group members
    d. repeated practice in rejecting prejudiced thoughts as they occur
    e. developing empathy

Essentials of Psychology Chapter 12

74. Which researcher conducted an influential study on conformity?
    a. Asch
    b. Bandura
    c. Zweigenhaft
    d. Donne
    e. Zajonc

75. Research evidence on romantic attraction suggests that the major determinant of initial attraction is
    a. perceived similarities.
    b. novelty.
    c. physical appearance.
    d. internal characteristics.
    e. proximity.

76. Junie is from a culture that values self-criticism and humility. Other factors being equal, Junie is ______ than someone from a culture that values the protection of self-esteem.
    a. less likely to show a self-serving bias
    b. more likely to show the actor-observer effect
    c. more likely to make the fundamental attribution error
    d. more likely to make dispositional attributions when explaining the behavior of others
    e. less likely to recognize the need to work harder in the future

77. Messages are more credible when they
    a. reflect the interests of the communicator.
    b. go against the interests of the communicator.
    c. are irrelevant to the interests of the communicator.
    d. are not accompanied by relevant counter-arguments.
    e. are not often repeated.

78. How does the recipient's mood affect persuasion?
    a. A good mood makes people more critical and questioning of persuasive messages.
    b. A good mood has no effect on persuasive messages.
    c. A good mood makes people more receptive to persuasive messages.
    d. A good mood makes it easier to ignore persuasive messages.
    e. A good mood leads to low elaboration likelihood.

79. Studies describing gender differences in conformity suggest that women are ______ men to conform
    a. much more likely than
    b. slightly more likely than
    c. equally likely as
    d. slightly less likely than
    e. much less likely than

Essentials of Psychology Chapter 12

80. Randy believes that all people from Cropilia are basically aggressive. When he meets a Cropilian, he acts more aggressive himself. The Cropilian responds with aggressive behavior, which strengthens Randy's impression of their aggressiveness and makes it harder to budge. This process is best described by the concept of
    a. cultural stereotyping.
    b. self-serving attribution.
    c. the fundamental attribution error.
    d. cognitive dissonance.
    e. a self-fulfilling prophecy.

81. All but which of the following may help explain the inaction of witnesses in the famous case of Kitty Genovese?
    a. diffusion of responsibility
    b. situational ambiguity
    c. perceived cost
    d. attributions of the cause of need
    e. prejudice

82. In attitudes, _______ are to cognitions as _______ are to emotions.
    a. beliefs; actions
    b. actions; feelings
    c. feelings; beliefs
    d. feelings; actions
    e. beliefs; feelings

83. Mischa believes she did well on her English exam because she is very intelligent but that she failed her Chemistry exam because her instructor is not very good. We may explain her beliefs in terms of
    a. the fundamental attribution error.
    b. reciprocity.
    c. self-fulfilling prophecy.
    d. the actor-observer effect.
    e. self-serving bias.

84. First impressions tend to become lasting impressions in part because of the role of
    a. social schemas.
    b. actor-observer effects.
    c. discrimination.
    d. cognitive dissonance.
    e. the fundamental attribution error.

Name:________________________ Class:________________ Date:_________

Essentials of Psychology Chapter 12

X

85. As discussed in the text, Milgram's findings raise important questions about all but one of the following?
    a. legitimization of authority.
    b. oversocialization of obedience in young people.
    c. social validation of immoral behavior.
    d. our capacity for destructive obedience.
    e. troubling effects of groupthink.

86. Which of the following best describes the role of heredity in attitudes?
    a. Genes play almost no role in developing attitudes.
    b. Genes are directly responsible for developing attitudes.
    c. Genes account for similarities, but not differences, in attitudes.
    d. Genes contribute to factors such as intelligence and personality traits that affect the development of attitudes.
    e. Genes account for differences, but not similarities, in attitudes.

87. Jamal is in a situation where another person needs help. According to the bystander intervention model, Jamal's first step will be
    a. choosing a way to help.
    b. interpreting the event as an emergency.
    c. assuming personal responsibility.
    d. recognizing a need for help.
    e. implementing his decision to help.

88. The relationship between attitudes and behavior is best described as
    a. nearly perfect.
    b. almost zero.
    c. modest.
    d. unclear.
    e. significant.

89. Regarding research evidence on aggression, which of the following statements is FALSE?
    a. Research suggests that males are generally more aggressive than females.
    b. Aggressive behavior generally increases with increasing temperatures, although it may decline at extremely high temperatures.
    c. Children learn aggression through modeling that occurs in the home, at school, and in the media.
    d. The fighting instinct is a basic survival mechanism in many animal species.
    e. Because of its depressant effects, alcohol use curbs impulsive behavior, including acts of impulsive violence.

Essentials of Psychology Chapter 12

90. Christine does not like country music. This reflects which component of her attitude toward country music?
    a. attribution
    b. cognition
    c. emotion
    d. behavior
    e. expectation

91. Frida is a CEO who must make an important decision regarding the future of her company. When Frida meets with her Board of Directors to discuss this decision, she should do all but which of the following?
    a. plan on holding several group meetings
    b. ask one of the Board members to play "devil's advocate"
    c. avoid bringing in any outsiders
    d. avoid stating her initial preferences early in the meeting
    e. subdivide the group into smaller units to independently review issues before the larger group

92. Attitudes may be described as comprising which components?
    a. emotions, cognitions, and expectations
    b. emotions, behaviors, and cognitions
    c. cognitions, expectations, and bodily arousal
    d. cognitions, emotions, and bodily arousal
    e. behaviors, expectations, and cognitions

93. All but which of the following are factors that influence the process of impression formation?
    a. social identity
    b. social schemas
    c. stereotyping
    d. personal disclosure
    e. self-fulfilling prophecies

94. What is the primary reason that people's behaviors do not always match their attitudes?
    a. genetic influences
    b. self-serving bias
    c. the actor-observer effect
    d. stereotyping
    e. situational constraints

95. Personal identity is to ______ as social identity is to ______.
    a. self-concept; group identity
    b. individual identity; group identity
    c. self-concept; groupthink
    d. self-esteem; group identity
    e. individual identity; groupthink

Name:______________________ Class:______________________ Date:______________

Essentials of Psychology Chapter 12

96. People use a central route of processing information when
    a. elaboration likelihood is high.
    b. cognitive dissonance is high.
    c. they are uninterested in the issue.
    d. motivation is low.
    e. they lack evaluation skills.

97. Regarding attitudes, which of the following statements is FALSE?
    a. Attitudes are acquired from a variety of sources in the social environment.
    b. Genetic factors are less important determinants of attitudes than environmental factors.
    c. Attitudes are more strongly linked to behaviors when the attitude can be readily recalled from memory.
    d. Attitudes are not especially strong predictors of behavior.
    e. Twin studies suggest that people inherit particular genes for particular attitudes.

98. Toula, who is Greek, has a negative bias toward members of other racial groups. What is Toula's bias called?
    a. authoritarianism
    b. stereotype threat
    c. discrimination
    d. universalist orientation
    e. racism

99. The hormone _________ has been linked to increased aggressive behavior.
    a. amphetamine
    b. testosterone
    c. GABA
    d. serotonin
    e. norepinephrine

100. When people make dispositional attributions for their successes and make situational attributions for their failures, they are demonstrating
    a. the fundamental attribution error.
    b. the actor-observer effect.
    c. a self-serving bias.
    d. a self-fulfilling prophecy.
    e. the elaboration likelihood model.

101. Miguel is asked to describe himself. Which of Miguel's statements represents his personal identity?
    a. I am a Mexican American.
    b. I am Buddhist.
    c. I am intelligent and creative.
    d. I am Carla and Manuel's son.
    e. I am a college student.

Essentials of Psychology Chapter 12

102. Regarding persuasive appeals, which of the following statements is FALSE?
  a. Messages that run counter to the perceived interests of the communicator tend to be perceived as more credible.
  b. Those of low intelligence or low self-confidence are generally harder to persuade.
  c. People in a good mood tend to be more receptive to persuasive messages than those in a bad mood.
  d. The more often people are exposed to a message, the more favorably they evaluate it, but only up to a point.
  e. Communicators who are similar to the audience are perceived more favorably than those who are dissimilar.

103. The "cover story" in the famous obedience research presented in the text was that the researcher was investigating
  a. the effects of group size on conformity.
  b. attribution errors.
  c. cognitive dissonance.
  d. the effects of punishment on learning.
  e. deindividuation of crowd members.

104. Which researcher(s) is/are associated with the study of bystander intervention?
  a. Bandura
  b. Milgram
  c. Fishbein
  d. Janis and Zajonc
  e. Latane and Darley

105. The tendency for people to reduce their efforts when working as part of a group is called
  a. social inhibition.
  b. social facilitation.
  c. social intervention.
  d. social loafing.
  e. groupthink.

106. In groupthink, group members emphasize ______ over thoughtful consideration of the issues.
  a. diffusion of responsibility
  b. social loafing
  c. impressions
  d. individual opinion
  e. consensus-building

107. The contact hypothesis suggests that prejudice
  a. can be reduced by bringing groups into contact with each other.
  b. is the result of groups being brought into contact with each other.
  c. results in increased group interaction.
  d. results in decreased group interaction.
  e. will be more apparent in situations of intergroup cooperation.

Essentials of Psychology Chapter 12

108. Generalizing from research, we can predict that the presence of others will _______ performance on well-learned tasks and ______ performance on novel or challenging tasks.
   a. decrease; have no effect on
   b. increase; have no effect on
   c. decrease; increase
   d. have no effect on; decrease
   e. increase; decrease

109. People with a high need for consistency are more likely to be susceptible to which compliance technique?
   a. bait-and-switch
   b. switch-and-pay
   c. foot-in-the-door
   d. low-ball
   e. door-in-the-face

110. Other factors being equal, which person is likely to identify more strongly with their personal identity than their social identity?
   a. an Asian American female
   b. a European American female
   c. a Hispanic American male
   d. an African American female
   e. a European American male

111. A ______ is a mental image or representation that a person uses to understand her/his social environment.
   a. situational attribution
   b. fundamental attribution error
   c. dispositional attribution
   d. social schema
   e. self-fulfilling prophecy

112. Which recipient variables have an influence on persuasion?
   a. intelligence and confidence
   b. confidence and mood
   c. credibility, likeability, and similarity
   d. intelligence, confidence, and mood
   e. credibility and similarity

113. Willem is a skilled pianist. He has recently started playing the violin. When an audience is present, Willem probably
   a. performs better on both instruments.
   b. performs worse on both instruments.
   c. performs better on the violin only.
   d. performs better on the piano only.
   e. performs worse on the piano only.

Name:______________________ Class:______________________ Date:______________

Essentials of Psychology Chapter 12

114. Regarding research on physical attractiveness, which of the following statements is FALSE?
   a. Faces having symmetrical features and a clear complexion tend to be perceived as more attractive.
   b. There appears to be little variation across cultures in the ideal facial features of females.
   c. Women and men tend to agree that the faces of men with more masculine features are more attractive than the faces of men with more feminine features.
   d. Women and men tend to agree that the faces of women with more feminine features are more attractive than the faces of women with more masculine features.
   e. Judgments of physical beauty for females typically include features such as high cheekbones, widely spaced eyes, fuller hairstyles, and a large smile.

115. In order for intergroup contact to have a desirable effect on prejudice and intergroup tension, all but which of the following conditions are necessary?
   a. opportunities for members to become acquainted
   b. equal status for all group members
   c. members with high levels of empathy
   d. social and institutional support
   e. intergroup cooperation

116. Regarding Milgram's research on obedience, which of the following statements is FALSE?
   a. Ethical concerns resulting from this research played a large role in the profession's adoption of ethical guidelines to protect research participants.
   b. Some people have interpreted Milgram's findings as suggesting we do too good a job in our culture at socializing young people to be obedient to authority.
   c. Milgram found that placing the "learner" in the same room as the "teacher" reduced obedience somewhat.
   d. Subsequent research revealed that the majority of "teachers" in Milgram's experiment did not believe that the "learners" were truly receiving significant levels of pain.
   e. When Milgram repeated his study in a dingy storefront setting rather than a university setting, nearly half of his subjects complied with the experimenter's demands.

X 117. Discrimination represents which attitudinal component of prejudice?
   a. cognition
   b. behavior
   c. feeling
   d. emotion
   e. belief

118. On their first date, Angelo told Robin detailed stories of his relationship with his last girlfriend. As a result, Robin
   a. will probably feel very comfortable because of Angelo's honesty.
   b. might be flattered that Angelo confided in her.
   c. will want to know even more on the next date.
   d. will likely feel that Angelo is mature and well adjusted.
   e. will likely feel that Angelo is insecure and poorly adjusted.

Essentials of Psychology Chapter 12

119. According to _______, people are more likely to carefully evaluate a persuasive message when their motivational state is high and when they have the ability or knowledge to evaluate the information.
   a. the contact hypothesis
   b. prosocial behavior theory
   c. the elaboration likelihood model
   d. the groupthink principle
   e. the self-fulfilling prophecy

120. Paul believes his mother yelled at him because she had a headache. Paul's conclusion is an example of a(n)
   a. attitude.
   b. self-serving bias.
   c. stereotype.
   d. attribution.
   e. schema.

121. According to Sternberg, the strongest relationships can be described as those with
   a. high levels of all three components of love in at least one partner.
   b. high levels of commitment, regardless of levels of intimacy or passion.
   c. high levels of commitment and intimacy, regardless of levels of passion.
   d. a high level of commitment by both partners.
   e. partners that have love triangles that are closely matched.

122. Similarity is important in a relationship because it
   a. minimizes controversy.
   b. gives people something to talk about.
   c. provides for validation of each person's self-concept.
   d. helps the people in the relationship meet other similar people.
   e. reflects the inner qualities of each individual.

123. Attempting to reduce prejudice by transporting students from the majority group to minority schools is suggested by
   a. the fundamental attribution error.
   b. the matching hypothesis.
   c. the contact hypothesis.
   d. cognitive dissonance.
   e. in-group favoritism.

124. In persuasive messages, the careful evaluation of the content of a message is accomplished via which route of processing?
   a. central
   b. peripheral
   c. attributional
   d. dissonant
   e. relational

Essentials of Psychology Chapter 12

125. Of the following smokers, which one is choosing the route of rationalization to deal with the dissonance between their smoking behavior and their belief that smoking is unhealthy?
   a. Alejandro, who says, “Cancer doesn’t run in my family anyway.”
   b. Bhodip, who says, “I’ll worry about quitting smoking when I’m older.”
   c. Corbin, who quits smoking “cold turkey.”
   d. Damita, who develops and implements a plan to gradually stop smoking.
   e. Esperanza, who stops paying attention to messages that smoking is harmful.

126. Heika and Lucille were both passed over for a promotion at work. Heika is sure that the boss does not like him, but he believes that Lucille was passed over because she is really a poor worker. His attribution of the cause of the event can be explained in terms of
   a. the fundamental attribution error.
   b. the actor-observer effect.
   c. a self-fulfilling prophecy.
   d. cognitive dissonance.
   e. stereotyping.

127. A popular diet company hires a physician to advertise their weight-loss program. Which source variable is the company trying to influence?
   a. likeability
   b. similarity
   c. credibility
   d. originality
   e. attractiveness

128. Carlotta has recently befriended Phyllis, who has been driving Carlotta’s children to day care. The new friendship is most likely based on
   a. matching.
   b. proximity.
   c. similarity.
   d. prosocial behavior.
   e. reciprocity.

129. Which social psychologist proposed that people tend to focus more on the behavior of others than on the circumstances in which the behavior occurs?
   a. Solomon Asch
   b. Robert Sternberg
   c. Fritz Heider
   d. C. Daniel Batson
   e. Stanley Milgram

Name:______________________________ Class:____________________ Date:__________

Essentials of Psychology Chapter 12

130. Regarding stereotypes, which of the following statements is FALSE?
   a. Stereotypes are relatively easy to change when new, valid information is presented.
   b. Stereotyping is a normal cognitive tendency.
   c. Although stereotypes can include positive or negative attributes, they are usually more negative.
   d. Stereotypes influence first impressions.
   e. Stereotypes help people more efficiently use their cognitive resources.

131. When John and Mary go on their first date, John reveals extensive personal information to Mary. What is the likely result of John's self-disclosure?
   a. It will help their relationship become stronger.
   b. It will lead Mary to form a negative first impression of John.
   c. It will lead Mary to form a positive first impression.
   d. It will help strengthen Mary's stereotype about men.
   e. It will have no effect on Mary's opinion or their relationship.

132. Features of a communicator attempting to deliver a persuasive message are called
   a. source variables.
   b. attribution variables.
   c. message variables.
   d. recipient variables.
   e. elaboration likelihood variables.

133. A group of students discusses their grades on their first psychology exam. Which student is making a dispositional attribution?
   a. Arne says, "I'll never pass this course. I'm just stupid."
   b. Beck says, "I did well because the test was really easy."
   c. Claire says, "The professor thinks I'm cute, so he graded my essays easy."
   d. Donal says, "My lucky rabbit's foot worked!"
   e. Earl says, "I flunked; that professor just doesn't like me."

X 134. Which of the following individuals is making the fundamental attribution error?
   a. Alex failed his psychology test and passed his biology test. He says his psychology professor made an unfair test, and that he studied hard for the biology test.
   b. Bernard asks a girl in his class for a date, and she responds in a curt, rude manner. Bernard says that she's stuck-up, but doesn't realize the girl's mother just died.
   c. Courtney and her friend just received grades from their first English composition, on which they both earned A's. Courtney says that she earned her grade after working really hard, while her friend earned her grade because she's lucky.
   d. Dimitria works in sales. When she makes a sale, she boasts about her sales skills, but when she fails to make one, she has an excuse for why it did not work out.
   e. Eduardo believes that all Italians are emotional and criminal-minded, so he avoids making friends with the Italian foreign exchange student in his dorm.

Essentials of Psychology Chapter 12

135. A homeless woman asks Tyler for five dollars. After Tyler says no, the woman asks for a dollar and Tyler gives her a dollar. Tyler's behavior is a response to which compliance technique?
    a. social validation
    b. door-in-the-face
    c. foot-in-the-door
    d. bait-and-switch
    e. low-ball

136. Which subfield of psychology is concerned with how a person's thoughts, feelings, and behaviors are influenced by interactions with others?
    a. health psychology
    b. clinical psychology
    c. developmental psychology
    d. positive psychology
    e. social psychology

137. Which of the following is the best definition of social facilitation?
    a. the tendency for some people to have better social skills than others
    b. the tendency for some people to facilitate the social skills of others
    c. the superior ability of groups to solve problems compared to individuals
    d. the tendency for people to perform better when others are present
    e. the tendency for members of a team to work harder than when they work alone

138. All but which of the following is identified in the text as a factor influencing conformity?
    a. age
    b. self-esteem
    c. gender differences
    d. desire to be liked
    e. political preference

139. Jahrul's instructor was very rude the first day of class. Jahrul assumed the instructor was a rude woman. He did not know that she had woken up late, had a car accident on the way to work, and had been locked out of her office. Jahrul is demonstrating
    a. the fundamental attribution error.
    b. self-serving bias.
    c. cognitive dissonance.
    d. the actor-observer effect.
    e. the elaboration likelihood model.

Essentials of Psychology Chapter 12

140. Behavior that is beneficial to others is called ______ behavior.
 a. diffused
 b. prejudicial
 c. prosocial
 d. attributional
 e. reciprocal

141. Regarding research evidence on aggression, which of the following statements is FALSE?
 a. Investigators have found strong links between alcohol use and violent behaviors like rape, homicide, and domestic violence.
 b. Investigators have identified neural mechanisms associated with genes linked to violent or impulsive behavior.
 c. The relationship between alcohol and aggressive behavior is influenced by situational social demands as well as the user's biological sensitivity to alcohol.
 d. Research suggests that frustration consistently leads people to behave aggressively.
 e. The increased availability of serotonin in aggressive men's brains may create a tendency to make them more likely to respond to social provocation.

Name:______________________ Class:______________________ Date:______________

Essentials of Psychology Chapter 13

1. The secondary gain of conversion symptoms refers *most* closely to which of the following?
   a. The symptom prevents the individual from having to confront stressful or conflict-laden situations.
   b. The symptom symbolizes an underlying struggle between opposing motives.
   c. The symptom enhances the employment of defense mechanisms.
   d. The symptom causes the person to have a certain amount of indifference toward it.
   e. The maintenance of the symptoms as conditioned responses.

2. All but which of the following are myths about suicide?
   a. People who commit suicide are usually suffering from a psychological disorder, but are not insane.
   b. People who threaten suicide are only trying to get attention.
   c. If someone threatens suicide, it is best to ignore it so as not to encourage repeated threats.
   d. Talking about suicide with a depressed person may prompt her/him to attempt suicide.
   e. People who attempt suicide and fail aren't serious about killing themselves.

3. The sociocultural model explains abnormal behavior in terms of
   a. disturbed learning processes.
   b. failures of society.
   c. distorted thinking.
   d. the failure of certain cultures to promote self-actualization.
   e. social influences on underlying biological factors.

4. Dr. Tomlin is a therapist working from the cognitive perspective. She is likely to describe abnormal behavior in terms of
   a. the role of repressed thoughts and beliefs.
   b. failure to achieve self-actualization.
   c. classical conditioning.
   d. the combination of classical and operant conditioning.
   e. irrational or distorted thinking.

5. Hallucinations are
   a. perceptions that occur without appropriate external stimuli.
   b. false beliefs.
   c. long strings of disconnected words.
   d. patterns of agitated, purposeless motion.
   e. a breakdown in the logical structure of thinking and speech.

6. Perceptions are to _____ as beliefs are to ______.
   a. anxiety; depression
   b. delusions; hallucinations
   c. compulsions; obsessions
   d. obsessions; compulsions
   e. hallucinations; delusions

Essentials of Psychology Chapter 13

7. Which theory would attribute a person's depression to faulty interpretations of events and distorted thinking patterns?
   a. Cognitive
   b. Humanistic
   c. Psychodynamic
   d. Behavior
   e. Sociocultural

8. Other factors being equal, a person from which group is *least* at risk for committing suicide?
   a. A Caucasian-American male
   b. A Caucasian-American female
   c. An African-American male
   d. An African-American female
   e. A Latino-American male

9. The criterion of maladaptive behavior used in determining whether behavior is abnormal would likely to be applied to which of the following cases?
   a. Jonathan, who is hearing voices
   b. Quincy, who is experiencing some symptoms of depression but is still functioning adequately.
   c. Nate, who has developed a drug abuse problem that is affecting his health.
   d. Tricia, who behaves in ways other people consider deviant.
   e. Leslie, who believes he is hounded by demons.

10. Regarding major depressive disorder,
    a. men are more likely than women to be affected.
    b. men and women are equally likely to be affected.
    c. women are more likely than men to be affected.
    d. young women are more likely than young men to be affected, and the pattern reverses in middle age.
    e. young men are more likely than young women to be affected, and the pattern reverses in middle age.

11. After getting into an automobile accident while fighting with her fiancé, Chou reports that she cannot see. Examinations indicate no apparent medical condition. Based on this description, Chou may be suffering from
    a. dissociative identity disorder.
    b. hypochondriasis.
    c. dissociative amnesia.
    d. functional neurological symptom disorder.
    e. bipolar disorder.

Essentials of Psychology Chapter 13

12. The most common form of hallucinations in schizophrenia is
    a. visual.
    b. olfactory.
    c. auditory.
    d. tactile.
    e. kinesthetic.

13. Major support for the sociocultural model of abnormal behavior is provided by evidence that
    a. intelligent people are more likely to suffer from severe forms of abnormality.
    b. psychological disorders appear with equal frequency in all cultures studied.
    c. wealthy people rarely suffer psychological disorders.
    d. severe disorders such as schizophrenia and depression are more prevalent in impoverished and otherwise disadvantaged groups.
    e. severe disorders such as schizophrenia and depression are more prevalent in wealthy, industrialized nations.

14. Regarding gender and suicide, which of the following statements is *true*?
    a. There are no gender differences in suicide attempts and suicide acts.
    b. When attempting suicide, women tend to choose more lethal methods.
    c. When attempting suicide, men are more likely than women to choose pills or poison.
    d. More men attempt suicide, but more women complete the suicide act.
    e. More women attempt suicide, but more men complete the suicide act.

15. The Diagnostic and Statistical Manual (DSM) uses the term _____ to describe abnormal patterns of behavior.
    a. mental illness
    b. mental disorder
    c. psychological disorder
    d. psychological illness
    e. personality disorder

16. Dissociative amnesia is
    a. a loss of memory due to head trauma.
    b. another term for dissociative identity disorder.
    c. another term for multiple personality disorder.
    d. a loss of memory with no identifiable physical cause.
    e. a loss of memory due to a neurological condition.

Essentials of Psychology Chapter 13

17. A woman walks into a police station. She has no identification and reports that she was walking down the street with no sense of who she is or how she got there. She is referred to a neurologist who finds no physical explanation for her condition. This description sounds like a case of
    a. dissociative amnesia.
    b. dissociative identity disorder.
    c. multiple personality disorder.
    d. anterograde amnesia.
    e. bipolar disorder.

18. The earliest major psychological model of abnormal behavior was the
    a. cognitive model.
    b. humanistic model.
    c. behavioral model.
    d. biopsychosocial model.
    e. psychodynamic model.

19. Regarding the diathesis-stress model, which of the following statements is *false*?
    a. Diatheses are generally genetic in nature, although they may also involve psychological factors.
    b. Significant sources of stress may increase the risk of developing particular disorders.
    c. The stronger the diathesis, the less stress is needed to produce a disorder.
    d. Disorders may develop under benign life circumstances.
    e. Whether a person having a diathesis develops a particular disorder is primarily dependent on his or her cluster of personality traits.

20. Edwina is constantly worried. She cannot really identify why she feels this way, and she finds it nearly impossible to relax. Edwina's therapist believes her symptoms best represent
    a. obsessive-compulsive.
    b. generalized anxiety disorder.
    c. panic disorder.
    d. social anxiety disorder.
    e. dissociative identity disorder.

21. As described in the text, the diathesis-stress model is an example of which model of abnormal behavior?
    a. Humanistic
    b. Cognitive
    c. Psychodynamic
    d. Sociocultural
    e. Biopsychosocial

Name:____________________ Class:________________ Date:__________

Essentials of Psychology Chapter 13

22. In explaining the development of schizophrenia, the diathesis-stress model emphasizes
    a. the role of brain abnormalities.
    b. the interaction of genetic predispositions and stress.
    c. the role of stressful life experiences in creating a diathesis.
    d. the role of psychosocial influences in creating a diathesis.
    e. biochemical imbalances.

23. The American Psychiatric Association once considered homosexuality as a type of mental disorder, but no longer does today. This fact is an example of which way that culture influences ideas about abnormality?
    a. The same behavior may be judged abnormal at some points in time, but not at others.
    b. Some forms of abnormal behavior in a particular culture may have no direct counterpart in another culture.
    c. The same behavior can be normal in one culture but abnormal in another.
    d. Abnormal behavior patterns may be expressed differently in different cultures.
    e. Some behaviors may be abnormal in the majority culture, but normal in the minority culture.

24. Therapist Charlotte Maley is a behaviorist. She is *most* likely to suggests that depression is
    a. due to unresolved unconscious conflicts.
    b. the result of losses or shortfalls in reinforcement levels.
    c. a matter of how people interpret events.
    d. genetic in origin but influenced by early trauma.
    e. the result of interruptions of one's sense of self-actualization.

25. According to Freud, psychological symptoms
    a. arise from disturbed brain chemistry.
    b. are a conscious cry for attention.
    c. represent an outward expression of inner turmoil.
    d. are produced voluntarily to obtain sympathy.
    e. are learned through experience.

26. Charmaine Coltraine is preoccupied with fears that she has a terrible health problem. Coltraine's fears are characteristic of
    a. functional neurological symptom disorder.
    b. somatic symptom disorder.
    c. dissociative identity disorder.
    d. dissociative amnesia.
    e. hysteria.

27. Humanistic theorists contend that abnormal behavior
    a. is the result of unconscious processes.
    b. is the result of conditioning.
    c. develops from encountering obstacles on the road to personal growth.
    d. involves distorted cognitions as well as learning influences.
    e. results from the stress of coping with poverty and social disadvantage.

Name:____________________ Class:____________________ Date:____________

28. Gina believes that she is the secret love child of the late Princess Diana and singer Elton John. Since she really is not their child, Gina's belief would be considered a(n)
   a. diathesis.
   b. delusion.
   c. hallucination.
   d. obsession.
   e. compulsion.

29. Regarding major depression, which of the following statements is *false*?
   a. Major depression has a relatively high rate of recurrence.
   b. Many psychologists believe that the stressors faced by many women today contribute to their increased risk of depression.
   c. When left untreated, episodes of major depression can last months, or a year or more.
   d. Researchers have found that women and men tend to cope with depression differently, with men more likely to ruminate.
   e. About 16.5 percent of U.S. adults develop major depression at some point in their lives.

30. Exaggerating the importance of negative events or personal flaws describes which type of cognitive distortion?
   a. All-or-nothing thinking
   b. Misfortune telling
   c. Catastrophizing
   d. Dismissing the positives
   e. Misplaced blame

31. Fannie goes to a humanist therapist. When she talks about her frustrations with attempting to satisfy other people's demands, her therapist may suggest that Fannie's attempts could lead to
   a. a distorted self-image.
   b. an inability to learn from experience.
   c. an inflated ego.
   d. unconscious aggressive desires.
   e. irrational and distorted thinking patterns.

32. Angelique has not left her house for two years. She is completely terrified of going out. Based on this description, she is probably suffering from
   a. agoraphobia.
   b. social anxiety disorder.
   c. specific phobia.
   d. panic disorder.
   e. post-traumatic stress disorder.

Essentials of Psychology Chapter 13

33. The patterns of behavior in personality disorders are, in many cases,
   a. highly resistant to change.
   b. somewhat resistant to change.
   c. somewhat easy to change.
   d. relatively easy to change with psychotherapy.
   e. relatively easy to change with drug treatment.

34. Attempts to understand the biological basis of depression has linked it to imbalances in
   a. serotonin and dopamine.
   b. dopamine and norepinephrine.
   c. norepinephrine and serotonin.
   d. serotonin and acetylcholine.
   e. epinephrine and dopamine.

35. In a manic episode of bipolar disorder, a person might be characterized by all but which of the following?
   a. Extreme euphoria and energy
   b. Pressured speech
   c. Inflated sense of self-worth
   d. Difficulty committing to decisions
   e. Poor judgment

36. All but which of the following statements describes antisocial personality disorder?
   a. The majority of people with this disorder engage in criminal activities.
   b. People with this disorder are sometimes called psychopaths or sociopaths.
   c. Some people with this disorder can be charming.
   d. This disorder affects men more often than women.
   e. Some people with this disorder have a high level of intelligence.

37. Schizophrenia follows a _______ and typically develops _______.
   a. chronic but not lifelong course; in early adolescence
   b. lifelong course; in early adolescence
   c. chronic but not lifelong course; in late adolescence or early adulthood
   d. lifelong course; in late adolescence or early adulthood
   e. variable course; during the person's thirties

38. Different personalities in dissociative identity disorder may demonstrate all of the following *except*
   a. different genders.
   b. different ages.
   c. different traits and manners of speech.
   d. different eye colors.
   e. different memories.

Essentials of Psychology Chapter 13

39. Which of the following individuals exhibits behaviors that would be considered maladaptive?
    a. Michael, who wears women's clothing when no one is looking
    b. Stanley, who battles depression
    c. Gary, who believes that he is the son of George Washington
    d. Irving, who hears voices
    e. Roy, who is continues to use drugs despite the effects on his health and functioning

40. Although they have different symptoms and characteristics, dissociative disorders and somatic symptom disorders are often grouped together because they both involve _______ defenses against _____.
    a. physical; anxiety
    b. physical; depression
    c. psychological; mania
    d. psychological; depression
    e. psychological; anxiety

41. Individuals with antisocial personality disorder demonstrate all of the following *except*
    a. disregard for rules of society.
    b. psychotic behavior.
    c. lack of remorse for misdeeds.
    d. impulsivity.
    e. irresponsible behavior.

42. The cognitive model of panic disorder focuses on misinterpretations of
    a. childhood experiences.
    b. social cues.
    c. bodily sensations.
    d. others' intentions.
    e. irregular brain wave patterns.

43. Persistent anxiety that is not tied to any particular object or situation is called
    a. generalized anxiety disorder.
    b. obsessive-compulsive disorder.
    c. agoraphobia.
    d. social anxiety disorder.
    e. panic disorder.

44. Behavior that violates established social norms or standards describes which of the following criteria for determining abnormal behavior?
    a. Dangerousness
    b. Social deviance
    c. Maladaptive behavior
    d. Unusualness
    e. Emotional distress

Essentials of Psychology Chapter 13

45. Physical complaints that cannot be explained medically are characteristic of
    a. dissociative identity disorder.
    b. obsessive-compulsive disorder.
    c. somatic symptoms and related disorders.
    d. dissociative amnesia.
    e. bipolar disorder.

46. Bipolar disorder was formerly called
    a. manic-depression.
    b. hysteria.
    c. illness anxiety disorder.
    d. multiple personality disorder.
    e. schizophrenia.

47. Freudian theory contends that depression
    a. represents the defense mechanism of displacement.
    b. is genetically based.
    c. represents anger turned inward.
    d. is a form of attention-getting.
    e. results from a lack of reinforcement.

48. "La belle indifference" describes which feature of a psychological disorder?
    a. The tendency for people with functional neurological symptom disorder to be unconcerned about their symptoms
    b. The tendency for people with dissociative identity disorder to have been highly imaginative as children
    c. The tendency for people with depression to have a maladaptive attributional style
    d. The tendency for people with bipolar disorder to swing dramatically from one end of the mood spectrum to the other
    e. The tendency for people with depression to show indifference toward their future

49. Because the anxiety is not tied to any particular object in generalized anxiety disorder, this type of anxiety is often described as
    a. obsessive.
    b. compulsive.
    c. free-floating.
    d. neurotic.
    e. post-traumatic.

Essentials of Psychology Chapter 13

50. Delusions of ______ describe the most common theme among schizophrenia patients.
 a. waxy flexibility
 b. jealousy
 c. la belle indifference
 d. grandeur
 e. persecution

51. Regarding dissociative disorders, which of the following statements is *false*?
 a. Dissociative disorders can involve amnesia.
 b. Dissociative disorders include cases of people with "multiple personalities."
 c. Dissociative disorders are among the most mystifying of psychological disorders.
 d. Compared to other psychological disorders, dissociative disorders are relatively common.
 e. Some mental health professionals question the existence of dissociative identity disorder.

52. Which of the following statements about schizophrenia is *true*?
 a. Schizophrenia affects about 1% of the adult population.
 b. Schizophrenia is somewhat more common in women than in men.
 c. Schizophrenia affects fewer than 500,000 people in the U.S.
 d. Schizophrenia typically develops in late childhood or early adolescence.
 e. Men tend to develop the disorder somewhat later than women.

53. Ceci has a depressive attributional style. This means that when she fails, she is likely to make which types of attributions?
 a. Internal, global, and stable
 b. Internal, specific, and stable
 c. Internal, global, and unstable
 d. External, global, and stable
 e. External, specific, and unstable

54. Approximately what percentage of men could be classified as having antisocial personality disorder?
 a. Less than 1%
 b. 1 to 3%
 c. 3 to 6%
 d. 5 to 8%
 e. 7 to 10%

55. Perhaps the earliest idea regarding abnormal behavior was that
 a. supernatural forces or demonic spirits were at work.
 b. the brains of people displaying abnormal behavior were defective.
 c. it was the product of the inappropriate use of rewards and punishments.
 d. it was the result of a moral weakness.
 e. irrational thoughts or distorted thinking lead to emotional problems.

Essentials of Psychology Chapter 13

56. Personality disorders are a cluster of psychological disorders
    a. involving extremely rigid patterns of behavior.
    b. in which mood disturbances are the primary symptom.
    c. that all include psychotic symptoms.
    d. involving extreme anxiety.
    e. in which cognitive distortions result in impaired functioning.

57. Which of the following is *not* one of the criteria used by psychologists to determine whether a behavior is abnormal?
    a. Morality
    b. Social deviance
    c. Dangerousness
    d. Unusualness
    e. Emotional distress

58. Twin and adoptee studies provide strong evidence for a __________ factor involved in anxiety disorders.
    a. biochemical
    b. genetic
    c. biopsychosocial
    d. neurotransmitter
    e. prenatal

59. A breakdown in the logical structure of thinking and speech, revealed in the form of a loosening of associations, best describes which psychological disorder?
    a. Antisocial personality disorder
    b. Major depressive disorder
    c. Obsessive-compulsive disorder
    d. Dissociative identity disorder
    e. Schizophrenia

60. Which of the following statements regarding criteria for determining abnormal behavior is *false*?
    a. Psychologists use multiple criteria in determining whether behavior is abnormal.
    b. The one determining feature of abnormal behavior is unusualness.
    c. Most people feel anxious or depressed from time to time.
    d. The same behavior may be judged normal under one circumstance and abnormal under another circumstance.
    e. Psychologists take into account the cultural context when making judgments about abnormal behavior.

Essentials of Psychology Chapter 13

61. Phobias develop through associations of aversive stimuli with previously neutral stimuli. This expresses the ______ explanation of phobia development.
   a. cognitive
   b. classical conditioning
   c. operant conditioning
   d. psychodynamic
   e. sociocultural

62. Nagging, intrusive thoughts are called ______, and repetitive or ritual behaviors are called ______.
   a. diatheses; delusions
   b. compulsions; obsessions
   c. obsessions; compulsions
   d. diatheses; conversions
   e. conversions; diatheses

63. Ella finds herself extremely frightened whenever she sees a snake. This describes a form of
   a. panic disorder.
   b. specific phobia.
   c. agoraphobia.
   d. obsessive-compulsive disorder.
   e. social anxiety disorder.

64. The disorder that *most* resembles common notions of insanity, madness, or lunacy is
   a. major depressive disorder.
   b. dissociative identity disorder.
   c. generalized anxiety disorder.
   d. schizophrenia.
   e. bipolar disorder.

65. Fear of heights is to ______ as fear of enclosed spaces is to ______.
   a. claustrophobia; acrophobia
   b. acrophobia; claustrophobia
   c. agoraphobia; claustrophobia
   d. agoraphobia; acrophobia
   e. acrophobia; agoraphobia

66. In the diathesis-stress model of explaining schizophrenia, which of the following factors would represent a psychosocial influence?
   a. Childhood brain damage
   b. Prenatal brain trauma
   c. Failure in school
   d. Loss of a loved one
   e. Being raised in an abusive family environment

Essentials of Psychology Chapter 13

67. All but which of the following have been implicated in the development of borderline personality disorder?
   a. Abuse or neglect in childhood
   b. Failure to develop a cohesive self-concept in childhood
   c. Low levels of dopamine production
   d. Brain abnormalities
   e. Genetic factors

68. Schizophrenia may involve imbalances in nerve pathways that utilize which neurotransmitter?
   a. Serotonin
   b. Melatonin
   c. Dopamine
   d. Norepinephrine
   e. Epinephrine

69. In experiments with Little Albert, Watson demonstrated
   a. the need to consider cognitive, as well as learning, influences in abnormal behavior.
   b. the inability of young children to acquire phobias.
   c. the role of classical conditioning in the development of phobias.
   d. the ease with which instinctual fears are demonstrated in young children.
   e. the role of operant conditioning in fostering aggression.

70. Critics of the concept of dissociative identity disorder suggest
   a. it is really a form a schizophrenia.
   b. it represents a form of attention-seeking role playing.
   c. there are underlying physical causes that are unidentified.
   d. it is not really an abnormal condition.
   e. it fails to provide secondary gain.

71. Eleanor is a quiet 41-year-old housewife. Occasionally, she seems to "become" a 14-year-old male juvenile delinquent. Other times she "becomes" a 52-year-old, foul-mouthed alcoholic. This sounds like a textbook case of
   a. schizophrenia.
   b. manic-depressive disorder.
   c. dissociative identity disorder.
   d. conversion disorder.
   e. bipolar disorder.

72. Which of the following people can be described as having features of obsessive-compulsive disorder?
   a. Buckie, who locks and unlocks her door three times each time she enters and leaves her home
   b. Scott, who has a low-level state of anxiety that seems to travel with him wherever he goes
   c. Rick, who has an irrational fear of riding on escalators
   d. Mary Jo, who refuses to leave her house because going out in public makes her panic
   e. Guillermo, who experiences sudden, unexpected episodes of sheer terror

Name:______________________________ Class:____________________ Date:__________

Essentials of Psychology Chapter 13

73. Which of the following describes a negative symptom of schizophrenia?
    a. Hallucinations
    b. Delusions
    c. Thought disorders
    d. Social isolation
    e. Bizarre behaviors

74. Tatiana is a schizophrenia patient with delusional thinking. Based on this description, what is Tatiana *most* likely experiencing?
    a. Perceptions that occur without appropriate external stimuli
    b. False but firm beliefs
    c. Violent, aggressive outbursts
    d. Patterns of disorganized speech
    e. Removal of inhibitions resulting in violent outbursts

75. Which ethnic groups have relatively higher rates of suicide?
    a. Caucasian Americans and African Americans
    b. Caucasian Americans and Hispanic Americans
    c. Caucasian Americans and Native Americans
    d. African Americans and Hispanic Americans
    e. African Americans and Native Americans

76. Based on available evidence, which of the following brain regions appears to be the *most* affected in cases of schizophrenia?
    a. Prefrontal cortex and limbic system
    b. Limbic system and hypothalamus
    c. Hypothalamus and medulla
    d. Medulla and prefrontal cortex
    e. Thalamus and medulla

77. What is the approximate prevalence of bipolar disorder in the adult U.S. population?
    a. 1%
    b. 4%
    c. 7%
    d. 10%
    e. 12%

78. Genetic studies demonstrate that the concordance rate for schizophrenia is
    a. highest among family members.
    b. highest among monozygotic twins.
    c. highest among dyzygotic twins.
    d. highest among distant family members.
    e. similar across different groups.

79. George was committed to a psychiatric hospital after he was caught happily shopping at the local supermarket without any clothes on. By what criterion is George's behavior considered abnormal?
    a. Dangerousness
    b. Maladaptive behavior
    c. Social deviance
    d. Emotional distress
    e. Faulty perceptions or interpretations of reality

80. Whenever Fritz leaves his house, he has a nagging thought that he is forgetting something. He goes back to check that he has turned off the water and stove and locked the door. Some days, it takes Fritz over an hour to actually leave the house. This sounds like a case of
    a. somatoform disorder.
    b. obsessive-compulsive disorder.
    c. agoraphobia.
    d. panic disorder.
    e. acrophobia.

81. Steven has bipolar disorder. All of the following may occur during his manic episodes *except*
    a. flight of ideas.
    b. pressured speech.
    c. waxy flexibility.
    d. grandiosity.
    e. restlessness.

82. Dissociative identity disorder is commonly referred to as
    a. multiple personality disorder.
    b. neurosis.
    c. schizophrenia.
    d. generalized anxiety disorder.
    e. antisocial personality disorder.

83. Regarding causes of suicide, which of the following statements is *false*?
    a. Suicide may be linked to irregularities in serotonin functioning in the brain that leads to a disinhibition effect.
    b. Suicide is closely linked to mood disorders.
    c. Adolescents who have a friend who attempted suicide are less likely than their peers to attempt suicide themselves.
    d. Suicidal people may have fewer coping responses, leaving them especially vulnerable to exit events.
    e. Suicides are linked to exit events that leave people feeling stripped of social support.

Essentials of Psychology Chapter 13

84. Which of the following statements *best* captures the cognitive distortion of "mistaken responsibility"?
   a. My partner is going to have an accident when s/he goes skiing.
   b. I failed my first statistics exam. I'll never get into graduate school.
   c. I have to get an A in that class.
   d. I didn't get the grade I wanted in that class; I'm so stupid.
   e. My partner is angry today. I must have done something wrong.

85. Which theorists are associated with the humanistic model of understanding behavior?
   a. Sigmund Freud and Anna Freud
   b. Carl Rogers and Abraham Maslow
   c. John B. Watson and Ivan Pavlov
   d. Albert Ellis and Aaron Beck
   e. Erik Erikson and Carl Jung

86. Regarding panic disorder, which of the following statements is *false*?
   a. Panic attacks can last more than an hour.
   b. Panic disorder is characterized by intense physical symptoms.
   c. Some people with this disorder mistake their symptoms for a heart attack.
   d. Agoraphobia sometimes develops in people with panic disorder.
   e. Panic attacks initially begin because of their association with a specific situation.

87. All but which of the following have been implicated in antisocial personality disorder?
   a. Familial environment characterized by neglect and harsh punishment
   b. Underlying brain abnormalities
   c. Low levels of dopamine production
   d. Genetics
   e. Need for high levels of stimulation to maintain optimal level of arousal

88. Diana has borderline personality disorder. Which of the following *best* describes the major symptoms of her disorder?
   a. Tendency toward mood swings and stormy relationships with others
   b. Extreme suspiciousness or mistrust of others
   c. Pattern of avoiding social relationships out of fear of rejection
   d. Excessive need for orderliness and attention to detail
   e. Odd or eccentric, but not psychotic, behaviors

Name:____ Class:_________________________ Date:______________

Essentials of Psychology Chapter 13

89. Which statement would be made by someone supporting a cognitive explanation for somatic symptom and related disorders?
    a. People with these disorders are reinforced by others for adopting a "sick role" by drawing sympathy and support.
    b. Conversion symptoms help the person avoid anxiety-invoking situations.
    c. Conversion symptoms provide secondary gain.
    d. Conversion symptoms are an outward sign of an unconscious dynamic struggle between opposing motives.
    e. Like people with panic disorder, people with hypochondriasis tend to misinterpret bodily sensations as signs of catastrophic causes.

90. A loss of physical function that has no organic cause is the primary symptom of
    a. hypochondriasis.
    b. dissociative identity disorder.
    c. functional neurological symptom disorder.
    d. schizophrenia.
    e. dissociative amnesia.

91. As described in the text, psychological models of abnormal behavior based on classical conditioning were useful in developing explanations of
    a. personality disorders.
    b. phobias.
    c. schizophrenia.
    d. depression.
    e. self-actualization.

92. Tako occasionally finds himself in a state of sheer terror. The sensation lasts for several minutes, and he often believes he is "going crazy." His symptoms most closely describe
    a. agoraphobia.
    b. post-traumatic stress disorder.
    c. obsessive-compulsive disorder.
    d. panic disorder.
    e. generalized anxiety disorder.

93. Schizophrenia is best described as a type of ________ disorder.
    a. anxiety
    b. mood
    c. personality
    d. psychotic
    e. dissociative

Essentials of Psychology Chapter 13

94. Which of the following involves the removal of normal restraints that serve to keep impulsive behaviors in check?
    a. An exit event
    b. A cognitive distortion
    c. A negative symptom
    d. Waxy flexibility
    e. The disinhibition effect

95. A diathesis is a
    a. severely traumatic incident.
    b. gene linked to a psychological disorder.
    c. predisposition or vulnerability to a disorder.
    d. learned pattern of abnormal behavior.
    e. disturbance of mood, perception, or behavior.

96. All but which of the following people have a specific phobia?
    a. Joe, who is afraid of spiders
    b. Pat, who is afraid of heights
    c. Nicole, who is afraid of venturing out into open places
    d. Michael, who is afraid of snakes
    e. Meghan, who is afraid of flying in airplanes

97. Pablo has an intense fear of giving oral presentations in class. He also is very fearful of dating. Based on this description, he is probably suffering from
    a. agoraphobia.
    b. specific phobia.
    c. social anxiety disorder.
    d. generalized anxiety disorder.
    e. claustrophobia.

98. Jurgen has been diagnosed as having a phobia. This means that Jurgen experiences
    a. sudden episodes of sheer terror with no apparent cause.
    b. persistent anxiety without a specific focus.
    c. nagging, intrusive thoughts.
    d. an irrational or excessive fear of something.
    e. a loss of a physical function that defies explanation.

99. Which model of abnormal behavior is the most comprehensive?
    a. Medical
    b. Sociocultural
    c. Psychodynamic
    d. Biopsychosocial
    e. Humanistic

Essentials of Psychology Chapter 13

100. Felicia reports that she is hearing voices that continually demean and belittle her. By what criterion is her behavior considered abnormal?
a. Dangerousness
b. Maladaptive behavior
c. Social deviance
d. Emotional distress
e. Faulty perceptions or interpretations of reality

101. Which theorist is associated with the study of learned helplessness?
a. Aaron Beck
b. Albert Ellis
c. Albert Bandura
d. Carl Rogers
e. Martin Seligman

102. Bertram suffers from schizophrenia with symptoms of catatonia. Sometimes he seems to "freeze up" in an unusual body position for hours at a time. This particular symptom is called
a. hysterical neurosis.
b. disorganized thinking.
c. waxy flexibility.
d. psychotic frenzy.
e. la belle indifference.

103. Which anxiety disorder has the highest lifetime prevalence in the population?
a. Agoraphobia
b. Social anxiety disorder
c. Panic disorder
d. Generalized anxiety disorder
e. Specific phobia

104. Ted has antisocial personality disorder. It is likely that Ted shows abnormal functioning in which part of his brain?
a. Hippocampus
b. Amygdala
c. Prefrontal cortex
d. Temporal lobes
e. Corpus callosum

105. In schizophrenia, behavioral excesses are to ______ as behavioral deficits are to ______.
a. psychotic disorder; thought disorder
b. thought disorder; psychotic disorder
c. disorganization; paranoia
d. positive symptoms; negative symptoms
e. negative symptoms; positive symptoms

Essentials of Psychology Chapter 13

106. Reduction of anxiety that occurs when feared objects are avoided is the basis of which explanation of phobic avoidance?
   a. Biological
   b. Classical conditioning
   c. Operant conditioning
   d. Cognitive
   e. Humanistic

107. Regarding cross-cultural differences in schizophrenia, which of the following statements is *true*?
   a. Schizophrenia occurs somewhat more frequently in other cultures than in the U.S., and its symptoms are similar across cultures.
   b. Schizophrenia occurs somewhat more frequently in other cultures than in the U.S., and particular symptoms vary from culture to culture.
   c. Schizophrenia occurs much more frequently in other cultures than in the U.S., and particular symptoms vary from culture to culture.
   d. Schizophrenia occurs about as frequently in other cultures as in the U.S., and its symptoms are similar across cultures.
   e. Schizophrenia occurs about as frequently in other cultures as in the U.S., but particular symptoms vary from culture to culture.

108. Within the medical model, distinctive patterns of abnormal behavior are described as
   a. psychological oddities.
   b. biological disorders.
   c. mental disorders or mental illnesses.
   d. diatheses.
   e. attributional styles.

109. Bonnie has been feeling extremely sad for the last two months. She has difficulty getting out of bed to face the day and has lost interest in formerly pleasurable activities. Occasionally, she thinks about committing suicide. She sounds like she may be suffering from ________ disorder.
   a. manic
   b. antisocial personality
   c. bipolar
   d. major depressive
   e. functional neurological symptom

110. Approximately what percentage of American adults has a diagnosable psychological disorder at some point in their life?
   a. 20%
   b. 35%
   c. 50%
   d. 60%
   e. 75%

Essentials of Psychology Chapter 13

111. A stereotypical man with antisocial personality disorder is likely to have been raised in a home characterized by
   a. permissiveness and a general lack of rules.
   b. spoiling and excessive indulgence.
   c. neglect, abuse, and lack of warmth.
   d. excessive stimulation and constant excitement.
   e. moderate, authoritative discipline.

112. A class of psychological disorders involving changes in consciousness, memory, or self-identity is known as
   a. personality disorders.
   b. phobias.
   c. somatic symptom disorders.
   d. mood disorders.
   e. dissociative disorders.

113. The irrational or excessive fear of enclosed spaces is called
   a. acrophobia.
   b. social phobia.
   c. claustrophobia.
   d. obsessive-compulsive disorder.
   e. agoraphobia.

114. Which of the following biological factors is *most* likely to be considered in the cognitive explanation of anxiety disorders?
   a. Genetic inheritance
   b. Biochemical changes in the brain
   c. Disturbances in the functioning of neurotransmitters
   d. Heightened activity in certain regions of the brain
   e. Minor changes in bodily sensations

115. Regarding genetic factors in schizophrenia, which of the following statements is *false*?
   a. When one identical twin has schizophrenia, the other twin has a 45% to 50% chance of having the disorder.
   b. About 13% of people with a schizophrenic parent develop the disorder themselves.
   c. The closer the genetic relationship a person shares with a schizophrenic individual, the greater the likelihood that the person will have or develop schizophrenia.
   d. Investigators have identified a single gene that is responsible for creating a genetic predisposition for schizophrenia.
   e. Heredity plays an important role in schizophrenia, but biological and environmental factors also play important roles.

Essentials of Psychology Chapter 13

116. Regarding anxiety disorders, which of the following statements is *false*?
a. Such disorders involve excessive anxiety that may interfere with normal functioning.
b. Fear is a general feeling of anxiety or dread that is not specific to particular situations.
c. Anxiety disorders are some of the most commonly experienced psychological disorders.
d. Phobias are excessive or irrational fears of particular objects or situations.
e. Anxiety is an adaptive response in some situations.

117. Other factors being equal, which person is at highest risk for suicide?
a. Hugh, a 90-year-old male
b. DeeDee, a 70-year-old female
c. Frank, a 50-year-old male
d. Betty, a 50-year-old female
e. Jake, an 18-year-old male

118. As described in the text, behavioral models of abnormality assume that abnormal behavior
a. is learned in much the same way that normal behavior is learned.
b. is best explained by a different set of learning principles than those governing normal behavior.
c. is largely unlearned, but can be brought under the influence of the environment.
d. is the result of a blockage of a person's natural potential.
e. is largely the result of genetics, but can be influenced by learning.

119. Garth goes to a psychodynamic therapist for treatment of his anxiety. What will be the goal of Garth's therapy?
a. To unroot unconscious conflicts that give rise to his anxiety
b. To determine the biological cause of his anxiety and find the right drug to treat it
c. To become aware of his true feelings, fix his self-image, and come to accept himself the way he is
d. To identify and change the irrational thought patterns that have led to his anxiety
e. To determine how factors like his gender, social class, and ethnicity interact to make him anxious

120. Approximately how many people are hospitalized for schizophrenia in a given year?
a. Very few; most all are treated in community settings
b. Between 5,000 to 10,0000
c. Between 25,000 and 50,0000
d. Between 75,000 and 100,0000
e. More than 100,000

Name:_______________________________________ Class:_________________________ Date:_____________

Essentials of Psychology Chapter 14

1. Gestalt therapy frequently uses which of the following techniques?
   a. empty chair
   b. free association
   c. dream analysis
   d. reflecting back
   e. behavior modification

2. Associating objects that elicit an undesirable response with unpleasant or negative stimuli describes the key principle of
   a. systematic desensitization.
   b. aversive conditioning.
   c. in vivo exposure.
   d. gradual exposure therapy.
   e. virtual therapy.

3. The development of which class of drugs revolutionized the treatment of schizophrenia?
   a. MAO inhibitors
   b. phenothiazines
   c. serotonin-reuptake inhibitors
   d. minor tranquilizers
   e. tricyclics

4. The first class of antipsychotics were the
   a. MAO inhibitors.
   b. tricyclics.
   c. SSRIs.
   d. phenothiazines.
   e. minor tranquilizers.

5. Iqbal and his therapist have fallen into treating each other in a father-son manner. The therapist has started to react to Iqbal as if Iqbal was his son, while Iqbal plays out his troubled relationship with his own father with the therapist. In this case, Iqbal is experiencing ______, while the therapist is experiencing ______.
   a. repression; resistance
   b. insight; interpretation
   c. countertransference; transference
   d. transference; countertransference
   e. resistance; repression

6. In research reported in your text, an analysis of 400 controlled studies evaluating the effectiveness of psychotherapy found that the average person receiving therapy did better than approximately what percentage of people placed on waiting lists for therapy?
   a. 30%
   b. 50%
   c. 60%
   d. 80%
   e. 93%

7. In finding mental health help, the text recommends all but which of the following?
   a. getting recommendations from respected sources
   b. selecting a therapist from local advertisements
   c. obtaining referrals from local medical or community health centers
   d. seeking a consultation with a college health services center
   e. contacting professional organizations for recommendations

8. Juan suffers from alcoholism and has not responded to other types of treatment. Juan's therapist suggests aversive conditioning in which Juan will take a nausea-inducing drug at the same time he sniffs beer. In this treatment strategy, the beer is the ______ during conditioning and the _____ after conditioning.
   a. unconditioned stimulus; neutral stimulus
   b. unconditioned stimulus; conditioned stimulus
   c. conditioned stimulus; neutral stimulus
   d. neutral stimulus; unconditioned stimulus
   e. neutral stimulus; conditioned stimulus

9. Regarding the use of antidepressants, which of the following statements is FALSE?
   a. Tricyclics and SSRIs are about equally effective in treating depression.
   b. SSRIs are generally preferred over tricyclics because they are less dangerous in overdose situations.
   c. Antidepressants that target serotonin can help treat eating disorders like bulimia.
   d. Compared to tricyclics, SSRIs have more severe side effects.
   e. Antidepressants are helpful in treating a variety of anxiety disorders.

10. ______ describes the social policy of redirecting the care of people with severe mental disorders from state mental hospitals toward community-based treatment settings.
    a. Gradual exposure
    b. Systematic desensitization
    c. Meta-analytic movement
    d. Positive psychology
    e. Deinstitutionalization

Essentials of Psychology Chapter 14

11. Which of the following correctly describes the effects of deinstitutionalization?
    a. Deinstitutionalization has been a resounding success, as almost all mental patients have now been reintegrated into the community.
    b. Deinstitutionalization has been an unequivocal failure, as mental patients have not been helped at all.
    c. Deinstitutionalization has been predominantly a failure due to its overly aggressive outreach programs.
    d. Deinstitutionalization has been a mix of success and failure as many people have been helped but far too many have not.
    e. Deinstitutionalization has been predominantly successful since the vast majority of mental patients are now receiving help in their community.

12. Regarding traditional psychoanalysis, which of the following statements is FALSE?
    a. A major technique in psychoanalysis is dream analysis, and Freud thought the latent content of dreams was particularly important.
    b. Freud believed that the ability to understand transference is essential to a client's success in psychoanalysis.
    c. Freud's techniques of free association, dream analysis, and interpretation are designed to help clients repress negative aspects of their personalities.
    d. Freud believed when a client has self-insight her/his ego no longer needs to maintain defensive behaviors or psychological symptoms.
    e. In psychoanalysis, the therapist offers interpretations to help the client gain insight into the unconscious origins of their problems.

13. ______ is an empirically supported treatment for enuresis (bed-wetting).
    a. Interpersonal psychotherapy
    b. Behavior therapy
    c. Humanistic, Gestalt therapy
    d. Cognitive therapy
    e. Cognitive-behavioral therapy

14. According to Ellis, negative emotions are
    a. inevitable consequences of negative events.
    b. automatic reactions of the central nervous system.
    c. produced directly by life events.
    d. the result of irrational beliefs about life events.
    e. the logical result of overanalyzing one's life situation.

15. Regarding prefrontal lobotomy, which of the following statements is FALSE?
    a. Antonio Egas Moniz, who was later shot and paralyzed by one of his own patients, developed this technique.
    b. This technique was eliminated because of serious complications in patients.
    c. Compared to this technique, psychiatric drugs offer a less radical alternative to treating abnormal behavior.
    d. In this technique, nerve pathways between the frontal lobe and lower brain centers are severed.
    e. This technique was once used to treat extreme passivity or extreme aggressiveness.

Essentials of Psychology Chapter 14

16. Eclectic therapists
    a. do not believe in using psychoanalysis.
    b. generally adhere to behavioral principles.
    c. are most often humanistic therapists.
    d. are more often psychiatrists than psychologists.
    e. integrate approaches from many different schools of therapy.

17. Lakeisha has a snake phobia and decides to see a behavioral therapist. Her therapist suggests systematic desensitization. What is the second step Lakeisha will take in her therapy?
    a. touching a snake
    b. looking at pictures of a snake
    c. learning relaxation techniques
    d. being in the same room as a snake
    e. developing a fear hierarchy for snakes

18. Vanessa feels an attachment toward her therapist and the therapy process. Vanessa's experience is referred to as
    a. a specific factor.
    b. countertransference.
    c. the therapeutic alliance.
    d. a placebo effect.
    e. transference.

19. Which of the following is NOT a key idea from client-centered therapy?
    a. Conflicting parts of the client's personality should be integrated into a functional whole.
    b. Psychological problems develop from distorted self-concepts.
    c. Clients need a safe place in which to freely explore their feelings and be themselves.
    d. The therapist's primary role is reflection.
    e. In therapy, the client should be allowed to take the lead and set the tone of therapy.

20. In finding mental health help, the text recommends all but which of the following?
    a. getting recommendations from respected sources
    b. looking for an online therapist
    c. obtaining referrals from local medical or community health centers
    d. seeking a consultation with a college health services center
    e. contacting professional organizations for recommendations

Essentials of Psychology Chapter 14

21. Shannon goes to a cognitive therapist that gives her the following assignment, "Next time you have a negative thought, investigate it to determine if it is valid." Based on this description, which therapeutic technique is Shannon's therapist using?
   a. reality testing
   b. empathy
   c. empty chair
   d. gradual exposure
   e. interpretation

22. Regarding clinical psychologists, which of the following statements is TRUE?
   a. Clinical psychologists are graduates of medical school.
   b. In the majority of states in the U.S., clinical psychologists may prescribe medications.
   c. Clinical psychologists have passed a licensing exam.
   d. Clinical psychologists are specifically trained in psychoanalysis.
   e. Clinical psychologists mostly treat people with severe psychological disorders.

23. Jewel takes an antianxiety drug for the treatment of her panic disorder. She experiences a common side effect from her treatment. Which side effect is Jewel most likely to experience?
   a. sexual dysfunction
   b. memory impairment
   c. dry mouth
   d. drowsiness
   e. muscular tremors

24. Which of the statements about locating a qualified mental health professional is untrue?
   a. In many states, anyone can set up a practice as a "therapist."
   b. Ethical professionals will support efforts to get a second opinion.
   c. Professionals who take out large ads and claim to be experts in treating many types of problems may be suspect.
   d. A client should ask a potential therapist about his/her professional background and experience treating people with similar problems.
   e. A client should not inquire about the specific therapeutic methods that will be used because this will spoil their effects.

25. All but which of the following are reasons given in the text as to why racial and ethnic minorities have less access to mental health care than the majority group?
   a. They are less likely to have health insurance than the majority group.
   b. They have less access to treatment providers who possess the appropriate language skills.
   c. Their cultures have more of a stigma relating to mental illness.
   d. There are fewer treatment providers in locations where more racial and ethnic minorities reside.
   e. They are more likely to suffer from disorders that fall outside the range of available treatments.

Name:____ Class:__________________________ Date:_____________

Essentials of Psychology Chapter 14

26. Learning desirable behavior by watching and imitating others is known as ______, and ______ pioneered the use of this technique to help people overcome phobias.
   a. transference; Sigmund Freud
   b. modeling; John B. Watson
   c. modeling; Albert Ellis
   d. transference; Albert Bandura
   e. modeling; Albert Bandura

27. Regarding behavioral therapy, which of the following statements is FALSE?
   a. Aversive conditioning uses principles of operant conditioning to help people extinguish undesirable behaviors.
   b. Gradual exposure can help people overcome specific phobias, social phobias, and post-traumatic stress disorder.
   c. Behavior therapy is also referred to as behavior modification.
   d. In systematic desensitization, the goal is to use relaxation as an incompatible response to fear in order to weaken the bonds between the frightening stimuli and the fear response.
   e. Since behavior therapy is focused on directly changing problem behaviors, it tends to be relatively brief compared to other forms of therapy.

28. What is a primary disadvantage of the antianxiety drug Valium?
   a. It can lead to psychological and physiological dependence, and it can be deadly when mixed with alcohol.
   b. It is overused in the treatment of children with attention deficit hyperactivity disorder.
   c. Its overuse suggests that mental health professionals are too eager to find quick fixes for complex problems.
   d. Its use may lead to the development of a disabling movement disorder.
   e. A significant percentage of relapses occur in patients who use this drug.

29. Regarding the use of psychotropic drugs, which of the following statements is FALSE?
   a. Antidepressant drugs bring complete symptom relief in most patients who take them.
   b. Antidepressant use can increase the risk of suicidal behavior in children and adolescents.
   c. Clozapine, a newer antipsychotic, appears to be at least as effective as earlier antipsychotics in the treatment of schizophrenia, but has fewer side effects.
   d. Although large numbers of children take the drug Ritalin, little is known about the long-term effects of the drug on the developing brain.
   e. Some behavioral forms of treatment are as effective in treating depression as antidepressant medications.

30. Phenothiazines would be used to treat which of the following people?
   a. Tobey, who has schizophrenia
   b. Kirsten, who has bulimia
   c. Sami, who has bipolar disorder
   d. Michelle, who has an anxiety disorder
   e. Alfredo, who has major depression

Name:______________________ Class:______________ Date:________

Essentials of Psychology Chapter 14

31. Which of the following is NOT a key idea from psychodynamic therapies?
    a. Psychological problems are rooted in unconscious psychological conflicts.
    b. Restoring psychological health involves gaining insight into and working through unconscious conflicts.
    c. Childhood conflicts need to be understood in light of the individual's adult personality.
    d. Therapy will help people develop their unique potentials.
    e. Psychological problems are rooted in conflicts dating from childhood.

32. Regarding the effectiveness of psychotherapy, which of the following statements is FALSE?
    a. While the majority of people benefit from therapy, some may deteriorate.
    b. Meta-analysis is a statistical technique used to average the results across a large number of studies, and this technique has been used to evaluate the effectiveness of therapy.
    c. The greatest improvements in therapy are typically gained during the last few months of treatment.
    d. Research supports the overall effectivness of psychotherapy, marital therapy, group therapy, and family therapy.
    e. The average therapy client achieves greater improvement than the majority of people assigned to untreated control groups.

33. Electroconvulsive shock therapy is effective in treating
    a. schizophrenia.
    b. generalized anxiety disorder.
    c. severe depression.
    d. obsessive-compulsive disorder.
    e. dissociative identity disorder.

34. Antidepressants have therapeutic effects in treating all of the following EXCEPT
    a. bulimia nervosa.
    b. obsessive-compulsive disorder.
    c. social phobia.
    d. schizophrenia.
    e. depression.

35. According to a psychoanalyst, anxiety results from
    a. unacceptable impulses that threaten to leak into consciousness.
    b. the id's desire to meet the demands of the ego.
    c. the id's desire to meet the demands of the superego.
    d. the superego's attempts to satisfy the ego.
    e. a failure of the superego to control the ego.

Essentials of Psychology Chapter 14

36. All but which of the following are advantages of group therapy over individual therapy?
    a. Group therapy allows the client to see how others have coped with similar problems.
    b. Because it involves group interaction, group therapy is especially helpful for people experiencing problems like loneliness and shyness.
    c. Those in group therapy have the extra benefit of social support from the group.
    d. Clients feel safer expressing their feelings in a group setting.
    e. Group therapy is usually less costly than individual therapy.

37. Marjorie receives treatment for depression. In her treatment, Marjorie receives jolts of electricity through her head. What is Marjorie's treatment?
    a. aversive conditioning
    b. prefrontal lobotomy
    c. systematic desensitization
    d. psychosurgery
    e. electroconvulsive therapy

38. Critics of deinstitutionalization complain that contemporary public mental hospitals are like
    a. country clubs, high in cost and providing too many amenities.
    b. warehouses, storing patients away without helping them.
    c. maximum-security jails, taking inmates in for life sentences.
    d. revolving doors, repeatedly admitting patients and rapidly discharging them.
    e. "human snakepits," keeping patients in conditions that are deplorable.

39. Dr. Stevenson just began a job treating Hispanic Americans in a rural clinic. An important cultural consideration for Stevenson to consider is the tendency for Hispanic Americans to
    a. be reserved in display of emotion.
    b. view the therapist as an authority figure.
    c. place a strong emphasis on family interdependency.
    d. be guarded and secretive when interacting with other groups.
    e. express emotional problems through physical symptoms.

40. The Gestalt therapist Fritz Perls was most disillusioned with which aspect of psychoanalysis?
    a. implied superiority of males over females
    b. emphasis on the client's early childhood experiences
    c. lack of emphasis on the client's subjective experience in the present
    d. emphasis on confrontation
    e. the duration of psychoanalysis

Name:________________________ Class:________________________ Date:______________

Essentials of Psychology Chapter 14

41. Which of the following best describes the effectiveness of deinstitutionalization?
    a. a resounding success
    b. an unequivocal failure
    c. has not been in place long enough to evaluate.
    d. a mix of success and failure
    e. predominantly successful since most patients are serviced by the community

42. A general term for any psychologically based form of treatment to help people better understand their problems is
    a. psychoanalysis.
    b. behavior modification.
    c. psychotherapy.
    d. psychosurgery.
    e. counseling.

43. Tricyclic antidepressants raise brain levels of neurotransmitters by
    a. increasing production of neurotransmitters.
    b. reducing breakdown of neurotransmitters.
    c. interfering with the reuptake process.
    d. increasing receptors for neurotransmitters.
    e. making receptors for neurotransmitters more sensitive.

44. Psychoanalysts are typically which type of mental health professional?
    a. psychiatrists or psychologists
    b. clinical or psychiatric social workers
    c. psychiatric nurses
    d. psychiatric nurses or psychiatric social workers
    e. psychiatrists or psychiatric nurses

45. Common side effects of antidepressants are
    a. muscle ache and drowsiness.
    b. agitation and aggression.
    c. sexual dysfunction and dry mouth.
    d. muscular tremors and impairments in memory.
    e. rigidity and severe movement disorders.

46. All but which of the following has limited the effectiveness of deinstitutionalization?
    a. the lack of comprehensive community programs
    b. cracks in the system that leave patients to fend for themselves
    c. court decisions that reversed the policy of deinstitutionalization
    d. the problem of psychiatric homelessness
    e. the use of mental hospitals as "revolving doors"

Essentials of Psychology Chapter 14

47. Regarding electroconvulsive therapy, which of the following statements is FALSE?
    a. Though ECT can relieve depression, no one is really sure how it works.
    b. Before receiving ECT, patients are given muscle relaxants and anesthesia.
    c. For those who receive ECT, memories of events during the weeks or months preceding and following the experience are very strong.
    d. ECT is usually administered in a series of six to twelve treatments over several weeks.
    e. Many mental health professionals view ECT as a "last resort" treatment.

48. All but which of the following describes the practice of psychotherapy?
    a. involves a series of verbal interactions
    b. is limited to the treatment of individuals
    c. includes hundreds of different types
    d. reflects psychological models of abnormal behavior
    e. is often referred to as talk therapy

49. After Raymond described his dream to his therapist, efforts were made to figure out what the dream meant, or its
    a. latent content.
    b. manifest content.
    c. repressed content.
    d. transfer content.
    e. subjective content.

50. Victor Van Dusen takes an antidepressant to cope with his depressive disorder. On which neurotransmitters is his antidepressant likely to work?
    a. GABA and serotonin
    b. Serotonin and norepinephrine
    c. Norepinephrine and dopamine
    d. Dopamine and GABA
    e. Serotonin and epinephrine

51. In behavioral therapy, another term for gradual exposure is
    a. countertransference.
    b. token economy.
    c. in vivo exposure.
    d. transference.
    e. virtual exposure.

52. Humanistic therapists emphasize all but which of the following?
    a. the client's present experience
    b. the client's subjective experience
    c. the client's conscious experience
    d. free will
    e. irrational beliefs

Essentials of Psychology Chapter 14

X

53. Which of the following statements about the value of online therapy services today is untrue?
   a. The use of online counseling services is growing rapidly.
   b. Psychologists and other mental health professionals have expressed concern about online therapy.
   c. There is no system for ensuring that online therapists have the appropriate credentials to practice.
   d. There is no evidence that therapy can be effective when people interact with a therapist they have never met.
   e. Few psychologists believe that online therapy has any potential value.

54. Carl Rogers is to ______ therapy as Fritz Perls is to ______ therapy.
   a. behavioral; Gestalt
   b. Gestalt; client-centered
   c. Gestalt; behavioral
   d. client-centered; Gestalt
   e. client-centered; behavioral

55. Which of the following is NOT a feature of systematic desensitization?
   a. fear hierarchy
   b. relaxation training
   c. use of an incompatible response to anxiety
   d. observing non-fearful subjects interact with fearful stimuli
   e. imagining or viewing fearful stimuli

56. Roger has been convicted of sexually assaulting several young children. In prison he undergoes aversion therapy. He is presented with pictures of young children while receiving unpleasant electric shocks. Eventually, pictures of young children become aversive stimuli. In this procedure, the electric shocks are described as
   a. unconditioned stimulus.
   b. conditioned stimulus.
   c. conditioned response.
   d. unconditioned response.
   e. neutral stimulus.

57. Most of the antipsychotic drugs target which neurotransmitter?
   a. serotonin
   b. dopamine
   c. acetylcholine
   d. GABA
   e. norepinephrine

Essentials of Psychology Chapter 14

58. Meta-analyses of the effectiveness of psychotherapy suggest
    a. traditional psychoanalysis is generally the most effective form of therapy.
    b. behavior therapy is generally the most effective form of therapy.
    c. humanistic therapy is generally the most effective form of therapy.
    d. there is little difference in the effectiveness of the different forms of therapy.
    e. group therapy is generally the most effective form of therapy.

59. Regarding behavior therapy, which of the following is TRUE?
    a. It focuses on changing the client's thoughts and feelings.
    b. It focuses on exploring the client's feelings.
    c. It helps clients see how their past conflicts affect their current behavior.
    d. It is relatively brief, typically lasting only weeks or months.
    e. It uses learning principles to help clients achieve a state of self-actualization.

60. For which of her clients is behavioral therapist Dr. Williamson most likely to choose virtual therapy?
    a. Lucy has a fear of public speaking.
    b. Ricky has a fear of flying in airplanes.
    c. Ethel has a fear of riding in elevators.
    d. Fred has a fear of snakes.
    e. Desi has a fear of going outside into open spaces.

61. In client-centered therapy, the therapist demonstrates empathy when s/he
    a. completely accepts the client.
    b. can distinguish between latent and manifest dream content.
    c. accurately mirrors the client's experiences and feelings.
    d. maintains a direct, problem-solving focus during therapy.
    e. genuinely demonstrates her/his feelings during therapy.

62. Regarding cognitive therapies, which of the following statements is FALSE?
    a. Cognitive therapy techniques are based on the view that distorted ways of thinking underlie emotional problems.
    b. Cognitive therapies are relatively brief forms of treatment.
    c. Cognitive therapies focus more on what is happening in the present than on what happened in the past.
    d. Clients are given "homework assignments" in cognitive therapy.
    e. Cognitive therapists believe that emotional problems are caused by negative events and life experiences.

63. The majority of community-based mental health centers today would best be described as
    a. well-staffed and well-funded.
    b. well-staffed, but underfunded.
    c. understaffed, but well-funded.
    d. understaffed and underfunded.
    e. adequately meeting the mental health needs of their respective communities.

Essentials of Psychology Chapter 14

64. According to your text, all but which of the following are problems with using psychiatric drugs to treat psychological disorders?
    a. Not all patients respond well to psychiatric drugs.
    b. Drugs do not teach people how to resolve their problems.
    c. Relapses are common when patients stop taking drugs.
    d. Psychiatric drugs carry risks of adverse side effects.
    e. In the long run, psychiatric drugs are more expensive than psychotherapy.

65. Which type of therapy focuses on helping families focus on changing disruptive patterns of communication and improving the ways in which members relate to each other?
    a. group therapy
    b. marital therapy
    c. couples therapy
    d. family therapy
    e. behavioral modification

66. Behavior therapy focuses on
    a. changing thoughts to correspond to behaviors.
    b. helping clients achieve self-actualization.
    c. changing maladaptive patterns of responding.
    d. altering errors of thinking.
    e. the adaptive functioning of the ego.

67. Generalizing from research evidence, some forms of psychodynamic therapy are predicted to produce good results in treating which of the following?
    a. schizophrenia
    b. anorexia
    c. bulimia
    d. panic disorder
    e. obsessive-compulsive disorder

68. Dr. Gomez is a Gestalt therapist. What would you expect to be the emphasis of his therapy sessions with clients?
    a. uncovering clients' unconscious childhood conflicts
    b. helping clients achieve self-actualization
    c. changing maladaptive behaviors through systematic desensitization
    d. creating a warm and accepting atmosphere for clients to share their feelings
    e. integrating inner feelings into one's conscious experience

Essentials of Psychology Chapter 14

69. Wanda's therapy involves directly confronting fearful stimuli, little by little, until her fear of the stimulus is reduced or eliminated. Based on this description, which technique is Wanda's therapist utilizing?
   a. aversive conditioning
   b. transference
   c. modeling
   d. gradual exposure
   e. reconditioning

70. Minor tranquilizer drugs are also called
   a. antidepressants.
   b. antisomatic drugs.
   c. antipsychotics.
   d. tricyclics.
   e. antianxiety drugs.

71. According to Carl Rogers, what are three important components of therapy?
   a. placebos, ECT, and REBT
   b. activating events, beliefs, and consequences
   c. fear hierarchies, gradual exposure, and systematic desensitization
   d. interpretation, dream analysis, and free association
   e. empathy, genuineness, and unconditional positive regard

72. Which approach to therapy combines techniques like gradual exposure and modeling with efforts to challenge and correct faulty thinking patterns?
   a. humanistic
   b. psychodynamic
   c. cognitive-behavioral
   d. Gestalt
   e. Gestalt-behavioral

73. In a study reported in the text, which orientation was most often reported by a group of clinical and counseling psychologists?
   a. Eclectic
   b. Gestalt
   c. Cognitive-behavioral
   d. Psychoanalytic
   e. Client-centered

Essentials of Psychology Chapter 14

74. The first form of psychodynamic therapy to be developed was
    a. cognitive.
    b. behavioral.
    c. humanistic.
    d. psychoanalysis.
    e. client-centered.

75. Dr. Lau is a couple therapist. What is the most typical problem she is likely to target in treatment?
    a. sexual dysfunctions
    b. communication difficulties
    c. arguments about money
    d. disagreements about parenting
    e. infidelity

76. Gail suffers from bipolar disorder. Which drug is Gail's doctor likely to prescribe to help stabilize her mood swings?
    a. Thorazine
    b. Prozac
    c. Lithium
    d. Librium
    e. Cylert

77. In psychoanalysis, _____ describes blocking that occurs when the therapy touches upon anxiety-evoking thoughts or feelings.
    a. resistance
    b. transference
    c. countertransference
    d. interpretation
    e. insight

78. Of the following patients receiving treatment for depression, who is most likely to be a candidate for electroconvulsive therapy?
    a. Ang, who has a mild case of depression
    b. Bobbie, who has a moderate case of depression
    c. Courtney, who has a severe case of depression that seems to be responding to drugs and cognitive-behavioral therapy
    d. Damien, who has a severe case of depression that has not responded to other forms of treatment
    e. Edgar, who is suffering from schizophrenia

Essentials of Psychology Chapter 14

79. Behavior therapy and cognitive-behavioral therapies have demonstrated impressive results in treating all of the following EXCEPT
    a. panic disorder.
    b. bulimia.
    c. bipolar disorder.
    d. depression.
    e. social anxiety disorder.

80. All but which of the following describes the functions of the community-based mental health centers?
    a. crisis intervention
    b. protective living environments for long-term patients
    c. supervised residential facilities
    d. outpatient care
    e. day treatment programs

81. Psychotropic drugs are also known as _______ drugs.
    a. illicit
    b. psychological
    c. psychiatric
    d. hallucinogenic
    e. biopsychosocial

82. Which type of antidepressant has the lowest rate of severe side effects?
    a. SSRIs
    b. Minor tranquilizers
    c. Tricyclics
    d. Phenothiazines
    e. They all have the same rate of severe side effects.

83. Anticonvulsant drugs used to treat epilepsy have also proved useful in the treatment of
    a. bipolar disorder.
    b. attention deficit hyperactivity disorder.
    c. phobias.
    d. schizophrenia.
    e. somatoform disorders.

84. Psychosurgery is sometimes used today to treat severe cases of
    a. schizophrenia.
    b. antisocial personality disorder.
    c. generalized anxiety disorder.
    d. obsessive-compulsive disorder.
    e. conversion disorder.

Name:______________________ Class:______________________ Date:____________

Essentials of Psychology Chapter 14

85. During which decade did the community health system begin to take shape in the United States?
    a. 1940s
    b. 1950s
    c. 1960s
    d. 1970s
    e. 1980s

86. As discussed in the text, a popular term often used to refer to psychotherapy is
    a. talk therapy.
    b. verbal therapy.
    c. psychoanalysis.
    d. psychological therapy.
    e. psychodynamic therapy.

87. Regarding psychotropic drugs, which of the following statements is FALSE?
    a. Scientists have developed drugs that work on neurotransmitter irregularities that are involved in a wide range of psychological disorders.
    b. There are four major groupings of psychotropic drugs—antianxiety, antidepressant, antipsychotic, and antisomatic.
    c. Psychotropic drugs work as either agonists or antagonists.
    d. Limitations of psychotropic drugs include side effects and potential for abuse.
    e. Compared to other biomedical therapies, psychotropic drugs are less controversial.

88. Which of the following best describes the hope of the community-based care movement?
    a. That promising psychotropic drugs could help people deal more effectively with psychological disorders
    b. That mental patients could be reintegrated into society instead of being hospitalized for the long-term
    c. That mental hospitals would reflect the values of their community
    d. That the treatment of the mentally ill would be humanized
    e. That costs of caring for the mentally ill would be reduced

89. All but which of the following mental health professionals are psychotherapists?
    a. Cheryl, who works from the psychoanalytic perspective
    b. Tim, who is a couples therapist using behavioral techniques
    c. Lisa, who works from the humanistic perspective
    d. Frankie, who conducts therapy with groups using cognitive techniques
    e. Vernon, who administers electroconvulsive therapy to people experiencing severe depression

90. The idea that irrational beliefs lead to emotional distress is at the core of which approach to therapy?
    a. behavior therapy
    b. rational-emotive behavior therapy
    c. humanistic therapy
    d. Gestalt therapy
    e. client-centered therapy

Essentials of Psychology Chapter 14

91. During a visit to his therapist, Ishmael was asked to begin talking about whatever was on his mind even if it seems trivial or irrelevant. This example describes
   a. transference.
   b. interpretation.
   c. countertransference.
   d. free association.
   e. insight.

92. Brooke goes to a Gestalt therapist. In her therapy, Brooke will probably be encouraged to
   a. analyze early childhood traumas.
   b. focus on how she is feeling in the here-and-now.
   c. suppress uncomfortable feelings.
   d. accept other people unconditionally.
   e. develop a fear hierarchy.

93. In psychoanalysis, transference is when
   a. the client talks freely about whatever comes to mind.
   b. the therapist directs some of his or her anxiety toward the client.
   c. the manifest content of dreams evolves into latent content.
   d. the client begins acting toward the therapist in ways that mirror the client's conflict-ridden relationships with others.
   e. the client transfers material from the unconscious mind to the conscious mind.

94. Puge has just graduated from college as a clinical social worker. Which degree has Puge earned?
   a. R.N.
   b. M.D.
   c. Ed.D.
   d. Ph.D.
   e. M.S.W.

95. According to Freud, the most important use of interpretation in psychoanalysis is
   a. developing strong client skills in free association.
   b. helping clients understand the manifest content of their dreams.
   c. analysis of the transference relationship.
   d. exploration of countertransference.
   e. helping clients understand the latent content of their dreams.

Essentials of Psychology Chapter 14

96. Rachel's psychoanalyst asked her to talk about what she had dreamed about the previous night. In this case, Rachel is being asked about
    a. manifest content.
    b. latent content.
    c. transfer content.
    d. repressed content.
    e. subjective content.

97. All but which of the following describes the practice of psychotherapy?
    a. based on verbal interactions
    b. used to resolve emotional problems
    c. used to resolve behavioral problems
    d. involves the use of psychiatric drugs when needed
    e. comprises many different types

98. All but which of the following people are demonstrating an irrational belief, according to Ellis?
    a. Antoine believes that he must always have the approval of virtually all the important people in his life.
    b. Beatriz thinks it is awful and catastrophic when life does not go the way she wants it to go.
    c. Carmine believes that her past will invariably affect her and determine her behavior.
    d. Dominic believes that people must always treat him fairly, and it is horrible when they do not.
    e. Eduardo believes that life's problems don't typically have clear and quick solutions.

99. In the evaluation of different types of therapies, common characteristics of all types of therapy under study are referred to as
    a. core practices.
    b. expectancy effects.
    c. specific factors.
    d. nonspecific factors.
    e. placebos.

100. In client-centered therapy, unconditional positive regard is
    a. the therapist's complete acceptance of the client.
    b. accepting the client only when s/he behaves acceptably.
    c. accepting the client only when s/he approaches self-actualization.
    d. the therapist's ability to express genuine feelings.
    e. the ability to accurately mirror the client's feelings and experiences.

Name:__________ Class:__________ Date:__________

Essentials of Psychology Chapter 14

101. All but which of the following are examples of operant conditioning in behavioral therapy?
    a. Dr. Angelino instructs teachers to use time-out as punishment when children with ADHD misbehave.
    b. Dr. Barbarino teaches Bob and Judy to use a reward system when their daughter behaves in a desirable way.
    c. Dr. Chang develops a token economy for use with residents of a mental hospital.
    d. Dr. Dorian uses a nausea-inducing drug with his client Eduardo, who suffers from alcoholism.
    e. Dr. Eggleston teaches Edwina to withdraw attention when her child misbehaves.

102. Callie is participating in a behavior therapy method in which her therapist first teaches her relaxation techniques. Based on this description, what is most likely to be Callie's therapy of choice?
    a. aversive conditioning
    b. dream analysis
    c. systematic desensitization
    d. token economy
    e. REBT

103. Cognitive therapists such as Aaron Beck refer to errors in thinking as
    a. cognitive distortions.
    b. faulty attributions.
    c. cognitive appraisals.
    d. activating events.
    e. irrational beliefs.

104. Which of the following does NOT belong?
    a. thorazine
    b. antipsychotic
    c. prozac
    d. phenothiazine
    e. major tranquilizer

105. Computer technology has been used for a new form of exposure therapy called
    a. electroconvulsive therapy.
    b. rational emotive behavior therapy.
    c. virtual reality therapy.
    d. cybertherapy.
    e. online therapy.

106. Regarding client-centered therapy, which of the following DOES NOT belong?
    a. nondirective
    b. confrontation
    c. reflection
    d. genuineness
    e. empathy

Essentials of Psychology Chapter 14

107. Therapies that are judged to have demonstrated effectiveness in scientifically based studies are called
   a. substantiated treatments.
   b. eclectic treatments.
   c. scientific therapies.
   d. meta-analyzed treatments.
   e. empirically supported treatments.

108. In Freudian terms, the goal of psychoanalysis is to shine the light of the _____ on the unconscious recesses of the _______.
   a. ego; id
   b. ego; superego
   c. id; ego
   d. superego; ego
   e. id; superego

109. In psychoanalysis, Hannah seems to hesitate when talking about her relationship with her father. Hannah's hesitation may describe
   a. insight.
   b. resistance.
   c. transference.
   d. systematic desensitization.
   e. countertransference.

110. Which of the following DOES NOT belong?
   a. empty chair technique
   b. systematic desensitization
   c. modeling
   d. gradual exposure
   e. aversive conditioning

111. During her clinical internship, psychology graduate student Veronica Wiza will conduct therapy sessions with African American clients. An important consideration for Wiza to consider when treating African Americans is their
   a. tendency toward open display of emotions.
   b. history, as a people, of racial discrimination and oppression.
   c. willingness to share personal information.
   d. tendency to lack insight into the psychological origins of their problems.
   e. language preferences.

Essentials of Psychology Chapter 14

112. Dr. Thornton specializes in psychotherapy with a particular ethnic group. Compared to people from other ethnic groups, Thornton's clients are more likely to keep their feelings to themselves. Thornton understands that this should not lead him to interpret his clients as being uncooperative or avoidant. In addition, Thornton recognizes that people with this cultural background are more likely to emphasize collective values than individualism. Dr. Thornton is most likely to be working with which ethnic group?
  a. Latino Americans
  b. African Americans
  c. Asian Americans
  d. European Americans
  e. Native Americans

113. Hugo has major depression. He might be treated with any of the following EXCEPT
  a. Tofranil.
  b. Xanax.
  c. Elavil.
  d. Nardil.
  e. Zoloft.

114. Dr. Melfi is a psychodynamic therapist. Therefore, we can predict she believes that restoring psychological health involves
  a. increasing efforts toward self-actualization.
  b. gaining insight into unconscious psychological conflicts.
  c. focusing on changing behavior.
  d. suppressing unacceptable motives and desires.
  e. focusing on the client's experience in the here-and-now.

115. Which of the following describes the primary purpose of the modern mental hospital?
  a. to provide outpatient care
  b. to provide a supervised residential facility
  c. to serve as a halfway house
  d. to offer day treatment programs
  e. to provide a protective living environment for long-term patients

116. Which type of drug typically acts on the neurotransmitter GABA?
  a. antianxiety
  b. antidepressant
  c. antipsychotic
  d. antisomatic
  e. mood stabilizing

Essentials of Psychology Chapter 14

117. Major tranquilizer is to _____ as minor tranquilizer is to ______.
   a. antipsychotic; antianxiety
   b. antipsychotic; antidepressant
   c. antidepressant; antipsychotic
   d. antidepressant; antianxiety
   e. antianxiety; antipsychotic

118. Aaron Beck is to ______ therapy as Albert Ellis is to ______ therapy.
   a. rational-emotive behavior; cognitive
   b. cognitive; Gestalt
   c. operant-based behavioral; classical-based behavioral
   d. Gestalt; cognitive
   e. cognitive; rational-emotive behavior

119. Taylor takes Ritalin to treat his ADHD. The drug's effectiveness may be based on its ability to increase the activity of _____ in Taylor's cerebral cortex.
   a. dopamine
   b. serotonin
   c. GABA
   d. melatonin
   e. norepinephrine

120. Which drug can produce mild impairments in memory and must be closely monitored because of its potentially toxic effects?
   a. Clozapine
   b. Lithium
   c. Methylphenidate
   d. Pemoline
   e. Risperidone

121. Caleb Burke is a hyperactive child with a poor attention span and disruptive behaviors. Caleb is likely to be treated with which type of drug?
   a. antianxiety
   b. antipsychotic
   c. stimulant
   d. anticonvulsant
   e. antidepressant

Essentials of Psychology Chapter 14

122. Compared to traditional psychoanalysis, modern psychoanalysis includes all of the following EXCEPT
   a. less emphasis on sexual issues.
   b. less emphasis on the remote past.
   c. less confrontation.
   d. a briefer and less frequent therapy format.
   e. more dialogue between analyst and client.

123. Paul was not given a promotion. He feels upset and disappointed because he thinks of himself as a failure who will never succeed. From the perspective of rational-emotive behavior therapy, Paul's view of himself is the
   a. activating event.
   b. irrational belief.
   c. self-defeating behavior.
   d. consequence.
   e. outcome.

124. There are ______ major types of antidepressants, and they are called _______.
   a. 2; minor and major tranquilizers
   b. 3; MAO inhibitors, tricyclics, and selective serotonin-reuptake inhibitors
   c. 3; Valium, Librium, and Xanax
   d. 2; phenothiazines and neo-phenothiazines
   e. 2; stimulants and anticonvulsants